PUTTING ON THE DOG

The Animal Origins
of What We Wear

MELISSA KWASNY

TRINITY UNIVERSITY PRESS
SAN ANTONIO, TEXAS

The publisher appreciates the support of the Kendeda
Fund in publishing this book.

Published by Trinity University Press
San Antonio, Texas 78212

Book design by BookMatters
Jacket design by Rebecca Lown
Cover image: iStock/DenisDubrovin
Author photo by Donna Goode Rogers

ISBN 978-1-59534-864-7 hardcover
ISBN 978-1-59534-865-4 ebook

Trinity University Press strives to produce its books
using methods and materials in an environmentally
sensitive manner. We favor working with manufacturers that practice sustainable management of all
natural resources, produce paper using recycled stock,
and manage forests with the best possible practices
for people, biodiversity, and sustainability. The press
is a member of the Green Press Initiative, a nonprofit
program dedicated to supporting publishers in their
efforts to reduce their impacts on endangered forests,
climate change, and forest-dependent communities.

The paper used in this publication meets the minimum
requirements of the American National Standard
for Information Sciences—Permanence of Paper for
Printed Library Materials, ANSI 39.48-1992.

CIP data on file at the Library of Congress

23 22 21 20 19 | 5 4 3 2 1

Contents

Introduction ∼ 1

1 Leather ∼ 9

2 Wool ∼ 49

3 Silk ∼ 85

4 Feathers ∼ 122

5 Pearls ∼ 159

6 Fur ∼ 187

Conclusion ∼ 228

Notes ∼ 237

Acknowledgments ∼ 265

Index ∼ 268

Introduction

To be draped in the spun cocoons of silkworms, or warmed by piles of feathery down, to slip on sweaters, coats, hats, and gloves woven from the wool of sheep grazing in high pastures, to avoid rocks and thorns and cold by walking in the tanned and beaded skins of deer, elk, caribou, moose—or in spike heels made of alligator hide by Manolo Blahnik—is to be human. Though we may clothe our cats or dogs, *Homo sapiens* is the only species that makes its own clothing. According to the *Oxford English Dictionary*, *clothe* means (1) to put clothes on, (2) to provide someone with clothes, and (3) to endow with particular qualities, as in "You have been clothed with power from on high." Not included in these definitions, it seems to me, is a missing subject. Who is clothing whom? In many cases, throughout human history, that subject is an animal. As well, between the noun *clothing* and the verb *clothe* lies a whole universe of animal-human relations, of processes and trade, of traditional use and modern industrialization, of indigenous notions of reciprocity and contemporary ideas of sustainability. In effect, what we wear represents one of our most profound engagements with the natural world.

We are born naked—featherless and furless. Scientists speculate that we lost our body hair between one and three million years ago.

Subtropical Africa, where the first anatomically modern humans evolved, was warm and mild, its temperatures hovering between eighty and ninety degrees, the optimal thermal range for unclothed humans. We were nonetheless vulnerable, our feet callused but easily torn, our skin chapped by the wind and bitten by insects. Our first sunscreen may well have been animal fat, mixed with red ochre. We may have painted or scarred our bodies in imitation of the stripes, spots, and colors of the beasts surrounding us. Yet according to archaeologists, the making of complex clothing—material that is cut and sewn to fit the body—is a surprisingly recent innovation, an event that occurred only in the last one hundred thousand years.

Clothing is obviously an important event in our evolutionary history, yet its actual invention is shrouded in mystery because it was made of animal and plant materials, which rot and disintegrate quickly. As the *Encyclopedia of Human Evolution and Prehistory* notes, "Such substances as wood, hide, and vegetable fiber are preserved only in exceptional conditions, such as dry caves or waterlogged, anaerobic sediments." Almost all of what we know of prehistoric human life is from archaeologists speculating on what was done with the stone tools and stone artifacts left behind. The earliest chipped stone tools have been found in Ethiopia and near Lake Turkana in Kenya and date to three million years ago, indicating that the manufacture of tools was practiced by hominids long before the emergence of *Homo sapiens*. But scrapers and blades could have been used to scavenge animal skins for their flesh or fat, not necessarily for our ancestors to be able to wear them.

Once piercing tools—awls and needles—appear, we can be certain that complex clothing manufacture is involved. People used awls to puncture hides, perhaps to run sinew through them for shoes or to tighten the edges of a cape. Awls, choppers, and axes have existed since the early Stone Age. Bone awls, perhaps the oldest awl type in the world, have been discovered in caves in South Africa and dated to 72,000–84,000 years ago. Other evidence from the same period includes beads and buttons, as well as carved figures wearing what looks like fur. Eyed needles, however, only began to surface in the archaeological record around forty thousand years ago; the oldest examples were found in the colder climates of western Europe, Siberia, and northern China.

Another form of indirect evidence for clothing manufacture comes from an interesting source: lice, one of our oldest tormentors. The human head louse, *Pediculus humanus capitis*, has apparently been with humanity since our beginnings. It is a single species that now occurs as two distinct ecological types: head lice and clothing lice. By sequencing the DNA from both types of lice found on contemporary humans around the globe, researchers believe they can determine when the split between the two occurred, and thus, the origins of clothing. In other words, once we lost our body hair, head lice were restricted to our heads; a different type of lice evolved only when we started wearing the hides of animals. According to Ralf Kittler, Manfred Kayser, and Mark Stoneking, who in 2003 were the first to attempt this sequencing, "A molecular clock analysis indicates that body lice originated not more than about 72,000–42,000 years ago." Further studies by Melissa A. Toups and colleagues, in 2011, suggest that it might have been closer to 170,000 years ago: "Our analysis suggests that the use of clothing likely originated with anatomically modern humans in Africa." (There is no proof of other species of archaic hominids wearing or not wearing hides or furs: because they are extinct, we can collect no living lice from them to analyze.)

Collectively, these findings affirm the theory that, as humans encountered cooler temperatures brought on by another ice age and emigrated out of Africa and into harsher climates, the need to protect themselves from the cold probably brought about the invention of complex clothing. Humans, who are vulnerable to cold, have three responses to it: fire, shelter, and clothing. Only clothing is easily portable. In Paleolithic time the Northern Hemisphere was covered with growing and shrinking ice sheets and large bands of coniferous forests. "Specialized cold-weather clothing" must have been crucial for the multiple widespread migrations that took place across the globe for the next thousands of years, giving *Homo sapiens* a distinct advantage over nonmodern forms of hominids, such as the Neanderthals in Europe. In fact, archaeologists analyzing faunal remains in early modern strata have found that the bones of Canidae (wolves, foxes, dogs) and Mustelidae (wolverines, mink, weasels) at *Homo sapiens* sites greatly outnumbered those at Neanderthal ones, indicating that the wearing of fur may have made the difference in who survived. As Kittler, Kayser, and Stoneking state, "Clothing may have allowed early modern humans to colonize more extreme latitudes than their archaic predecessors, and hence might have been a factor in the successful spread of modern humans out of Africa."

This is not to say that protection from cold and wind was the only function of even archaic clothing. Psychological functions—for example, promoting modesty, avoiding shame, or displaying sexual attractiveness—must have been present even before the advent of complex clothing, as evidenced in the leaf aprons and loincloths depicted in artifacts and historical accounts of later hunter-gatherer societies. A desire for adornment is also apparent in the bone beads and perforated shells found in caves in what is now Algeria and Israel; these items are between ninety thousand and a hundred thousand years old. An equally ancient workshop for mixing red ochre with fat and other materials to create paint, possibly for body decoration, was recently excavated a few hundred miles east of Cape Town. Feathers were certainly a source of beauty and allure. As Ian Gilligan writes in "The Prehistoric Development of Clothing: Archaeological Implications of a Thermal Model," "In all likelihood, dress has its origins in the decoration of the unclad body, a function subsequently transferred to clothing." Today we are aware of the many social functions of our apparel, including as markers of identity—gender, rank, tribe or ethnicity, region, role, occupation, generation, familial relationship, age, and religious or spiritual belief—some of which may have been present before the invention of the needle and the awl. The Upper Pleistocene, however, is when Gilligan believes complex clothing "began to acquire psychosocial functions that have helped to maintain its continuing use up to the present."

⌁

In prehistoric Africa, elephants, rhinoceroses, and hippos splashed about in what is now desert. There were Cape buffalo and long-horned buffalo, horses, gazelles, wildebeests, and enormous herds of the elegantly named eland. Europe was home to cave bears, woolly-haired rhinoceroses, and mammoths, as well as the smaller red deer and reindeer. Humans shared the Americas with the giant ground sloth, camel, horse, tapir, wild boar, Saiga antelope, bison, mammoth, musk ox, caribou, 350-pound beaver, armadillo, condor, stag moose, the ten-foot-long armored glyptodont, the short-faced bear (weighing in at over a ton), and the smaller grizzly bear. Naia, the young girl whose 13,000-year-old skeleton was recently discovered at the bottom of a Mexican underwater cave, shared her crypt with saber-tooth tigers and a kind of extinct elephant called a gomphothere. Whether humans began fashioning gazelle capes to combat a cooling trend in Africa or picked up a needle to sew a wolf ruff onto a parka in any of the other cooler, and cooling, climates around the globe, it is certain that what we dressed ourselves in for millennia was a second skin.

The animals were here when we arrived. They were our predators and our prey. They were also our teachers and our kin. As philosopher and ecologist David Abram writes in *Becoming Animal: An Earthly Cosmology*, we must have made "the animistic assumption, common to countless indigenous cultures but long banished from polite society, that human beings are closely kindred to other creatures, and indeed have various other animals as our direct ancestors." Fire would not warm us once we left it. We saw, however, that the other animals, with their heavy coats, didn't die from the weather or even seem to suffer much from it. We followed them to water; we watched what they ate, and then tried it ourselves when we saw that they weren't poisoned.

We fashioned beads out of their bones and perhaps painted whiskers onto our cheeks. Men in the Arctic Circle who wore walrus ivory labrets pierced through their lips probably did so for the same reason that contemporary women wear pearls around their necks: to borrow some of the power, mystery, and color of the animal world around us.

One can gain a sense of this tutelary relationship in many of the American Indian, Alaska Native, African, or Australian aboriginal stories that have been handed down orally for countless generations. "The buffalo, elk, and birds in the air—they are just like relatives to us and we get along fine with them, for we get our powers from them and from them we live," the Lakota chief Black Elk said. Abram calls this relationship—of respect toward animals, of an age-old tutelage— *indigenousness*. He writes, "We fail to recognize that over the course of hundreds of generations, such participation with the enfolding earth [was] tuned so thoroughly by both the serendipities and adversities of this world, by its blessings and its poisons, its enlivening allies and its predatory powers, as to be wholly beyond the ken of any merely naive or sentimental approach to things."

A friend shows me her daughter's tortoise-shell barrettes, plastic-like in their smoothness. What species of tortoise? She hadn't thought about it; I wouldn't have either before I wrote this book. She shows me her great-grandmother's ivory bracelet, which is painted with a scene from royal India. *Ivory*: such a lovely word, smooth in the mouth like its namesake, procured by the slaughter of walrus, elephant, or mammoth. But which one? In medieval Europe, traders charged large sums for bits and pieces of the tusk of the narwhal—a small arctic whale with an ivory tusk "spiraling out of its forehead"— which they misrepresented as pieces of the unicorn's horn. Christians wore them as talismans to protect themselves from illness and evil spells. Likewise, trade, mass production, and an increasing distance from wild and rural life have obscured our relationship to the origins of much of our clothing, whether it is an ivory bracelet or the dyed coyote trim on our Walmart parka.

In this book I investigate the history and ongoing relationship forged between humans and the nonhuman animals whom we still depend on to clothe and adorn us: sheep, goats, rabbits, cows, seals, ground squirrels, salmon, silkworms, oysters, mink, foxes, coyotes, wolves, geese, ducks, chinchillas, and many more. One of my goals has been to meet and learn from people who spend their lives working with these animals—hunters, trappers, farmers, ranchers, and shepherds—and find out what their experience can teach the rest of us in a broader sense about our place in nature. Another is to offer a glimpse into the time-consuming processes of making and, therefore, *interacting with* the materials these animals provide, by hearing from tanners, spinners, weavers, dyers, sewers, and artisans of all kinds. The book is divided into six sections: leather, including fleece and rawhide; wool, including cashmere, angora, and mohair; silk; feathers, including down; pearls; and fur. For each chapter, I traveled to the animals—to Alaska's tundra, to sheep ranches atop Montana's Continental Divide, to silkworm farms in northern Japan and mink farms on Denmark's western coast, and to the pearl beds in the Sea of Cortés.

In "Fragments of the Heavens," Catherine Howard tells the story of an anthropologist in Brazil trying to purchase a marvelous feather headdress from the Waiwai. Before he could take possession of it, he had to listen to five hours of stories about how each feather and animal part was obtained. When he asked the villagers to skip that part, they couldn't. Every object had to be given with the story of "where its raw materials came from, how it was made, through whose hands it passed, when it was used." To not do so—to not impart those stories—disrespected not only the animal but also all the knowledge and skill that went into producing the desired garment. What has it meant for us, as individuals and consumers, to have lost a connection with the source of our clothing? To answer that question is to track a global and labyrinthine journey that involves many hands, enormous amounts of capital, and a trail of destructive practices that have harmed animals and humans alike. This book maps some of those mistakes and some of the solutions currently being presented: predator-friendly ranching, indigenous harvesting of seals, sustainable pearl farms, traceable down. Educating ourselves about what we use, I hope, provides an incentive—moral, spiritual, and yes, sometimes financial—to conservation and preservation.

At its heart, the book is about the clothing itself, the marvel and miracle of it: silk kimonos dyed in a soup of red cedar bark, pearls cast in the hues of the sea itself. *Putting on the dog* is an American phrase that means "donning fancy clothes for a special occasion." Although the idiom is relatively recent—one source traces it back to the expensive lap dogs wealthy people showed off in the nineteenth century, and another to the stiff "dog collar" shirts young men wore for formal occasions at Yale—it is ancient in practice in the sense that the materials that animals provide us *are* luxury products, *are* precious, given that they often require the loss of an animal's life and hours of care from those humans who have hunted it, raised it, and crafted painstakingly elegant and practical things from it. Few of us make our own clothing anymore; the origins of our clothing, in fact, are many degrees removed from the product we buy at the mall or order online. Most of us live in urban areas far from wild or domesticated animals. Yet that obscurity, in the end, is not a reality. In writing this book, I learned about Yup'ik women in the Arctic, who say they wear their furs, which they have sewn and decorated so masterfully, out into the world *so that the animals can see them.* The animals, as well as the farmers and hunters and the makers of our clothing, are all around us. They do see us, in that what we wear directly affects their lives. To see *them* is to bring us closer in the circle.

1 Leather

The Secrets of Skin Sewing

My friend Lorna is wearing an apple-green corduroy parka lined with
a recycled down one, the ruff around its hood made of wolf fur, sewn
for her by a Yup'ik woman she met when she was teaching in the
Alaskan tundra twenty-five years ago. Rarely is it cold enough even
here in Montana for her to wear it, but at noon today, when we meet
for lunch, it is ten below. She tells me that the woman had sent her to
the village store to get the trim, hearing that a relative had brought in
a wolf, a rare occurrence. The coat's ruff is thick, formidable, silver and
black, about a hand's length long. Lorna says she once wore the coat
into a nearby art museum, and the women in the gift shop glared at
her. People in the West have strong feelings about wolves, pro and con.

In Alaska, Lorna was once given a spotted seal by a Yup'ik hunter
from the Bering Coast. She skinned it, froze the meat, rendered the
oil, and distributed it to the villagers. She sent the skin to a tannery
in Seattle but had to order it under a villager's name, as she is *kass'at*
and, under the Marine Mammal Protection Act of 1972, it is illegal
for white people to traffic in seals, sea lions, whales, and walruses.
The sealskin, depilated, supplied the soles for the pair of boots she
is pulling out of a plastic bag to show me. The haired skin, scratchy,

white with gray spots, forms the almost knee-high sides. Decorated with traditional red tassels, which some villagers called "bumblebees" and others (more appropriately, given the habitat) "flies," the boots are waterproof and were often stuffed with grass for warmth. The mukluk has been a crucial element in arctic survival for millennia and serves as the model for the brand-name Muck Boots and Sorels that have replaced them.

During the last glacial period—between twenty-six and ten thousand years ago—when North America lay covered by sheets of ice, a "bridge" formed from eastern Russia to coastal Alaska across the waters of the Bering Strait. Over it, thousands of early peoples moved back and forth between Eurasia and the Americas. This area, called Beringia, has been the traditional home to the Yup'ik and Inupiaq people for hundreds, perhaps thousands, of generations. An archaeological site in nearby northeastern Siberia is the oldest known evidence of human occupation in the Arctic Circle, dating to thirty thousand years ago. Hundreds of mammoth, bison, lion, and horse bones were found within it, many with marks of butchering; in addition, a trove of walrus ivory jewelry, as well as what could possibly be an awl made from wolf bone, indicate the use of clothing and a desire for adornment.

White explorers early on adopted the name Eskimo for all circumpolar peoples, a term whose origins, like the people, is clouded in myth. Some say it means "raw fish eaters." Some linguists say it derives from southern Algonquin neighbors and meant "to net snowshoes." Today many Alaskans use the terms Eskimo or Alaska Native interchangeably to designate the two major language groups of Inupiaq and Yup'ik. The adjectives Yup'ik and Inupiaq (or nouns Yupiit and Inupiat) are what the indigenous people use; as with many tribal names in the lower forty-eight, these terms simply mean "the real people." With approximately twenty-three thousand enrolled members spread among small villages, the Yupiit are the largest Native population in Alaska. Along with the more northern Inupiat, they are one of the few hunter-gatherer or "subsistence" societies still functioning today and among the most traditional Native Americans. They are also, Lorna tells me, renowned for their skills in "skin sewing." When she invites me to accompany her in August back to her tundra village, there is no question that I will say yes.

✎

Before my trip I spend hours looking at photographs: a boy's loon-skin "socks," glossy black and green and white, feathers out to shed the rain. An entire adult coat made of the pure white bodies of fifty-six seabirds, mostly the breast feathers of common murre—the skins of eiders, long-tailed ducks, and emperor geese are said to be the warmest. A child's parka and pants made of swanskin, worn feathers-in, so that when she emerges, naked cygnet, she is hot and sticky with down. Fish-skin gloves with palms made of sealskin, completely waterproof. Inupiaq women in the 1930s, their full faces framed with "sunshine ruffs" made of wolverine and tipped with wolf hairs. I try to imagine them: caribou people on the land, seal people on the sea, their smell— the overly strong smell of the human—disguised by burning grass. Loon-capped, beaver-shouldered, wolverine tails trimming their chests, the stiff hair of seal coating their legs: dressed up as animals, creeping through the land, they were created figures, not natural ones. They must have seemed incomprehensible to the other animals, so that they had no choice but to accept them.

In turn, it must also be an animal wish to become transparent, *see-through*. Naked, where would we not stand out? As disguise, Yup'ik clothing did not call attention but deflected it. Moving slowly across the winter tundra, parka feathers flaring and settling in the winds, the hunters were invisible, so that the caribou were convinced they weren't there. A disturbance in landscape, perhaps; an intuition, not yet of harm. Or when the men in kayaks, their hunting caps painted white with clay, their gut parkas the color of salted air, approached a seal, what the seal saw was not a danger but instead an iceberg floating toward it. As a hunter crept on his belly over the ice, he often held his elbow-length sealskin mittens to his face; if the seal looked up from its nap, the man disappeared in much the same way as the hunting polar bear does when it covers its black nose with its paw.

In autumn, the Yupiit and Inupiat hunted caribou and trapped mink, otter, muskrat, fox, arctic squirrel, even marmot. In the winter, they sewed clothing made of the animals' fur. In the spring, the first to come were the "bearded seals," then the smaller ringed seals, spotted seals, and ribbon seals. Sealskins were scraped and then soaked in fermented men's urine to remove the fats and oils. Thread was made from the twisted sinews of moose or sea mammal. Six to eight rabbits are needed for a child's parka, creating the look of a tiny snowman or an upright lamb; thirty-two muskrat skins for a woman's "fancy parka," fur side out to block the cold. Swan feet, which are black, were split and appliquéd on the hem, in designs that often depicted tributaries of the Kuskokwim or Yukon Rivers. For the Yupiit, who, until recently, spent almost every moment outside, on the sea, in strong winds, snow, and rain, a sealskin parka might last five or six months, a bird skin a little more than a year.

Skin sewing, ingeniously, also meant organ sewing. One of the most unusual—and essential—inventions of the Yupiit and Inupiat is the "gut raincoat," or *imarnitet,* made from the intestines of seal or walrus or sometimes beluga whale. Women removed the linings from the intestines with their fingernails, washed them of blood, then inflated them like balloons and hung them to dry. More recently they used air compressors, but in the old days they used their breath. In the photograph I am looking at, a grandmother holds a long loop of intestines, which look uncannily like the foam "noodles" used in water aerobics classes. Once they are dry, the guts are cut into panels and pieced into a parka and a hood, each seam rendered waterproof by inserting a blade of grass on either side of the running stitch.

The hem of the *imarnitet* is cut extra large to fit over the cockpit of a kayak and be fastened there in bad weather; the body becomes an extension of the kayak or the kayak an extension of the body, all completely impenetrable. "The seams are so airtight...if the parka is closed too tight, it will inflate from the air inside the kayak," writes Ann Fienup-Riordan, an anthropologist who lived with the Yupiit for many years. Because of this, a small hole is left in its back. The transparent parchment of the men's seal-gut parka shrinks into itself when dry, a stiff ball the color of yellowed newsprint, and is easily torn, but when moistened, it can be slipped on over the head. Wet, the parkas are as quiet as the kayak, which is also manufactured out of skin.

For the Yupiit, clothing was shelter from cold and wind; it was thus house, boat, nursery, and, in emergency, food. People slept in their clothes, rode out storms in their clothes. Some of the fish-skin parkas of king salmon were so large that they doubled as tents for up to three people. In this sense, clothing was a tool, the making of it a technology, like scrapers and spear points and woven baskets. The need for it was not frivolous, not fashionable, but absolute.

✦

Flying into Bethel, Alaska, with Lorna, I suddenly understand how all manner of secrets could be lost below. My first glimpse of the tundra—of puddles, pools, lakes, rivers, sloughs, streams, inlets, outlets—makes me wonder at its strangeness. Completely roadless, seemingly uninhabitable, the flat water-and-marsh stretches to the far horizon, where I am pretty sure I can see the curve of the earth, fluid and shimmering. Lorna says the tundra is 40 percent water. What land there is, is yellow, rust, green, like a fall-themed, tie-dyed blanket or a spreading sea of giant algae, land created from silt flowing down the Yukon, Kuskokwim, and Nushagak Rivers. No hills. No landmarks to navigate by. Soon I will learn that summer is when people leave—visiting relatives in Hawaii, Oregon, Seattle—because winter, when the land is frozen, enables travel.

On our way to Bethel from Montana, we had used our six-hour layover in Anchorage to take a bus downtown. Questions of prehistory (mammoths, musk oxen, the Bering Strait) and questions of people (subsistence, suicide, alcohol's fairly recent destructiveness) are so present there that they collide within the ten blocks of the small downtown. In Anchorage, in addition to earrings made of walrus ivory and musk ox horn, one can buy beads made of mammoth tusk unearthed from recent drilling, or carvings made of whalebone or baleen, the black, stiff bristle filters in the mouths of some whales. On the front page of the *Alaska Dispatch News* is the story of Andrew Harrelson, who found a seventy-five-pound mammoth tusk in the same curve of Fish River where his mother, exactly ten years earlier, had found one. It could be anywhere from 12,000 to 400,000 years old. I try on a string of brownish-cream beads dug out of the muck of prehistory.

Running across the tarmac, we arrive in Bethel amid a monsoon that even the locals admit is irregular. We are spending the night in this border town, the last stop before the bush planes that serve the sixty or so villages that line the Bering Coast and inland rivers, one of which will take us tomorrow to Kusigluk. Here *village* means an Alaska Native village. Bethel is half Native, with the rest of the population made up of Chinese Americans or Korean Americans who run the restaurants, and whites, craggy and eccentric, the men bearded, devoted to fishing, sled dogs, or hunting. Bethel is built on the tundra. The houses sit on stilts, not because of flooding, as I had imagined, but because the heat and weight of a house and its people will eventually melt the permafrost, causing the whole town to sink. The sewer lines are above ground, silver barrels that snake out of the back of each home and run above the sloughs looking like roller coasters. The tiniest shacks have "open" signs in their windows, even this late: a Chinese restaurant, a Native craft store with baskets made of river grass, a couple of boat repair shops.

The next morning, breakfast is canned pineapple, white toast, and "man eggs," meaning hot dogs and frozen potato cubes fried with fake eggs. Lorna's friend Cauline Ferguson arrives with gifts: a quart jar of salmon and a box of Pilot Bread—oversized, hard crackers that originated as boat food. She has agreed to take us on a quest for clothing sewn from skins, but first she shows me photographs on her cell phone of her granddaughter in one of the fancy parkas she made for her. No, she didn't trap the muskrats; she shot them, going out on the water each week and adding what she got to her pile. "Do they sink?" I ask. "No, you just grab them." "But what if they're not dead?" But now I've made her suspicious. Who am I, an animal rights crazy? "I smack them against the boat," she says, gauging my response.

When I tell her I am interested in what indigenous people tell themselves when they have to kill for a parka or meat, she says I should be careful asking people that. They aren't going to talk freely to a white person, she says, who might misinterpret or make judgments without knowing anything about their lives. The most important thing, Ferguson adds, is that people believe the animal gives itself to the hunter. The worse thing is to not appreciate that gift or to turn it down—even when it isn't hunting season or you've already reached your limit. This attitude presents all kinds of problems in the cultural clash that is Native–White Alaska.

Our first stop is someone's mudroom, where we find rabbit mittens and three children's seal-gut parkas. "An old lady from one of the villages came through last week selling them," the merchant explains. At the gift shop at the airport, run by Lucy Crow, we find the hides of two red foxes ($350 each), a large arctic wolf ($650), and an arctic fox, white and spotless ($450). Crow collects traditional clothing, and on the walls hang at least twenty pairs of sealskin mukluks in various stages of wear, an impressive set of thigh-high fish-skin boots, and a child's parka of arctic squirrel, with its characteristic decorative spots. "My mother," Crow says, pointing at the parka, "always scraping, scraping squirrel hides." Another parka, slightly larger, is mottled snowy and dark brown, and long-haired like a litter of exotic kittens. Crow says it is a rare bird parka once common on the Lower Kuskokwim River, the front made from scoter and swan. She finds a postcard of Maggie Lind, its maker, wearing it, and gives it to me. Lind looks to be seventy or eighty.

We move on to the Saturday Market at the Yupiit Piciryarit Cultural Center. Although we get there a bit late, the elder ladies come later, their hair under brightly knotted hairnets called *kaapaaq*, a hybrid of Russian babushka and Yup'ik fishnet. I buy a pincushion made of sealskin, with real ptarmigan feet attached, from Mary Thomas. She and her friend are selling hats hand-sewn of *mouton*—sheepskin dyed to look like beaver or seal—trimmed with red fox or sea otter, and men's hats of mink and beaver. Each hat costs $250 or more. We buy Christmas decorations (tiny mukluks made of sealskin) from Ella, who says she hadn't sewn for a very long time. She was too busy working "by the hour." Even now, she says, she will make more of these "little things" instead of survival clothes that take so much time and cost too much for the tourists. Though there is a revival of skin sewing, it is now viewed as a craft. The hides are bought, no longer hand-tanned, ordered from a shop in Seattle.

ⱱ↗

"It's like no place else you've ever been," the pilot remarks as we disembark the next day in the village of Kasigluk. We drag our roller suitcases from the runway onto the boardwalks that serve as sidewalks crisscrossing the village, past the many government-built houses on stilts and toward the Akula School, red and sprawling. Although it is after 8 p.m., the light is still luminous, the sun suspended in the sky. After storing our things in the school—where we will be sleeping on the floor of the teacher's lounge—we go walking. Up a rise is the graveyard, separated by sect: Orthodox, Moravian, and perhaps simply a family's, marked by whitewashed plywood crosses. Beyond that, the tundra, a heathered, lovely mess of reindeer moss, miniature firs, and scalloped leaves of long-gone salmon berries, the ground so soft we sink at every step, a mattress that soon exhausts us. Past the airport, a man keeps his sled dogs. At Fox Lake, we see fox tracks in the sand. Berry-pickers return on ATVs, whole families, including a grandfather, perched precariously atop them. A day ago someone saw a brown bear. We hear this from everyone we pass.

At the Akula grade school, half the day is taught in Yup'ik and half in English. In middle school, students learn to write and read their native language. *Waqaa*: hello. *Evineq*: island of grass. Although Yup'ik, like many other Native languages, was endangered for a time, it is now the second-most-spoken Native language in the United States, after Navajo. There are an estimated ten thousand Yup'ik speakers in Alaska. Every day for a week we sit in on Charlie Issac's middle school class, listening as they go over the word lists: *clouds, berries, burlap, sleep.* "Charlie, what is 'ice flow'?" a student asks. When they are unsure, students silently leave their seats and move closer to the front of the class to be near him. "What is *stair*," someone asks, "*s-t-a-i-r*?" How to spell *fish eggs, river, hunger, berries, clouds (not one, more than one), sled*? "After nine, the moose sit down and you never see them," Charlie begins his story. "Once, three boys got up early and left to go moose hunting. They saw a canoe beached along the shore and pulled up next to it. There was a tent there, with three boys still sleeping in it. There was also a moose beyond the tent, which they shot and killed. This is a true story from our village," he says. "If you sleep, good things won't come to you but to someone else who wakes up early."

It is a cliché that the Eskimo have a hundred words for snow, but most of us want to believe it. We want to believe there are people who pay that much attention to nature, who know their environment so intimately. We imagine the words as nuanced and soft as the snow itself. Apparently the cliché itself originates from a misinterpretation. Yup'ik has the same number of words for snow as the English language, yet it has more ways to modify those words for prevailing conditions. There are Yup'ik words not only for each species of seal, correspondent to Western scientific taxonomies, but also for each seal by age: adult bearded seal, subadult, adult with small body, adult in rut, young, two-year-old or pup. In addition, there are eight names based on the bearded seal's behavior and appearance: how they sleep, for instance, or what color they appear when they surface from the sea. There are forty-five different words for wood—not species of trees, but states of being: waterlogged wood, shavings, chips, wood that is hard and burns well, soft unburnable wood, wood for various jobs such as smoking fish or carving kayak spines. It is a language of makers, I realize, of a people who know the *material world*.

Anna Barbara Charles, one of Lorna's former students, arrives for berry-picking late mornings in a blueberry print *gaspuk* and pink cotton pants, both hand-sewn. She wears store-bought Muck boots on her feet. She comes from the old village by boat with only a berry bucket—no purse, no pack, no plastic water bottle. Her hair is short, thick, and going gray. One can see she was an adorable child. She is fifty now, four and a half feet tall, and very quiet. "Do you want to go over there? Do you want to visit Gertrude?" Questions are all she will speak in English. We pick berries, not talking, for hours, the morning warm and mosquito-filled. Charles has a learning disability, yet she knows all the villagers: the parents' and children's names, the people they are related to, the exact dates of each death. The blueberries will be frozen for later feasts to honor those who have passed away. They are the special ingredient in *akutag*, "Eskimo ice cream," which isn't cold at all: it's a mixture of berries, beaten Crisco, and powdered sugar, and sometimes fish or fiddlehead fern.

Charles lives with four of her twelve sisters. We visit them in the old village, fifteen minutes by motorboat, a trip accomplished by simply standing on the dock in Akula and waiting for someone who is going over. The sisters' house is large and clean. Incense burns on the inside porches in the old village, perhaps to deter insects or to mask the odors of houses with no sewers or running water. Along the boardwalk there are "honey pots" where people empty their waste, which is eventually dumped in the lagoon. A light but not unpleasant sewer smell hovers in the air outside. None of the sisters is married. Edith, they say, "does not like the men." She fishes, drives the boat, hunts geese and ducks.

A nephew has killed a moose and left part of it on their porch. Men and women often stay unmarried in order to take care of others. The sisters' mother, who lived here, recently died at 105.

Villages, too, sink on the tundra, and the US government must help them move. Before Alaska became a state on January 3, 1959, and before schools, which the new government required children to attend, the people lived in small, nomadic family units. They had summer fish camps, winter camps, fall hunting spots, and places to go in the spring. The land could recover. The old village is increasingly a sinking island, its boardwalk level with the water. As we walk, I feel like a shorebird moving through tall grass. It is a hauntingly quiet place filled with water-light. In each house, those surviving hold on to the old life. One of Lorna's old friends, Gertrude, sits immobile and rail thin from rheumatoid arthritis. Her many pairs of walrus ivory earrings lie on the end table next to her, but she is no longer able to put them on. On the table sits a bowl of boiled potatoes and smoked salmon bellies, untouched. "I don't want a dog house inside my house," Gertrude complains, by which she means having to move to a new home with a toilet.

One day we hire Wassillie Berlin to take us by boat to Nunachuk, the *oldest old* village. Berlin is partially disabled, walks unbalanced, and is hard to understand. Yet once in the water, he is transformed, agile and fast, master of the boat and the topography. Our route disappears quickly behind us, and then we are boating for hours. Periodically, he has to stop to clean grass from the propeller. Sun, water, *evineq*— islands of grass. Berlin slows as we approach a long shoreline, and I have no idea why we are stopping. Suddenly, on the right, what had looked like a solid piece of land separates into a narrow lead just large enough for the boat, and we are soon zooming down its curves. I am astonished to see a path where there was none apparent. "I would never have seen that!" I exclaim to Berlin.

"I was born here!!!" he yells over the motor, incredulous that I would even think I could do it, and the ridiculousness of what I have said, along with his response, makes us all laugh.

Lead, as in a lead opening up in the ice, allowing passage for hunters and seabirds, denotes the revelation of opening. The word evokes a childhood fantasy of moving through walls, sticking an arm through the solid. Yet a lead can be serious, life-threatening. To follow the leads, to sense them, one must have experience, practice, mentors. Without them one could get fatally lost. "A good knowledge of the local landscape and the ability to draw a detailed map are two very different cognitive skills," writes Barry Lopez in *Arctic Dreams*, his book about the far North. "Nevertheless, many Eskimos, both men and women, produced highly accurate maps of the coastal and interior regions of their homeland." Lopez tells of leads closing behind ships maneuvering open water through ice, of whales being backed in by increasingly frozen water.

Berlin produces a long stick of driftwood with which he tests the solidity of the bank before we step out at Nunachuk. He ties the boat not to a branch but to a more stable root. The island is a long, grassy knoll with water on both sides. From it the newer villages gleam like Oz in the distance. (A tip in the local paper warns not to try to swim to shore if overboard: "It is usually much farther than it looks.") We have arrived at Daisy's fish camp, but no one is here: a shed, a "steam house," everything in its place, ready to work when the fish run again. Nunachuk is where Vivian Beaver was born and lived until she was eight, she told us, when they were all forced to move to the newly built school. Beaver did better in school than most because she had already learned English from the biologists who hired her father to guide for them. The others, especially the boys from Bethel, could not help blurting out Yup'ik words, for which they were made to hop around the classroom like rabbits so the teachers could hit them on their bottoms as they went by. Dancing was forbidden. Singing was forbidden. It wasn't until the mid-1960s, she said, that they quit beating Indian children.

In 1959, Nunachuk split into two villages, Nunapitchuk and Kasigluk. In 1980, with the houses of the new Kasigluk sinking, half the population moved to the even newer Kasigluk, which is built on sand. The graves of those buried before the Russians invaded, before the missionaries and their crosses, have long sunk. The crosses are now waist-deep in their disappearing. Berlin points out depressions in the earth, all that's left of where families lived.

Yesterday, when I asked Sam Twitchell about subsistence living, he showed me photos on his smartphone of this year's salmon harvest: his shed full of bright red fillets hanging from the rafters, willow branches with their summer leaves slipped into the bodies to keep them from curling. All day, he said, they fished the Kuskokwim with a drift net, back and forth maybe five or six times, each time catching about twenty fish, then boating back to the village, where they cut, split, washed, and hung them, then started the fire to smoke them. A good life—enough fish for the winter caught in one day. When I complimented Twitchell on his family's good fortune, he looked puzzled. "All summer, everywhere in the village you see salmon hanging. It makes me happy to see it." For him, Twitchell wanted to make clear, fortune is good if everyone shares in it, if there is enough for everyone.

Subsistence: salmon, whitefish, blackfish, lush, pike. Driftwood that comes down the river in spring breakup. Berries—wild crowberries, blueberries, salmonberries, raspberries. And "mouse food," the cut greens the mice harvest and store in preparation for winter. Beaver said her mother advised leaving enough in the holes they raided for the mice to survive; otherwise they would not do this work for them in the future. "When we go anywhere," she said, "we go there for a purpose."

For the past week, when Lorna told people I am a writer, they immediately quit talking. Who can blame them? So much continues to be stolen from them. Yet when I explained that I am interested in the secrets of skin sewing, everyone brought out a coat or pair of mukluks their mother or grandmother had made for them. Bertha Hoover showed me her own "fancy squirrel parka" but said she never wears it. She is too shy, and everyone would stare at her. It is *too fancy*. And probably too old-fashioned. "We can buy things now," she says. She lets me try it on; despite its bulk, it is miraculously light. A cook at the school, Bertha Brink, told me that people do wear their fancy parkas when it gets really cold, say minus thirty. But they are too hot most of the time now. She showed me her mother's "fur inside" parka, made of rabbit fur covered with corduroy. She borrows it, since her mother, who is in her eighties, doesn't go out much.

In Edna Wilder's book *Secrets of Eskimo Skin Sewing*, she writes that after the squirrel skins were harvested, fleshed, and dried, women would spend an entire morning turning them inside out and back again to soften them, pulling and stretching all the while: "The women with good strong hands usually did 18 to 20 a day." For thread they used sinew from caribou or beluga whale, but it had to be split and twisted to become strong and pliable. "Learning to twist sinew is rather difficult," she says. "Eskimo women used to make up sinew in packs about an inch thick and keep it ready, so that during the daylight hours they could spend more time sewing and less time getting ready." Work parkas like Brink's mother's were worn fur side in, but people's wealth was judged on the quality of their fancy squirrel parkas, which required weeks of work and generations of knowledge. Wilder says that if someone was gifted a wolverine and wolf ruff, it was so prized that, when they died, the family was required to cut it off and give it back to the original owner.

I think of the arctic peoples' invention of the parka, muck boot, kayak, anorak. Even the hoodie might be an appropriation of the *kasput*, with its hood to ward off mosquitoes and its large pockets for berries. Victoria Dewar, president of the Pauktuutit Inuit Women's Association of Canada, claims that the Inupiat and Yupiit have never been given credit—or money—for the invention of this ingenious cold-weather clothing. She writes, "We are no longer willing to be treated like artifacts in museums, and that includes our living culture which is embodied in our clothing." Her concern is that, if used ignorantly, the clothing will become "meaningless."

Men living north of the Kuskokwim used to insert walrus ivory labrets in holes pierced on either side of their lower lip. In old photographs, with their chopped bangs, fur parkas trimmed with white gussets, and the heavy "tusks" that pull their mouths open, they look uncannily like walruses. Many Yup'ik women used to tattoo stripes across their faces or hands, animal markings that make them resemble bobcats or lynx. For a people who spent all their time procuring food and shelter, what about this need for ornamentation is functional? It is true that style of clothes or shape of kayak often denoted membership in a specific family or village. But beauty on its own also had a use for the Yupiit, one rooted in their philosophical relationship to the animals they killed. It is said that they decorated their clothing to pay respect to the animals it came from. As Fienup-Riordan relates, one important Yup'ik teaching is "The ocean has eyes and the world knows."

"The Boy Who Lived with the Seals" is a traditional Yup'ik story that illustrates this concept. The story begins in a remote village near the coast of the Bering Sea, the home of a young couple who were able to have only one son. They wanted him to become a great hunter, of course, so he could supply meat and skins for them as they grew older. They went to speak to a shaman who said he would send the boy to live with the seals, but they would have to be willing to give him up for a year. They almost agreed a few times but at the last minute backed out. He was their only son, after all, and they loved him. But finally, at the spring Bladder Festival, when the bladders of all the seals the villagers had caught in the previous year were deflated and returned to the ocean via the river, the shaman led the boy to the water and pushed him through the ice. The boy suddenly found himself swimming with a great number of seals, who led him to their underwater lodge.

Once there, he was befriended by a bearded seal who taught him what he knew about hunters. Sea mammals, the Yupiit believed, live in an underwater *qasgi* or ceremonial house, just as the men and boys did in their villages. As in the *qasgi*, there was a skylight at the top from which they could observe human beings, deciding if they were acting rightly and who they would sacrifice themselves to in the spring. Seals come willingly, it is said, only to those who keep the animals foremost in their minds and who honor and respect them. When the spring came, the boy swam out with the seals and was harpooned by one of the men of the village. The next day, the shaman found the boy lying by the river, back to himself. He did indeed become a great hunter because he understood what the animals wanted from humans, which was a greater *reciprocity*.

Implicit in this story are a number of beliefs intrinsic to many indigenous worldviews: the belief that nonhumans and humans used to be able to understand each other, even change into each other; the concept that animals "give themselves" to the people, whether for food or clothing or spiritual help; and the idea that all actions have consequences for the cohabitants of the earth. Though a shaman is sometimes needed to mediate conflicts between humans and non-humans, each person is responsible for keeping the lines of communication open and being aware that one's unwise actions can cause harm not only to oneself but to an entire people by alienating the plants and animals, the waters and the winds, on which they depend for their survival. According to Fienup-Riordan, "People believed that thoughtful actions cleared a path for the animals they would someday hunt."

Reciprocity? My friend from the city scoffs, in late-modernist despair over what humans have done to the earth: "I know what animals have given us, but honestly, what good have we ever provided for them? We've just hunted and crowded them into extinction." She believes any human attempt to mitigate the fact that we have had to kill animals to survive is merely a transparent attempt to excuse our own rapaciousness. Even Lopez, when pondering the unease he had felt participating in an arctic walrus hunt, writes, "No culture has yet solved the dilemma each has faced with the growth of a conscious mind: how to live a moral and compassionate existence when one is fully aware of the blood, the horror inherent in all life, when one finds darkness not only in one's own culture but within oneself."

The Yupiit, as well as many hunting and gathering cultures, seem to have formulated an answer that might serve as we continue to reflect on this dilemma. In an interview with Fienup-Riordan, Yup'ik elder Paul John says, "Our ancestors took great care of everything around them as they lived their lives because they fully understood that everything had awareness. They knew that even fish bones were conscious and perceptive." If one believes, as many indigenous cultures do, in what Fienup-Riordan calls "the essential personhood of animals," as well as their "responsiveness...to human thought and deed," what would that require of us? What would it mean to ask *who* instead of *what*? For instance, *who* are we killing in order to eat? *Who* are we wearing?

"It was the gift rather than the death that was preeminent in the Eskimo view of hunting," Lopez writes. Thus, the killing of any animal is done with extreme gratefulness and regard, as well as accompanied by ritual. He writes, "Such [acts] of propitiation [are] sometimes dismissed as 'superstition.' 'Technique of awareness' would come much closer to the mark." For Paul John, awareness meant one did not step on a skin or fish bones lying on the ground. One did not waste or overuse or let things rot. Furthermore, one paid attention to the habitat that the fish swam in. Was the water clean enough? How would the salmon come back if the rivers were dammed? The continuance of the animals, in effect, became a human responsibility. The soul of the seal, it is said, is located in its bladder. For that reason, bladders were returned to the sea in the spring, so they could ensure the birth of new seals.

Included also in lessons passed down through stories such as "The Boy Who Lived with the Seals" is the lesson of the passing down itself. The Yup'ik relation to the dead, a relation some may think of as "spiritual" and thus dismiss, is practical. According to the Yupiit and Inupiat, when an animal dies, its soul or *inua* enters an unborn animal of the same or similar species. The animal's death—or gift of life—is seen as a passageway between the future and past, the web of living and dying. Yup'ik lessons were not written but bestowed on the very young, lessons that would save their lives on the ocean or the tundra: tool knowledge, hunting knowledge—"never approach a seal from behind"—and a larger knowledge, so wise that it looks to us like myth, conveyed in stories like "The Boy Who Lived with the Seals." In order to ensure the continuation of the animals the Yupiit depended on, they developed a set of responsibilities to them: attention, respect, gratitude, conservation, care.

Hides

Hide, a verb: to put or keep out of sight, conceal from view or notice of others. Or a noun: camouflaged shelter used by hunters to get a close view of wildlife. From the Old English *hÿden*: the skin of an animal, especially when tanned and dressed. We say *to tan someone's hide*, meaning to put it through excruciating manipulations, to beat it enough to soften it and make it yield. We say we *couldn't find hide nor hair of her*, or he has a *thick hide*, meaning he doesn't feel insult or pain easily. He is protected as the first *Homo sapiens* were when they hid from the weather under a mammoth hide.

Until the sixteenth century in England, the word *leather*, from the Celtic *lethar*, meant the skin of both humans and animals. We now use the term to distance ourselves, rather than admit that our shoes are made from the same delicate material that covers our own feet. The hide and fur industry has terms for what happens to skin once it is flayed from the animal; being is translated instantly into product: pelt, shearling, fleece, leather, chamois, kid, suede, and fur. Given that clothing has been made out of the skins of just about every animal alive, domesticated or wild—fish, seal, elephant, ostrich, alligator, horse, sheep, goat, cow, deer, elk, beaver, mink, fox, even dog—naming that product can be extraordinarily confusing for the layperson.

What, for instance, is the difference between a vest made of calfskin with the hair side removed and a top hat made out of the shaved hairs of a beaver? The downy nests of the fleece slippers I slide my feet into each morning: do I call that leather? Because my slippers were handmade by a small craftsman in a nearby town, I decided to ask the maker himself.

"*Fleece*, we don't use that word," says Gary Thomas, proprietor of High Plains Sheepskin. "Fleece is made of plastic, like those fleece jackets everyone wears. I call it wool, whether with the skin on or not. It's the American Wool Growers Association, not Sheep Growers." My original idea that sheepskin is a kind of leather, and that wool is a textile, is obviously confounded here. "But you don't call these wool, do you?" I ask, pointing to a large table piled with twenty or more "fun rugs," which he frowns at cynically. Each has been decorated with faux faces and feet so that the white wool looks like the animal it has been bleached and shaped to not resemble. Thomas makes it clear that these are not *his* favorite. He just sells them. "You could call them pelts," he says. He throws a rougher-looking brown and white spotted sheepskin over the others. The pelt is larger than expected, wider even than my skin, if I were split open from neck to pubic bone and spread. He points out where the sheep's "underarms" are, free of wool, ashy like the skin at my elbows.

Thomas has agreed to talk to me about contemporary "skin sewing." His storefront is on Main Street in East Helena, Montana, a small western town of a couple thousand, six miles from the state capital. The brick building, circa 1900, is long and narrow and stacked to the ceiling with hundreds of rolled pelts. On racks near the front are his products: sheepskin-lined mittens, bomber hats with flaps over the ears, and his signature slippers, a brown tea color lined with fluff, sewn with leather soles or without, all made for our harsh Montana climate. The shop is overcrowded with tools and hides, the air dusty with errant fibers. Most of the space serves as storage or workroom; two black sewing machines, looking like ancient Olivetti typewriters, sit in a corner where he also cuts out his patterns. Except for around the holidays, High Plains Sheepskin is a one-man operation.

Thomas brings a storm-gray pelt from the back and tosses it on the floor. Biggest sheep I've ever seen, he says. It looks like a bear lying there, face down. "Is this what is called a black sheep?" I ask. "Any sheep not white is called black," he answers. We measure the pelt; it is fifty-six inches long.

A middle-aged man and woman come into the store while we are talking. I am curious how they found it, since there is only a small sign above the door, and the shelves and walls where Thomas has haphazardly hung his wares are hardly a showroom. Most of his sales are through the internet. "These've lasted me twenty years," the man says, holding up a pair of mittens large as a welder's. "Guess it's finally time to get a new pair." The couple, who are from Billings, four hours away, are laughing at the husband's frugality as well as the wonder of mittens lasting so long. While Thomas takes his order, I examine a stringer of beaver hides, each round like a flattened beaver balloon. I've recently read that the shape is because one slit is made, and the body is turned inside out of its skin. The beavers' coats are richly hued, changing color depending on how I smooth them or hold them to the light: bronze, saffron, cinnamon.

Skin seems to long to be touched, and I can't help touching everything. The beaver's coat is so smooth it feels almost greasy, and as the hairs move, they shimmer. Fur-bearing animals—beaver, mink, ermine, fox, even muskrat—feel different than wool-bearing, but why? "Feel this," Thomas says, leading my hand to the curved edge of the beaver pelt. It is buttery but fibrous, and he tells me that it is the belly of the beaver, which has no guard hairs as the back does to protect its softness. Machines have been invented that shear off these guard hairs, a process used in making "shorn beaver coats." This beaver's tiny leather ears peek out from the glorious brown, indicating where the head was. Its eyes are dried out, like wood pith. Suddenly I can understand why someone would want to take it home. It is luxurious.

From the back storage room, Thomas retrieves a cap made of beaver felt, dyed black, sleek. Beaver felt is even more confusing to classify. It is made from the underhairs of the beaver, shaved and mixed into a matted fabric that is boiled and then pressed into shape, not exactly a skin, not exactly a fiber. Felt top hats, Wellingtons, D'Orsays were worn by all gentlemen, even Abe Lincoln, until silk took over. In fact, the European craze for beaver hats almost wiped out the beaver population in the New World. Trapping beavers made the Hudson's Bay Company one of the richest companies of its time.

Thomas hands me a small black pelt, which he calls *mouton*, French for "wool," and also specific for the French-bred sheep it is made from. I test it against the ordinary wool, which previously was soft and now feels scratchy. I realize that to understand sheepskin I will have to invent a new vocabulary of softness: the softness of its leather (a worry stone), ordinary wool (warm sand through my fingers), *mouton* (soft as sudsy water). Wool, apparently, is defined by the density of its fibers. In fact, I can't pry the mouton apart far enough to even see the skin.

The most important thing to understand about skin, Thomas is saying, is it is an *organ*, which is a collection of tissues joined together to fulfill a function of the body. In fact, skin provides a number of functions. In addition to protecting and containing all of our other organs, it rids the body of toxins, and it regulates the body's water and cooling through perspiration. It is also a sense organ; all animals who have skin, including ourselves, feel temperature, pressure, moisture, and texture, as well as pain, via our overall body covering. For most animals, skin is made up of 65 percent water and 35 percent collagen, and it consists of three layers, although all are tightly connected. The top layer, the epidermis, "carries" the hair or wool; it sheds, forms horns in deer, goats, caribou, and musk ox, and is what enables us to sense. It synthesizes vitamin D and prevents the entry of pathogens or harm to the lower layers. The middle layer, called the corium, or dermis, is what leather is made of. It contains hair roots, sweat glands, blood vessels, and fibrous tissue. Its job is to feed nutrients to the epidermis and to regulate temperature. The bottom layer—the subcutis, which means "below the skin"—is connective tissue, made of fat and blood. Most animals have this membrane between the flesh and hide, which makes skinning easier. When hides are kept for later tanning, the subcutis is removed in the slaughterhouse.

The middle layer, the corium—again, what leather is actually made from—can be further divided into what are called the reticular and papillary layers. The reticular layer is netlike, with fibers twisting around each other. This is the layer that gives leather its strength. It regulates temperature and also attaches the skin to its deepest tissues. The papillary layer contains papillary glands and pores. Papillary glands are the small protrusions or follicles at the root of hairs and feathers. Pores are small openings that allow for perspiration. The roots and pores are responsible for the different "grain" patterns of certain leathers. Professional buyers, Thomas says, can look at a piece of leather and determine exactly what kind, and sometimes the age, of animal it came from. A calf's skin is smoother because its pores are smaller. The typical grain pattern of goatskin is a half moon. Close up, cattle grain looks like mountain ranges seen from space, the ridges cast with a thin line of snow; sheep grain is pebbled. The pig is the animal whose skin most closely resembles ours.

Thomas passes me a cowhide. It is so heavy I can't fold it into a manageable shape, so I stand there holding it as if a large man had fainted in my arms. I look closely at the grain. All leather, after the skin is washed and stripped of its outer and inner layers, is white until tanned and dyed. This cowhide is dyed a flat gray, industrial and masculine. "Shoe leather," Thomas says. Earlier, he had shown me three or four small calfskins, thin as paper, spotted brown and white, their hair short as if coming back after a shave. Hereford. They were delicate like calves would be next to this bull. Their skins, where they had been scraped at the packing plant, were uneven, nubbed. It seems as if it would be easy to tear through them. Barbed wire had cut into one side of the cowhide, and here is its brand, still visible, burnt into the skin. "Leather flaws" are what a tannery would call them, as all cuts, burns, tears, bites, or skin diseases are called.

At this point I can't help looking at my own skin. Because I have no wool or hair, mine does not have a heavy grain pattern but rather a crosshatch of fine lines and the many tiny star bursts that are pores. There are moles and warts and deep wrinkles. Like most skin, mine is flexible, strong, resistant to tearing, abrasion, water, and wind. It can be stretched and compressed. It has insulation value. To retain these qualities past my demise, however, my skin would need to be tanned.

Leather

It is ninety degrees in San Antonio when I pull up in front of a block-long, windowless building with *Hide Drop Off* stenciled on the side. I have driven far south of downtown, through a Mexican American district of fruit stands and taco stands, across a set of railroad tracks, and to the end of an eerily empty dead-end road. I am here because Thomas has set up a tour for me with the Nugget Company, a tannery from which he orders his sheepskin pelts. Stepping out of the rental car, the stench accosts me—raw, meaty, sour—and I suddenly wonder if I will be able to stomach this. In Marrakesh, I have heard, guides at the medieval tanning pits give tourists mint leaves to stick in their noses to block the smell. I suspect I won't be so lucky.

The custodian, a sad-looking man my age whose clothes are filthy from the work, peers out from behind the locked gate of the dock. I say the name of the owner, "Colin Wheeler," and he lets me into a dimly lit warehouse, crowded with pallets piled high with fleeced skins, most of them dyed a pumpkin orange. The smell and heat are even heavier inside, enormous industrial fans blowing them about. On my way to meet Wheeler, another worker passes me pulling a cart with the eviscerated bodies of twenty bobcats, heads attached, flattened and stacked, as if they were costumes a child might try on. I recognize their spotted fur, their tufted ears. Thomas told me that in 1973 there were twenty-four or so sheepskin tanneries operating in the United States. The Nugget Company is one of the only ones left.

The real history of leather is the history of tanning. Untreated animal skins quickly harden, or, if kept humid, rot. Insects and bacteria move in to do their damage. An ancient human technology, the tanning process stops the natural process of death, which is decay. The word *tanning* comes from the word *tannin*, a naturally occurring chemical found in bark and leaves of plants. People have used oak, beech, sumac, and chestnut, as well as smoke, ammonia, pigeon excrement, animal brains, marrow, wheatmeal, and salt—anything, it seems, that will enter and biochemically merge with the skin fibers to soften and stabilize them. The Blackfeet might have been so named because the phenol in smoke blackened the buckskin they used for moccasins. The Yupiit collected alder bark, boiling it to use as a tanning agent and a deep red dye.

The Egyptians tawed their goat or pigskins, a method using alum and salt that results in skin that is white and stiff, although tawing does not result in a true leather. (Tawed skin will return to rawhide if soaked in water, as does unsmoked brain-tanned "buckskin.") The grave of Tutankhamun, who was buried in 1550 BCE, contained alum-tawed sandals; the figures of his enemies, which are engraved on the inner soles so he could trample them, are still perfectly visible. (The outer soles of the more fabulous shoes—the grave contained eighty-one pairs—were unsoiled, perhaps because servants carried Tutankhamun when he wore them.) A large-scale tannery has been discovered under the ruins of the first-century city of Pompeii, as well as in archaeological digs throughout Ireland and England. The tanner's guild, in fact, is among the oldest guilds in Europe: tanning was the first organized industry of medieval times. In the nineteenth century, manufactured chemicals were introduced as tannins, including chrome alum and chromium sulfate.

Wheeler greets me in his small air-conditioned office, jumping up from his computer to shake my hand. A tall, dark-haired man in his thirties, he wears fashionable thick-framed glasses, jeans, and a red T-shirt and seems open and friendly. Mike, on the other hand, whom he introduces as his general manager, sits, lacing a pair of blue suede shoes and scowling. "Most of our employees have gone home for the day; you should come back Monday when you can see them in action." (He clearly sees me as an intruder. Because I am a woman? Because I might be an inspector?) "Do you have rubber boots?" he asks. "Because there'll be mud and blood and water all over."

We begin the tour, starting at the shipyard, Wheeler leading me through the overheated rooms with loud fans and damp concrete floors, the floor drains clogged with membranes and hairs, the steel machine edges strung with stringy pasta-colored shreds of skin. The place is clean, but not exactly hygienic. We stop in an open-air back room, stacked with bundles of "raw skins." Wheeler explains that most of the sheepskin processed in the United States is lambskin, since few people eat mutton anymore. Although two million lambs are harvested annually in the United States, the number has been slowly declining by 2 to 4 percent, mostly because people's taste for lamb has diminished. The skins have come from the company's "raw skin procurement facility" (aka "slaughterhouse") in Colorado. He says in the 1940s and '50s, when Texans ranched a lot of sheep, his facility had a packing plant attached, but now that oil's been found, it is hard to find anybody who wants to ranch, let alone work in a tannery, the hottest, smelliest work there is: "Most people last half a day and say, 'This isn't for me.' Those that stay, stay for twenty-five years or more. But they are aging."

Lamb, by the Nugget Company's definition, is any animal up to ten months old. Lambs apparently grow larger than I had pictured them; each of these pelts is big enough for a cloak. The bundles are bulldozer-bucket-size, mud-colored and layered like the silt in an archaeological dig, and labeled on the side with a series of numbers that identify up to fifteen grades, according to thickness of skin, number of fibers in the wool, length of it, color, or tears, marks or other wounds. The Nugget Company processes twenty-five thousand lambskins a year. (It also does a side business catering to the local hunters, hence the bobcat skins.) Wheeler says he has just returned from China, where he toured a tannery in Shanghai. There they processed forty-five thousand skins a week.

Raw skins arrive from the Colorado facility sprayed down, salted, and packed to dry so the moisture leaves the skin quickly. A spray of pesticide is sometimes used to keep bugs at bay. Raw skins can only be suspended in this state a few months before parasites will find a way in, destroying the leather. I finger the salt beads embedded in the wool, which is dirty—full of seeds, soil, and manure—as the coat of any animal living in the outdoors would be. Behind this pile is a pallet of "black" sheepskins, charcoal to a faded gray, the wool an inch and a half thick. I part it. Next to the skin, the fur is a clean apricot and cream. Wheeler says the grade determines what can be done with it. Being in Texas, one of the company's biggest clients is the saddle maker, who needs large, fat, American sheep and who wants them dyed orange. Black sheep are often dyed "cappuccino" and used for boots. The popularity of Ugg boots has been a boon for the industry.

Wheeler is proud of his family's company, and he seems to have had practice representing it. "When people ask me what I do for a living, I have to gauge their level of knowledge. Most people have no idea what a tannery does. I simply say I am in the leather business." There are at least twenty-nine steps from salted skin to the finished product, he explains, a process that can take three weeks or more. After soaking in big rotating tanks to rewet and wash them, the skins are run through *sabreuse* machines, which rinse the wool and further scrape the skin. This is also where the first clipping occurs. (A shearling is a sheepskin or a lambskin that has been tanned with the wool on the skin. For other leathers, such as cowhide, the skins would also be soaked in a lime solution to facilitate dehairing.) The huge vats serve a number of functions: dyeing, washing, tanning. They are expensive, manufactured in Turkey or Italy—old-country centers of tanning—and were shipped at great expense. Surprisingly, all the work is still done by hand. I watch two men who have unloaded one of the tanks and are feeding the slippery skins through the *sabreuse* machines, one by one, controlling the speed by foot pedal.

Once the skins have been washed and defleshed, they enter a pickling solution of salt and sulfuric acid that "shocks" them so that they are receptive to the tanning agents. Some hides are vegetable tanned, a more natural process that uses tree bark, resulting in the stiffer, browner sheepskin that Thomas, in his Montana shop, uses for the soles of his slippers. Worldwide, however, 85 percent of skins are chromium-tanned, which turns them from white to a silver blue. These are the proverbial "wet blues," or semiprocessed skins, that tanneries often ship off to other countries to be dyed and finished. (In this state, they are no longer susceptible to rot.) Every major tannery has a chemist on duty, Wheeler says, regulating the pickling, tanning, and dyeing agents depending on the state of the skins and the product that is to be made from them, adjusting for moisture content and seasonal temperature.

The stacked skins are wet, slimy as fish bellies. Because so much water is used in tanning, the drying process is crucial to the quality of leather obtained. I follow Wheeler into a room open to the air on all sides. This is where the "toggling machine" will dry and stretch each skin. (Because hides are sold per square foot, stretching is also crucial.) The toggling machine operators are gone for the day, but Wheeler shows me the specialized ringlike tool they slip their fingers into, the other end of it clipped to the edge of sheepskin. A tough job, he says, one man on either side pulling as hard as he can, then attaching the stretched hide to a metal screen which, overnight, will dry and stretch it incrementally further, a process akin to Native people staking the hide out in the sun. Wheeler and I are sweating profusely. I feel my jeans stuck to my legs. Mike comes out of the air-conditioned office and again invites me back on Monday to see the finishing crew. "Phew, worst it gets," he says about the heat, but I can see he's impressed that I've stuck it out so long. Me too. I've only been here an hour and a half. I would be one of those new employees who quit by noon.

◆

The spotted sealskin slippers, trimmed with beaver, which I bought in Fairbanks for my lover; my Italian, hand-tooled, wingtip ankle boots, which my lover bought me on our trip to Rome—I hadn't seen them as bodies flayed, flattened, salted, stacked, and piled on pallets. But one can smell the truth in a tannery. That is why packing plants, tanneries, and stockyards have always been located on the outskirts of town. Every major city in the world has an old Tannery Row, and many now have new ones. "Five years from now hides will never be lifted—seldom touched," reads the 1970 edition of the National Hide Association's *Hide and Skin Handbook*, perhaps optimistically. Tanning is more mechanized, but it is still a dangerous, labor-intensive, hands-on operation. Speaking to its fellow tannery owners, the handbook adds, "Five years from now where are we going to find men to stand shirtless and sweating knee deep in chrome loading a pile of wet blue stock?" The question as to where people in the future will be found to perform this difficult work, though, has been answered. Standing shirtless and often barefoot in chromium sulfates and poisonous dyes, they live in the poorest and most populous countries on earth.

The number of major tanneries in the United States has dropped from 250 in 1978 to fewer than a dozen. Currently, China and India lead the world in leather production, which is now a $77 billion industry. Two conditions have caused tanneries to move overseas: cheaper labor costs and fewer environmental regulations. One would think the tanneries would be a boon for employment in these countries, and they are, though the statistics are disturbing. Often, half the employees at these tanneries are child laborers, fourteen and fifteen and sometimes younger, working twelve-hour days seven days a week for minimum wage, which in India is about thirty-nine dollars a month.

Occupational safety standards don't exist. Because of journalists like Sean Gallagher, who won a Pulitzer for his investigations into the health hazards of tanneries in Kanpur, India, or Raveena Aulakh, who reports on Bangladesh, we have learned of children standing barefoot in open gutters of chromium waste, handling hides with no gloves or other protective gear. Women and adolescents, their faces and hands peeling into horrific splotched patterns of purple and blue, work long hours, until they are too sick to continue. In addition to contact dermatitis and melanoma, chromium sulfates used in the tanning process cause respiratory illnesses (including asthma), blindness, leukemia, and, in studies done with tannery workers in Belarus, high instances of pancreatic cancer. A health assessment of 197 men working in Kanpur tanneries found their mortality rate to be 40.1 percent compared to 19.6 percent for nontannery workers. The average life expectancy of any child working in the Bangladeshi tanneries is fifty years. As one can imagine, there is no system in place to deal with occupational injuries or illnesses. People simply lose their jobs, and others take their places.

Chromium salts, the central ingredient in chrome-tanned leather, are the cause of most of this illness. Why use chromium if it has so many dangers? The answer is simple, one we have come to expect from global capitalist industries: tanning with leaves and herbs takes time—up to forty-five days. Chrome tanning can be accomplished in less than three. In addition, vegetable tans produce stiffer, less luxurious leather.

Health hazards at work are not the only problem with chromium. Tanning is a water-intensive industry. Just as in Wheeler's tannery, skins must be washed and fleshed, pickled, and soaked in chromium and dyes mixed with water. Processing 100 kilograms (220 pounds) of hides uses over 845 gallons of fresh water. This water must, in turn, go someplace. Kanpur, called the "Leather City of the World," sits on the banks of the Ganges River, India's holiest river. In 2014 there were three hundred tanneries operating on its outskirts, employing an estimated twenty thousand people. The Ganges not only provides drinking water to millions but also irrigates cropland. Its water, which is crucial for crop production, is poisoning what food still grows there. Bangladesh has also emerged as one of the tanning capitals of the world. Hazaribagh, on the outskirts of Dhaka, the nation's capital, has two hundred leather tanneries, employing fifteen thousand people. It sits on the banks of the Buriganda River. It is estimated that only about 20 percent of water flowing into the river is treated.

There is also the problem of solid waste. "Seventy percent of an untreated hide is eventually discarded as solid waste," writes Andrew Tarantola in "How Leather Is Slowly Killing the People and Places That Make It." In the city of Hazaribagh, which means "The Thousand Gardens" in Bengali, 5,547,613 gallons of untreated waste are released into the Buriganda River every day, making it one of the most polluted rivers in the world. In videos I've watched, bubbles appear in the gray water, like those in a witch's cauldron. There are no longer any fish. It is, in effect, a dead river. Tannery runoff contains high levels of fat and other solid wastes, as well as the pesticides that are sometimes added in the early stages of getting skins to the tanneries. Hazaribagh is rated one of the five most toxic, heavily polluted sites on earth. Children are increasingly born with severe disabilities, and the groundwater has been found to be contaminated with chromium VI. "Short of binding U.N. arbitration or a massive international boycott against chromium tanned leather," Tarantola writes, there is not much to be done, as the profits to be made are enormous.

"When customers call me and want me to match the price they got from China or India," Wheeler says, "I tell them I can't. Our people won't work for those wages. See all these tanks? Those are wastewater treatment tanks. They're expensive. The process of filtering is extensive. If people want to buy from places where they dump chemicals directly into the rivers, where workers are paid practically nothing, I say 'Go ahead.' What can I say? I say it's up to them."

As I should have predicted, when I return to the Nugget Company on Monday morning, Mike isn't there, but Wheeler sighs and interrupts his work on the computer to take me around to see the processes that occur after tanning. *Maroquinerie*—the fashion industry's term for fine leather goods, named after Morocco, which is famous for them—is merely skin until it has been dyed, split, conditioned, polished, and perhaps painted. These steps are collectively called "finishing." As the last process in the already multistage art of tanning, finishing has its own encyclopedic vocabulary. *Full grain* means that the skin is presented as is, replete with the animal's scars and stains. *Corrected grain* is sanded for uniformity; *hot-stuffed* is conditioned with grease. *Split* means the skin is sliced into thinner layers, for use in gloves and garments. To make suede, split leather is sanded on both sides. In the case of sheepskin, the skin side might be subjected to any of these treatments; the wool side might be sheared, electrified, tipped, curled, straightened, or plumped.

Before ending up in the finishing section of the factory, Nugget Company pelts have been dyed, sometimes multiple times, in the large rotary tubs used for tanning and pickling, or sprayed with a "stony" or "tonka" glaze, the latter so-called because it is favored for Minnetonka moccasins, one of the sheepskin industry's biggest customers. In the past—and still in Marrakesh and Fez, where tourists can watch tannery workers trample goatskins in vats of bell pepper, red poppy, rose, henna, mint, and pomegranate—most leather was dyed with plants or other naturally occurring materials, including indigo, made from flowers native to Asia (*Indigofera tinctoria*); green span or verdigris, a copper acetate; saffron; and yellowwood. The makers kept their recipes under lock and key. Now over 70 percent of leather is dyed with plastic or "aniline" dyes produced from coal tars.

The finishing area of the factory consists of six machines, each about the size of an upright piano. An employee stands in front of each of them, a pallet of skins at his or her side. I watch as a woman deftly feeds a pelt under the roller, where the skin is heated and sheared to produce a spongier, springier wool, sort of like human hair after a hot conditioner. Wool lengths can be adjusted anywhere from one-half to one inch and curled or "electrified" by ironing out the kinks. Oils, waxes, and creams are applied, depending on whether the order is for slippers, coats, rugs, saddles, or even lambskin paint rollers. Sheepskin, like any leather, is eventually *a made thing*, no longer sheep or skin. In the end mouton is, at least at the Nugget Company, a sheepskin tanned, dyed black, sheared, hot-combed, and fluffed into a material that much resembles mink. Life comes and goes, here in the tannery, into a multiplicity of forms.

Take shell cordovan—the name of a rich burgundy or dark rose leather from which men's expensive shoes are made. Park Avenue Cordovan Oxfords, which Presidents Ronald Reagan, George H. W. Bush, Bill Clinton, and George W. Bush wore to their inaugurations, cost $650 a pair. The most nonporous leather in the world, lasting twenty years or more, shell cordovan is derived from the subcutaneous layer that covers a horse's rump. Each horse provides two hides, or shells, enough for two pairs of shoes. According to the Horween Leather Company, which is famous for it, the leather itself can take up to six months to make, including vegetable tanning and retanning, shaving and reshaving, hand-oiling and dyeing. In between, the leather has to rest. And good horsehides are rare. They are obtained from places where people still eat horsemeat, namely Canada and Europe.

The Horween Leather Company is the only tannery left in Chicago, processing about four thousand cowhides and one thousand horsehides a week. (Besides being known as the cordovan capital of the world, the company is also the sole maker of footballs for the NFL.) Its product is rightly expensive, given the hours and expertise to produce it. "If you came to me and said, 'Wow, I need a million of something in a really big hurry,' you're probably in the wrong place," says owner Skip Horween III.

While the United States is the top producer of bovine hides in the world, it is also one of the top importers of leather goods, along with

Germany, France, and the United Kingdom. To put this in perspective, in 2012, according to the US Hide, Skin, and Leather Association, we exported 1.6 billion raw cowhides. In turn, we buy a lot of these hides back as shoes. According to the World Statistical Compendium for Raw Hides and Skins, Leather and Leather Footwear, compiled by the United Nations, 4,504.8 billion pairs of leather shoes were made worldwide in 2011. Of those, the United States imported 608.4 million pairs. That's almost two pairs (1.92) for every man, woman, and child.

Until recently, leather was considered a *luxury good*, meaning extravagant and treasured, whether it is a fancy parka made of squirrels or the president's cordovans. Today almost everyone, at least in America and Europe, expects to buy cheap or reasonably priced leather goods, whether shoes or handbags, belts or wallets. Leather's transformation from precious to cheap commodity has come at the expense of severe environmental problems, health hazards for workers, and poorer, even unnatural, quality, in that some leathers now consist of up to 20 percent chemical additives. We have, as economists say, externalized the costs. In addition, although leather has always been justified as a by-product of human meat consumption, its production depends on a growing international industry that relies on that consumption. As journalist Fran Hawthorne, author of *Ethical Chic: The Inside Story of the Companies We Think We Love*, states, it "requires killing cows."

The Abattoir

The *Hide and Skin Handbook* begins, rightly, with the killing floor. Before the oak tannins or chrome, the vegetable or aniline dyes, before piecing the leather into a Louis Vuitton bag or a Timberland boot, there is the animal—in most cases, one that was domesticated a thousand years ago—descending from the wilds of Scotland and England. The word *cattle* comes from *chattel*, meaning "that which one owns."

Herefords. Black Angus. The dairy cows and the drafts. I am standing in my living room, looking down at the red Natuzzi couch I bought secondhand a few years ago, wondering for the first time how many cows it took to make it. Five? Six? Also, there are the two ottomans. This morning, about to leave for my appointment at a slaughterhouse, I reflect on how I've never asked myself this before.

"Leather is made in the beamhouse," goes a saying in the trade, meaning where the initial processes of flaying, washing, fleshing, demanuring, and salting down the animal's body happen. These processes will determine the quality of the leather. The name *beamhouse* derives from the original stone or metal beams the skins hung from or over in order to scrape them. Since the handbook was written, the process has been mechanized, using rotating brine tubs and fleshing machines. "This process eliminates smelly old hide cellars," the handbook says. "With the manure, flesh and blood removed, the element of bacteria is eliminated and odor with it. Often, these procedures occurred in the same area in which the cow was killed and skinned." I realize now I have been working backward to this.

Driving through the Peace Valley in Montana, mid-October, cottonwoods turning yellow, snow already on the peaks of the distant Tobacco Root mountains, I am trying not to think of what's coming. Brent Richman, proprietor of Milligan Canyon Meats, has agreed to let me watch him flay a cow. Ranchland spreads out on either side of me, grass in its white, burnt phase. Today is Tuesday; "we slaughter on Tuesdays," Richman had said. Richman deals in "country hides," the by-product of cows sent to him by local ranchers who are selling beef to their neighbors as a favor; most of their cattle are shipped to feedlots in Iowa or Nebraska, where they are fattened and then butchered in large slaughterhouses. My drive takes an hour, through a valley I know very well but today am noticing differently. Instead of the deer I am usually scanning for, a coyote or northern harrier skimming the cut hay, at least a thousand Black Angus punctuate my sight in that still-life pose that always distinguishes the domesticated. I reach for my green leather handbag; it is made of cows. How have I never made this connection?

Milligan Canyon Meats is housed in an aluminum building, far from any town, on a dirt back road surrounded by sagebrush. When I pull up, a man in a rubber apron is standing outside in what looks like a holding pen, a few chickens tripping over his feet. *Run!* I would have said to the black cow standing passively next to him, knowing what I know now, but at the moment I am too nervous to think. I have bludgeoned trout with rocks and once hit a packrat that was caught, not dead, in a trap. I can bone a chicken, and I have no problem with blood. But I have never seen something so large be killed. "Brent?" I call out, and the man shakes his head. "Go to the front," he points, somewhat urgently. Unlike the tannery, which smelled like death, this place smells like fresh blood, potent but not spoiled. Brent Richman waves to me from behind a glass door and comes to greet me. He is in his early thirties, blond, white, Montana-looking. He's suspicious already, though he's also trying to be polite. How did I hear about him? he asks. I tell him about the rancher down the road from whom I buy meat, about the tannery I have just visited in San Antonio. He seems to relax. "So how much of this do you want to see?" he asks.

"All of it," I say. "I think."

"He just shot one," he says. "Let's go in."

Inside the slaughter room, two skinned and beheaded sides of beef hang from the ceiling on hooks, extra-large complete versions of what we see packaged in plastic in grocery stores, marbled with fat and pink, except that the nerves in both shoulders are still twitching. A man, slim, dark, serious, opens a bin connected to the outside, and a gigantic black steer flops out onto the floor. There is another man holding a hose, and neither of them will meet my gaze. Richman straps a shackle around one of the steer's legs and begins to hoist it up, but the animal begins jerking frantically. "It's not dead," he says to me. "I have to shoot it again." He aims a .22 at its head. The other men plug their ears. It continues to thrash for another few minutes, and we wait in silence until the nerves quit. "Look at its eyes, all glazed over," Richmond says, I suspect to reassure me. "That's dead."

When the steer finally stops jerking, he hoists it, and the "knife-man"—Richman never introduces me to either of the men—slits its throat. The blood gushes, the body jerks, and the knifeman, sharpener in one hand and blade in the other, cuts off each ear, then slices around the neck and pulls the hood off. Next the body is lowered onto a "cradle." On its back, its legs flapped open, the steer looks like a large teddy bear, vulnerable, furry, and big-bellied, still animal, still something I can identify with. Still flesh and blood, as we say. Quickly, the four legs are sliced off below the knees. "Both the fell cutter and the rumper do most of their work by holding the hide tight with one hand and by working inside with the other hand. In other words, about 50 percent of their work is done by feeling rather than seeing," says the handbook. I watch Richman and the knifeman slip the skin expertly from the flesh. The entire process is done in less than fifteen minutes.

Spreading the hide on the floor, Richman explains that the tanners want a "square product," following the industry standard. Steers are what the tanneries want, he says; cows' skins are thinner, and bulls are tough. But he gets the same price for all of them: thirty dollars each. A "hide guy" picks them up weekly, washes, fleshes, and cures them with salt, then sends them by truck to "a tannery in Chicago." I try to imagine these three men without me here, killing and skinning and separating cows all day, the boom box playing country and western, cow after cow, the third man rinsing the carcass and floor with a hose, each one knowing what to do, what comes next, and doing it silently. I ask Richman how he learned to do this; he points to one of the men. Where did you learn it, I ask, and Richman answers for him: Oregon, Montana, all over the West.

For the employees at Milligan Canyon Meats, slaughtering fifteen to twenty cattle once a week, all from the ranchlands that surround them, at a pace that enables them to work conscientiously, the job is not unpleasant. They clearly work in an environment that is safe and that operates under the rules of the US Humane Methods of Livestock Slaughter Act. (Under these terms, the animal must be rendered "insensible to pain" by a single blow before hoisted or cut; these terms don't, however, apply to birds—chickens, turkeys, etc.) I am well aware that most people don't obtain their meat from places like this. I am also aware that cattle ranchers, including the one who sells his beef to me, could not keep their thousands of acres free from development if it were not for selling their cows each year to the nationwide supply chain of beef or selling hides to a global market that processes them.

Recently, films depicting horrific animal cruelty in industrial slaughterhouses have proliferated: animals skinned or plucked before being killed, crowded into cubicles or feedlots and force-fed pesticide-laden corn, an energy exhaustive and polluting process in itself. For the thousands of people employed in these packing plants, whether here in the United States or in Brazil or China, the killing of cattle or chickens or pigs is not the worst part of it. According to Human Rights Watch, one of the most dangerous jobs in America is industrial slaughterhouse work: "After slaughter, the carcasses hurl along evisceration and disassembly lines as workers hurriedly saw and cut them at unprecedented volume and pace." Most of the workers in the major US packing plants are immigrants, fearful of demanding occupational safety standards or even compensation for injuries. Describing Nebraska Beef Ltd., the seventh-largest beef packing plant in the country, located on the outskirts of Omaha, the report states, "Nebraska Beef has annual sales of more than $800 million and capacity for slaughtering three thousand head of beef per day. The company employs 1,100 workers, none of whom are union-represented."

In addition to the suffering of animals and workers, the industrial killing of cows presents another problem. This is the fact that cattle need cattle ranches. A 2009 Greenpeace study found that the Amazonian rainforest of Mato Grosso, Brazil, is being cleared at alarming rates in order for farmers to run cattle. Despite the Forest Code of 1965, which asks ranchers to maintain a ratio of eighty trees to twenty head of cattle, one hectare of rainforest is lost to ranching every eighteen seconds, and by 2018, Brazil wanted to double the herds. Brazil is second only to the United States in exporting bovine hides, yet neither is known as a major manufacturer of leather goods. *Italian leather*, a phrase that connotes high quality, does not mean Italian cows. As Lucy Siegel writes in the *Guardian,* if all the accessories and shoes—eleven billion pairs a year—that claimed to be Italian "really were from Italian cattle, they would overrun the country. They would drink from the Trevi fountain and chew the cud in Piazza San Marco."

Ethical leather? It is a question complicated, as many writers have said, by our expectation of cheap meat and cheap shoes, and by a global market system that expects gigantic returns. It is a question complicated by the ancient history of domestication—none of these cows or sheep would be able to survive on their own—and by our growing population and diminishing rural areas. Add the energy and environmental costs of manufacturing nonleather shoes, which depend on the petrochemical industry for their plastic material, and there is no easy answer.

Some companies in the United States and in Europe, however, are working together to come up with better methods. For instance, shoe manufacturers—which use 85 percent of leather worldwide—have formed the Leather Working Group, which monitors tanneries for occupational and environmental health and whose members, including Timberland, New Balance, Clarks, and Nike, agree to use only the top-rated tanneries and to refuse leather coming from places such as Hazaribagh. This has put pressure on other tanneries to clean up their plants and on the fashion industry to learn what happens at each stage of their production (most clothing manufacturers in Europe and the United States subcontract their work outside their own countries). After the 2009 Greenpeace report that revealed major leather manufacturers' complicity in rainforest destruction, a few designers initiated the Green Carpet Challenge, to raise the profile of ethics in the global fashion industry. Run by a company called Eco-Age, it promotes sustainability and social welfare as a value. Gucci, for instance, is making bags guaranteed not to be from a deforested rainforest and to be made in Tuscany, not a foreign sweatshop. The fact that "sustainability" has become a selling point, albeit only for more expensive brands so far, moves the industry toward better environmental standards.

Tonight, after my trip to the abattoir—an elegant-sounding word that brings to mind a piece of furniture one might find in a French bedroom—I try to sleep, and the half-dead steer keeps flopping onto the concrete floor. I was impressed, as I always am, by the skill and intelligence of workers like Richman and his employees. That there are men and women working on the outskirts of cities like San Antonio, in the ghetto of Kanpur, on the edge of a hayfield in southwestern Montana—all around us, if we but ask—to make our shoes and our wallets and our coats, our *luxury goods*, is something most people don't think about, and now I do. I had driven home, made lunch, read a few articles, all ordinary activities. Yet the death of the cow, now that it is over, keeps crossing my mind. Tonight, sleepless, as I turn on the light, the first thing I see are my two pairs of leather boots lined up along the wall, my two leather bags, a black belt lying on the floor, as if they had all come out of hiding to awaken me. When had I—or had I?—arranged them thus?

As an educator in my younger days, I was always astonished at how little urban students knew about where their food came from. "Where does milk come from?" I would ask third-graders, and, of course, they would say "The store." Ignorance about the origins of our clothing is much more extensive. Leafing through a collection of fourteen academic essays examining the cultural, psychological, and sexual significance of shoes, I search the index for some reference to the animal, any animal: *animal, cow, hide, goat, skin*. There is none. There are examinations of fetishism, to be sure: of Imelda Marcos's twelve hundred pairs of shoes and Marie Antoinette's five hundred. We don't see the cow as a source of our shoes, nor the child who tanned them, because, by the time they get to us, they are no longer skins but...something else, an expression of sex or job, politics or status. Like Tutankhamun, whose fanciest slippers glided through air because he had people to carry him, we, too, have lost touch with the ground.

2 Wool

Little Lamb who made thee
Dost thou know who made thee
WILLIAM BLAKE

Domestication

Twenty to thirty thousand years ago in Babylon or Sumer or Persia, a woman must have sat in a summer meadow overgrown with tall grasses, idly picking two or three blades and rolling them together against her thigh. Within seconds, she had string, something to tie back her hair or weave a basket or thread through holes in animal skins to cinch them. The knowledge of string-making—twisting a few pieces of fiber together to make them stronger—must have come like this, simply, by picking up the materials at hand: grass, flax stems, goat hair caught on a barbed branch of raspberry. "So powerful, in fact, is simple string in taming the world to human will and ingenuity," writes Elizabeth Wayland Barber in her comprehensive history of textiles, *Women's Work: The First 20,000 Years*, "that I suspect it to be the unseen weapon that allowed the human race to...move out into every eco-niche on the globe in the Upper Paleolithic."

Spinning supplies one of our oldest metaphors. Spider Grandmother spun the Hopi world into being by gathering the dew into her web and flinging it into the night sky to become stars. Arachne, on the other hand, was changed into a spider for daring to boast that her talent in spinning and weaving wool was greater than that of the goddess Athena. Clotho, one of the three ancient Fates, spun thread that was sometimes golden but more often blood-red. And then there is Rumpelstiltskin, who spun straw into gold for the daughter of a miller, bartering for first her necklace, then her ring, and finally the promise of her firstborn child. (Spinning animal hair into fibers that can be knitted or woven has, indeed, been like gold to many people. "The English word *robe* comes from *rob* because clothing was one of the most frequent forms of plunder in the Middle Ages," says Barber.)

It might even be that women were largely responsible for domestication itself. Because they needed to stay close to home to care for the children rather than to venture abroad to hunt, they would be the ones to notice the molting wool left behind, the friendlier wolf, the sprouts growing from the pits of rotting fruit under the tree. Animal hair, made out of the same proteins and amino acids as our own, was gathered from shrubs and thorns after the goat or sheep or yak's annual molt. The spinning of those fibers into thread was also uniquely suited to women's lives. It was mindless (their minds had to be on the safety of the children), it could be done while walking from camp to camp, and it could be picked up and put down in an instant. It took a lot of animals shedding their hair or wool in the spring, and a lot of hands gathering it, cleaning it, and then spinning it with a stick and a dowel—the earliest spindles—to supply enough fabric for a family. In this sense, women's work must have been endless.

Let me tell you about cashmere. It is spun from the softest undercoat of goats, the hair closest to its skin, functioning much like the down under the feathers of geese. In the Himalayas, in Mongolia, in the cold high desert climates where most are raised, the inner coat mitigates the harsh weather, but once the weather warms, the goats begin to shed. For generations, they have been herded by nomads, as they still are, the shedding hairs raked out by female hands. The finest fibers come from the neck and are crimped rather than wavy, which gives the fabric its characteristic lightness and lift. It takes the hair from three goats, producing four ounces each, to make a cashmere sweater. Today

I am wearing three goats, their naturally lustrous white or tan hairs dyed black. It is the first thing I reach for on cold mornings.

The word *cashmere* comes from the Vale of Kashmir, where, in the fifteenth century, more than fifty thousand people were employed in its processing after the goat hair was carted down from the mountains of Ladakh. Eight times warmer than sheep's wool and about that many times softer, cashmere clothing was once only available to royalty. Before continental Europe discovered it, it was wound in Egyptian turbans, fitted into robes of honor in Iran, and given by the Mongols to their allies. The characteristic "teardrop with bent tip" pattern that we now call paisley—which has been variously described as a flower, a pine, a cone, or a palm—was brought to Kashmir by immigrant Persian weavers. Their weaving was introduced to the French court in 1796 when Kashmir's governor gave a shawl to a visitor from Baghdad, who in turn gave it to an Egyptian royal family, who then gave it to Napoleon. The pashmina shawl (*pashmina* is Persian for wool) became a craze in Europe when Josephine began wearing it. Napoleon is said to have given his second wife, Marie-Louise, seventeen of them.

Another prized fiber, mohair, is made from a distinctive, single-coated goat, the Angora, which originated in Ankara, Turkey, hence its name. The Angora is a fuzzy-looking goat that resembles a sheep. These goats, which can produce up to a quarter of their body weight in wool, are usually sheared twice a year. The resulting fiber is warm, with a high luster. The original Ankaras were small and white. During the Industrial Revolution they were bred with big, colored goats so there would be more wool to sell. Then they were bred back to white to meet the demands of the dyers—a one in five thousand chance, given that color is a recessive gene. My mohair blend V-neck is dust-colored and whiskery; it has no holes, though I have worn it outside and in for ten years. The Angora goat is not to be confused with the product called *angora*. That material is collected from domesticated Angora rabbits, which look like fluffy couch pillows, peeking out from the satiny, long, white plumes they were bred for. Highly sought after, Angora rabbit fur is used in the finest sweaters, scarves, and baby clothes.

And then there are the outliers. *Alpaca* is made from the hair of a smaller cousin of the llama, bred high in the Andes. Wool sheared from alpaca has no lanolin; it is thick and thermal. Most alpaca fiber, when not made into blankets, is blended with silk or cashmere to make it softer. The vicuña is a wild camel, related to the llama and alpaca, which lives in Peru, Bolivia, and the mountains of Argentina and Chile. Elegant, lithe, weighing less than 140 pounds, it has the finest and most expensive fleece in the world. (Unprocessed wool from the vicuña averages $300 to $350 a kilo [2.2 pounds].) Vicuñas were almost extinct in the 1960s, due to overhunting and poaching, but a concerted effort by the countries of Chile and Peru has established national preserves, where they are now thriving. Every two or three years, villagers in Ucha Ucha, Bolivia, and Lucanas, Peru, round up the vicuñas on foot or by motorcycle, shear them, and release them. Descendants perhaps of the Incas who used to herd them, these villagers sell the wool to support themselves and promote conservation efforts for the vicuña.

The musk ox, which survived the ice age, still lives in Alaska and other areas within the Arctic Circle. A prehistoric-looking animal weighing between six hundred and a thousand pounds, with long, molting layers of brown dreadlocks, it grows an undercoat called by its Yup'ik and Inupiaq name, *qiviut*. For obvious reasons, it is one of the rarest fibers in the world. Qiviut is so delicate it can only be used for scarves and hats. I have a handful of it I purchased in Anchorage. Mouse-colored, it sits weightless and quivering in my palm. Besides the vicuña, the musk ox is one of the few undomesticated animals from which we gain fiber. But how to shear a musk ox? According to the Oomingmak Musk Ox Producers' Co-op, which contracts with Yup'ik villagers to knit their products, most qiviut is collected by Alaska Natives when the animal sheds in the spring, gathered at the large Animal Research Station in Fairbanks, or bought from the

Palmer Musk Ox Farm, where workers carefully comb an animal that "cannot yet be reliably called domestic." The Oomingmak Co-op is not the only place to buy qiviut fiber, yarn, or clothing made from it, but it is one of the best, given that its proceeds supplement the mostly subsistence lifestyle of Native women in very remote villages on the Alaskan tundra.

And finally, let me tell you about sheep's wool, which accounts for the majority of the world's animal fiber. Wool has several qualities that distinguish it from goat hair or rabbit fur, though it is made out of the same protein—keratin. Wool grows in clusters called staples, and its fiber is crimped, which makes it easier to spin because the crimps stick together. This also creates air pockets when the fiber is spun that retain heat, which allow it to breathe. Wool is water-absorbent and fire-retardant. It can absorb almost a third of its weight in water, and it smolders rather than flames when torched. Unlike bast fibers (produced from plants like flax and cotton), wool comes naturally in a range of colors and can also be easily overdyed. Plus, it smells good. No one has been able to find a synthetic fiber—though most synthetics have been modeled after wool—that is as cool when hot, as warm when cold, as fast-drying and as insulating.

And wool has another advantage: it comes from sheep. Unlike goats, which are recalcitrant, or musk oxen, which are dangerous, or cattle, which are large, domesticated sheep are docile and small enough for a small man or woman to manage. They are easily herded and, as long as one has access to grassland, cheap to raise. "Most people think sheep are dumb because they flock," says Kammy Johnson, one of the many local sheep women I've met in Montana, "but what would a sheep be most afraid of? Predators. They can't run fast, they have no defenses, but together they can form a formidable mass that's hard to penetrate." Sheep have a highly refined social structure and are consequently loyal. "A grandmother ewe can recognize her confused granddaughter at a gate and will wait to guide her through," Johnson says. "Twins are close forever. A mother will call them in to feed at the same time." Sheep have provided *Homo sapiens* with milk, meat in the form of mutton and lamb, hides, and fiber since the Neolithic revolution, over twelve thousand years ago. It is their fiber, though, that has transformed the course of human history, its trade enabling the expansion of cities, the founding of empires, the turn from wild grasslands to pasture, and the beginnings of the Industrial Revolution. Along the way, the animal too was transformed.

➤

Wild sheep and goats originated in the steep mountains of Europe and the dry steppes of North Africa and Eurasia. Two major species of sheep, the long-haired Mouflons (*Ovis aries*) of Europe and the "steppe sheep" or Urials (*Ovis orientalis*) of Southwest and Central Asia, are thought to be the ancestors of the more than 1.2 billion domesticated sheep we now find grazing all over the world. As the ice sheets melted about eleven thousand years ago, the wild sheep quickly spread or were herded to Eastern Europe, Russia, and India. (Merino, one of the most popular breeds, in Spanish means "a fugitive without a regular home.") Sheep are ruminants; they have a four-chambered stomach that functions as a big fermentation vat, allowing them to eat grass. They have split, or cloven, hooves that give them incredible dexterity and traction on steep slopes. Like the goat, camel, yak, and the early forms of cattle, initially sheep were herded not for their coats but for their meat, milk, and hides. As they became domesticated, starting around 10,000 BCE, they became smaller, retaining qualities such as the docility for which they are known and the child's propensity to be happy in close proximity to its kin. Like children, they prefer moving from a dark area to a lighter one. Like most of us, they prefer moving downhill. Animals with these qualities are much easier to tend and, consequently, to own. Sheep and humans proliferated.

Paging through a field guide to sheep breeds, I am amazed at how different the animals appear in real life compared with my stereotypical image of them: the cloud-outline that depicts sheep in children's picture books or the dun-colored lumps grazing slowly and forever across the arid miles of eastern Montana and Wyoming. In contrast to its distant cousins, each breed seems distinct, an individual, not at all like the homogeneous, passive flocks that serve as a metaphor for people who are blind followers and lack will. In the photographs, I encounter rams with curved horns and Dalmatian faces and ewes with long dreadlocks, their white or striped spats showing under a curtain of twisted gray rope. In one picture, six Cheviots move across a green pasture in Wales, their bodies round as balls. The sheep's coats range from the brown velvet of the Moorit, "red as the moors," to the funny shag rugs of the Shetland; the Devon Longwool, with so much hair in its eyes it looks like it wouldn't be able to see; the Cotswold, with its curled bangs used for dolls' wigs; or the Faroese, with its dirty blond, long permanent waves, all of them stuffed into their coats so tightly that their coats don't seem to grow from them but to have been sewn around them, making it look impossible for them to even move.

Sheep are the species with the most diversity: their over five hundred different breeds make up 25 percent of all the animal breeds on earth. How this happened is not a simple matter but a millennia-old process directed by both the sheep and the shepherds. "It is a mistake," Anne Perkins says, "to think that we are in control of the domestication process. The reintroducing of domesticated animals into the wild—such as the wolves—has shown that certain animals participate in their own domestication. In anthrozoology, we call it 'partnering with the animal.'" Perkins is an intense, wiry woman in her sixties, with long silver hair and a penchant for extravagant hats. She founded and directs Carroll College's anthrozoology department in Helena, Montana, the only undergraduate degree program of its kind in the country. Anthrozoology, a new cross-disciplinary field, is the study of the "human-animal bond" over time.

When Perkins began her studies, the field of anthrozoology didn't exist. Many biologists didn't even regard humans as animals. "They saw a definite split," she says, "human and nonhuman." I set up an interview with Perkins because I have been thinking about breeding. Wool, unlike leather, is a direct result of domestication, hence its use must have signaled a sea change in how human beings see our place in nature. What I mean is that most wild sheep were covered with hair, called *kemp*—not the soft material that is now spun into our suits, scarves, and sweaters. Sheep had to change a lot for us to use their wool. That change took thousands of years. It changed us, too. In an essay titled "Ten Thousand Years of Crisis," deep ecologist Paul Shepard claims that the human turn from hunting animals to taking care of them precipitated for us a cycle of "drudgery and catastrophe," turning our attentions from the movement of animals in the wild to the movement of the seasons, which invariably bring drought or flood, changing our nomadic days to the tedium of repetitive labor. If that is true, what did animals lose or gain when we tamed *them*?

"*Domesticated*," Perkins corrects me, "does not mean *tamed*. Tamed means that an animal is no longer frightened of or dangerous to humans. It sometimes means that we have trained them to obey our commands. Domestication, on the other hand, means we *genetically alter* a species, breeding for certain characteristics that are useful to us, which might be taste, appearance, color, tame-ability, as well as other behaviors, such as, in sheep, the propensity to flock." Unlike taming, she says, domestication requires many generations. And not all species are suitable for it. "The difference between domestication and taming is that, with the former, the animal is bred to *thrive* in captivity, not only to *survive*," Perkins says. There are only a handful of species that actually thrive under human care, including animals that have been crossbred. Some, such as horses and cats, can revert at a moment's notice back to the wild. Some, like the zebra and buffalo, are untamable.

Most archaeologists believe that the domestication of key plants and animals occurred within ten thousand years across Eurasia and the Americas. Our seemingly instantaneous transformation from hunter-gatherers to farmers and shepherds—the so-called Neolithic revolution—happened between ten thousand and fifteen thousand years ago, a fraction of the millions of years that humans have roamed the earth. Biologists claim that dogs began to diverge from the gray wolf, *Canis lupus familiaris*, between fifteen thousand and forty thousand years ago. Of the larger mammals, next came sheep and goats in West and Central Asia, encompassing the modern countries of Iraq, Turkey, Jordan, Syria, and Israel, nine thousand to eleven thousand years ago. Then came the ancestors of the present pig and cattle (the famous aurochs painted on the cave walls of Lascaux) in Eurasia and North Africa.

For those ancestral animals that could be domesticated—bred for human use, not simply tamed, though taming probably came first—the process went surprisingly smoothly. Wolves, for instance, the only direct progenitor of the domestic dog, are naturally curious about people and followed them from camp to camp. They are capable of eating bones left behind by humans in their middens, and, as great hunters themselves, they led our ancestors to game. Historically, those animals that were less afraid of humans found themselves better fed, and those that were easier to herd or corral or live with were the ones humans didn't eat first. Perkins explains that scientists call this type of symbiotic relationship between animals *mutualism*. Unlike a parasitic relationship, where one species benefits at the expense of another, or *commensalism*, when one benefits but does not hurt the other—such as the flea feeding on feathers of a bird, egrets and other birds feeding on insects turned up by grazing mammals, or, in the plant world, vines, orchids, and ferns growing in a host tree—in mutualism both species benefit from their relationship.

Animals, interestingly, also participated in their own domestication in a less conscious way. Most mammals, including humans, go through a long developmental period in which they grow out of their juvenile characteristics and become more adultlike. Within any population, however, there are those whose immature traits don't progress, locking them into a state they don't grow beyond. *Neotony* refers to the retention of juvenile traits into adulthood. In the case of wild animals, it might mean that the individual is smaller, with a shorter snout and smaller teeth, and a larger head in proportion to its body. These traits render it less harmful to humans, and thus would have made it an animal we would more likely consider domesticating. Other qualities that we preferred, and still prefer, hint at our maternal instincts: cuteness and smallness, as well as playfulness and docility—childishness, in other words. Those animals that exhibit "care-soliciting behavior," such as begging for food, also got our attention.

Often, Perkins says, biologists don't see animal-people relationships as evidence of mutualism because they don't regard humans as animals, yet she thinks mutualism could be a way to think about domestication as advantageous to both species. Domestication has allowed both sheep and humans to expand and to thrive. According to *Biology Online Dictionary*, to thrive, as opposed to merely to survive, is "to increase in bulk or stature; to grow vigorously or luxuriantly, as a plant; to flourish; as, young cattle thrive in rich pastures; trees thrive in a good soil." The population of most animals in the wild is circumscribed by limited availability of food and water, as well as dangers from illness, weather, and predators. Domestication eliminates most of those uncertainties as people tend to their animals, feeding, watering, and sheltering them, even inoculating them against disease. Although the milk and meat from domesticated sheep and goats certainly contributed to many early humans' survival, they could not have been a strong driver of population growth—they could not have allowed humans to *thrive*—given that shepherding is an exhausting, time-consuming task with meager rewards. Selection of sheep for qualities inherent in their wool doesn't seem to have happened until around 6000 BCE in Iran. It was then that raising sheep began to pay off for us.

Wild sheep, as I mentioned earlier, were predominantly hairy or "kempy." These short, coarse kemps would shatter if one tried to twist them. (Some primitive breeds still have an overcoat of kemp.)

Over time, some sheep developed coats that were softer, straighter, and longer—in other words, woolier—and that would molt in the spring. Because these sheep supplied fiber that could be spun, they were the ones that were not eaten. Eventually, after a couple thousand years of breeding, the kemp disappeared, the sheep no longer molted, and their coats could be shorn. These new "woolly sheep" made their first appearance in the Mediterranean around 3500 BCE, where they became instantly coveted.

As a fiber, wool differed from plain flax (linen) in that it could be easily dyed. In addition, it already came in a variety of shades: cream, charcoal, black, brown. This meant that suddenly weaving could incorporate pattern. By 2300 BCE, according to Barber, Crete had become famous for herding and weaving, exporting wool dyed yellow with saffron, crimson from the insect cochineal, blue from the flower called dyer's woad, and purple from an extract of murex sea shells (which made purple so precious that only royals could wear it). It was the days of women out on a saffron hunt and of Helen of Troy spinning purple cloth in Sparta. Once trading began, however, women couldn't keep up with the demand. Crete began to use slaves, mostly women and children captured in war, to spin and weave, and so it goes—an ancient precursor to woolen mill workers in the Industrial Revolution, one of whom was my own grandmother, who met her husband, a mill mechanic, while weaving suit cloth for practically nothing in the woolen mills of northern Indiana.

Wool trading began in earnest in Europe around 476 CE and, as in Crete, became a source of wealth. Trading fairs across continental Europe lasted for weeks. England and Spain were the main producers, Italy and Belgium the main processors. Wool made England, already a great source of numerous breeds of sheep, into a powerful nation. The Lord Chancellor of the British House of Commons today literally sits on a sack of wool, the "woolsack," symbolizing the fiber's role in the spread of the British Empire. To wear wool was to be patriotic. Consider this trajectory:

1571: An English man could be fined for not wearing a wool cap.

1662: Mourning clothes, by law, had to be made of wool.

1667: Everyone had to be buried in wool.

In the twelfth century a tribe of Arabic Moors introduced a breed of fine-wool sheep, the merino, to Spain. The merinos' soft wool became so coveted that anyone caught smuggling one of the sheep out of the country's borders received the death penalty. Eventually Spain relinquished some of its stock to its European neighbors, who crossbred them with sheep in their African colonies. In 1492, Columbus brought a flock of Spanish sheep to the shores of North America. Cortés was responsible for spreading sheep across Mexico and the West. In 1788, the Dutch in South Africa sent a load to Australia. By 1810, there were thirty thousand merinos thriving there. Today wool production is a highly lucrative international industry. For the sheep, domestication has equally been propitious. In 2006, there was one sheep for every six people on earth.

Wool Making

The Hilger Ranch lies right under the Sleeping Giant, a mountain that eerily resembles a woman sleeping on her back, her craggy nose and large breast profiled against the skyline, seemingly capable of rising and lumbering through the Helena Valley thirty miles south of it. Bordering the ranch is the historic Gates of the Mountains, a portion of the Missouri River that flows through high sandstone cliffs marked with pictographs and thousand-year-old trails, so named by Lewis and Clark, who camped along its banks in 1805. When I arrive for the annual sheep shearing, it is an unusually warm afternoon in early March, at least sixty degrees.

Outside a large, weathered barn, I meet a group of four women standing around what I recognize from books as a "skirting table." Jeanne deCoster, tall and tan, with long white hair and a young, open face, introduces herself first. She is the owner of a yarn company based in California called Elemental Affects. Dressed in a patchwork vest, hand-knitted with alpaca, a smoke-colored cashmere sweater, and jeans, she says has been coming here to buy the ranch's wool for fourteen years. Though she is here to hand-select what she wants and reject what she doesn't, the atmosphere seems one of camaraderie and shared information. DeCoster's company, she tells me, specializes in developing yarns from "primitive breeds of sheep," the North American Shetland and an heirloom Romney, as well as a blend of merino and silk. Cathy Campbell, who is owner and manager of the ranch, raises over four hundred Shetland sheep, making hers the largest flock of Shetlands in North America.

Shetlands are an ancient breed from the Shetland Islands off the northern coast of Scotland. Their wool is known for being so fine that traditional shawls knit from them could pass through a wedding ring. Like the original wild sheep, they still produce two coats, a soft inner one and a longer, coarser outer one. In addition, they come in multiple colors. Stapled to a fence post nearby is a list of eleven of them, some in the old Norse language still used for grading: *emsket* (a bluish gray), *shaela* (a charcoal gray), *musket* (a pale grayish brown), *mioget* (yellowish brown), and *moorit* (reddish brown). Behind me under a temporary tent, bins are filled with airy piles of shorn wool labeled with these names, as well as with the words *white*, *black*, and *fawn*.

Huddling together in the barnyard nearby, naked, white-skinned, and nicked, are several dozen poodle-sized sheep. I hear the buzz of the shearing tools begin and proceed to the dark, cool barn where, over the noise, I introduce myself to a stout, gray-haired woman in overalls who I assume is Campbell. Three men—two Peruvians and one Montanan, I learn later—each bend over a pregnant ewe, wedged on her backside between his legs. Their little tummies straddled, the sheep stare ahead unblinking and don't flinch.

Most large ranches in the West employ shearers and shepherds from Peru or Chile, whose ancestors learned their trade from Spanish Basques. It is estimated that about fifteen hundred shepherds spend the winter in the American West, working on guest visas under three-year contracts, flying back home, as these two do, a couple of times a year. Like much agricultural work in America, sheepherding has become an immigrant's job—low-paying, dirty, physically demanding—one that most Americans aren't willing to do if they have other options. Denis, who has been working for Campbell for sixteen years, is fast and expert, shaving the fleece so that it falls all in one piece, the ewe barely moving until he lets her go and she runs out through the chute into the corral with the others. Master shearer, shepherd, and adviser, he leans forward over a swing attached to the ceiling, a tool that I imagine saves his back from injury and allows him to shear sheep after sheep for hours without a break. His apprentice seems to be having a harder time getting his *emsket* mother to stop squirming. There are tricks to shearing—placing a boot just so next to a sheep's leg to steady her, pressing down on a hip to quiet her—that take years to master. The apprentice leaves a sheep full of small nicks that bleed, but she, too, doesn't grimace and sprints out the door when she is done. "They don't seem traumatized by it," I say to Becky Weed, owner of a spinning mill and sheep ranch a couple hours southeast, who has joined us inside because she is curious about Shetlands. She smiles widely: "I think they like it." By the time this day is done, Campbell says, they will have shorn 136 bred ewes.

When a fleece is shorn correctly, it comes off the sheep in one piece, looking like a sheepskin rug, though without the skin, remarkably larger than the small creature now quivering outside without its coat. An expert shearer will also cut out any unusable parts, such as soiled lower leg wool, butt bits, or groin and belly wool. Weed gathers the fleece from the floor, taking it outside, and Campbell sweeps so that no shreds of *emsket* will get mixed up with the *moorit* to be shorn next. I follow Weed out to the skirting table. In an expert motion, she unfurls the fleece onto the table, the side closest to the skin down. Skirting is the process of hand-removing stains, cuts, and vegetable matter from the wool before it is ready to sell. Consequently, the skirting table is a frame with an open top across which PVC pipes have been spaced an inch or so apart, allowing the wool debris to fall between them. Inspecting the wool she may buy or decline, deCoster immediately begins picking at it, pulling out tufts around the neck that are too short or stuck with manure or stained with blood. We flip the fleece over. Topside are the tufts of long hair, sometimes three or four inches long; on the other, the dense fur of the undercoat.

Each fleece is pinned with a slip of paper recording the sheep's name, age, and shearing history. DeCoster is in charge of "grading" each fleece. "Too long," she says, examining the three-inch guard hairs. (Shetland wool is processed with both hair and wool.) "Like last year," says Mackenzie, a young field hand, who is holding the clipboard and doing the recording. "Fair"; "strong"; "small, consider culling": deCoster takes less than three seconds to determine the grade. She will be paying the same amount per pound for all the wool she selects, whether excellent or good, black or white; this grading helps the ranch make decisions regarding future breeding or culling, and provides the buyer with higher-quality wool to choose from in the future.

Because breeding sheep involves producing more and more sheep— it's not an old folks' home, sheep breeders are known to say—the ranch naturally has to decide which sheep won't make it to the next year. Some will be sold as lambs for food. For the older ewes, rams, and werthers (castrated males), their meat will be processed by a local butcher and, since, as Campbell says, hardly anyone eats mutton in America, it will be given to the homeless.

"High veg," deCoster calls out, fingering a large black sheep clotted with straw, thorns, and seedheads. "Consider culling." Half the weight of wool is not wool at all, she explains. It is lanolin (sheep grease), burrs, dirt, twigs, and sheep sweat weighted with salt. The black fleece is as foamy as fiberglass insulation. (In fact, wool, known through history for its thermal properties, is sold as highly effective and biodegradable house insulation, albeit more expensive than the conventional kind.) Its smell is disagreeable, like human sweat gone stale. Grass clippings, tiny dried leaves, thorns, bark, and mud are flecked through it. The wool is viscous to the touch, almost wet, though it doesn't compact. I ask if some sheep get dirtier than others or if it is just that they unintentionally wandered into a thicket. "You know those people who seem to always look disheveled, as if they had just gotten out of bed?" deCoster asks. I laugh. "There's a saying in the industry: 'Dirty children hang out with dirty children.'"

Wool refers to the entire fleece but also to the extra-fine fibers it consists of. Fibers are measured in micron counts (a micron is one-millionth of one meter). Most usable wool falls between 10 and 35 microns. In comparison, a human hair averages 50 microns. Some sheep "locks," which is what a tuft of wool comes out as, are crimped, some straight. Some are an inch long, some seven, eight, up to sixteen inches, the tips sometimes darker, as if a blond's dyed hair was growing out. Meticulous records of breeding and of the resultant fleece are kept by most serious breeders, in what Campbell calls the "world's biggest genetic experiment." Shetlands are called "primitive" because their breed has somehow escaped the push for improved breeds that swept the market in the wake of the nineteenth century. "Improved" usually means bred to have qualities friendly to industrial production: uniformity and stability.

There used to be few true black sheep on the Hilger ranch, Campbell tells me, but tastes have changed, and buyers like deCoster are more interested in naturally occurring colors rather than toxic dyes. "There is a growing awareness," deCoster explains, "of where our food and now clothing comes from. Ten years ago, about 2 percent of the market wanted natural colors or primitive blends. 'It's not soft!' they'd complain, those who were used to commercially bred, soft, white merino. But people are asking more often about the animal, how it was raised, how it was treated; though that percentage is still low, I'd say it's about 25 percent now."

By the end of the week, much of the fourteen hundred pounds of sheared fleece will be loaded onto a flatbed and trucked a hundred miles west to a ranch in Drummond that will scour it. Next it will be sent to a spinning mill in Massachusetts that has machines that can handle the long and short fibers of the Shetland. It will then be sent to California, where deCoster will dye and sell the yarn over the internet, when it will again be shipped in skeins to knitters across the world, knitters who are willing to pay the price that these individualized and local steps require, who are concerned about the land, the process, the people, even the individual animal from which their fibers come. "They want to be assured their wool is 'green,' that the processing of their wool has low impact on the earth. They like to think about what flock it comes from," deCoster says.

"Instead of saying 'It's good with gravy,' as I do," teases Randy, a volunteer.

⌇

Thirteen Mile Lamb and Wool Company lies below the snow-capped Bridger Mountains outside of Bozeman, Montana. The two-lane road I take to get to it is surprisingly busy for being bordered by thousands of acres of ranch and farmland dotted with grazing sheep and cattle; the university town, ten miles distant, is spreading into suburbs. Off-road: two eagles; a handful of antelope; a rough-legged hawk on every power pole; two deer curled against each other, still as lawn ornaments, below the cottonwoods; and, in a stubble field, a large herd of feeding elk, richly brown.

When I pull into the driveway, Becky Weed, whom I met around the skirting table at the Hilger Ranch a week ago, is already waiting to greet me outside her stately old whitewashed barn, which is peeling and lovely in the spring light. Her farm, which she co-owns with her husband, Dave Tyler, was one of the first three pioneer ranches in the valley. It now houses one of the only three remaining woolen mills—or "natural fiber processing mills"—in the state. Weed waves, a flushed, small, fit woman in her forties with blond hair, wearing jeans, a hand-knit plum woolen vest, and under it, a tan wool sweater. Shreds of fleece cling to her shoulders and hair. Setting up this tour has been challenging, requiring at least ten phone calls with my beginning, "Is this a bad time?" and her answering, "Yes."

We enter the barn, where, in a small alcove, her "storefront" racks are filled with hanks of yarn plant-dyed the color of straw, alfalfa, mint, thistle, and soft blue. On the floor against the wall sit fifty or so garbage bags of raw wool: white, darkest brown, a mottled gray. Weed shows me to the back of the barn, to the washing vat, a stainless steel tank where the raw wool is bathed in very hot water to release the lanolin. All sheep are greasy to a greater or lesser extent. Washing releases the lanolin—the same product in some of our hand lotions— as well as manure, twigs, and dirt. Becky switches the tank's cycle into gear, and a gentle motion agitates the wool without muscling it into felt. Some wool has to be washed two or three times. A biodegradable cleanser is used, with a mild citric base, because the water is recycled into her fields. Thirteen Mile Lamb and Wool Company has a bank of solar panels mounted on the roof, a system they designed, which provides most of the hot water they need.

There are two ways to prepare clean wool for spinning, Weed explains to me. One is to card it, with either a hand carder or an industrial machine. I watch as she spreads the raw clean fleece evenly over a flat screen that then moves into the carder by conveyor belt. Inside are tiny bristles that pull the fibers apart as wind might tease apart a cloud. (The word *card* comes from the Latin word for "thistle," which is what ancient women used to separate the fibers of wool or goat.) Carding creates a fluffier, warmer product because of the air pockets it creates. When the carded fleece comes out the other side, in long, narrow, diaphanous ribbons, it is called *roving*. Spun into thread, the roving becomes *woolen yarn*.

Weed pulls a bit of fiber from a bag of unwashed wool and begins twisting it as teenage girls do a strand of hair. "Now pull on it," she says. With all my strength I pull, and it doesn't break. Wool that is combed rather than carded is called *worsted*. Combing, with either a

smaller pin-draft machine or a larger industrial comber, aligns the
wool fibers in the way a comb straightens our hair; rather than stretching the fibers apart, as in carding, combing results in a tighter-spun
thread that is more durable than woolen fabrics but not as warm.

All of Weed's machines are curious-looking: eccentric, anachro-
nistic. The spinning machine, a Gordian set of revolving spindles
and bobbins, each determining the tightness and length of the
thread, is about the size of a school chalkboard. A plying machine
spins two to three threads together to make them stronger. Each
machine is just manageable for one small person. Not so long ago, all
clothing was made in the home and by women. The invention of the
flying shuttle, which mechanized weaving, and the spinning jenny,
a machine that allowed eight spools of thread to be spun at once,
moved these tasks from the living room to the factory. Run first by
water and then by steam, the flying shuttle, the spinning frame, and
the spinning jenny ushered in the Industrial Revolution. Suddenly
fabric could be made a hundred times as fast. The knowledge of how
to hand-process wool was lost in a generation. But not completely.
Clearly there is something deeply pleasurable to people, if not profitable, about every aspect of wool-making: small flock sheep-rearing,
hand-spinning, natural dyeing, weaving, and knitting seem to be
having a resurgence.

Weed processes the wool from her own hundred sheep and accepts
wool from independent farms all over Montana and beyond. She
washes, cards, combs, and spins, depending on the customer's order,
and she also dyes. We head out to the greenhouse where, Weed
explains, the dyeing and drying are done. It is so arid in Montana that
here, unlike elsewhere, there is no need for electric dryers. In summer,
the washed wool is ready to be dyed in a few hours. Spread on trays
suspended from the rafters are drifts of fleece the color of faded ink,
red willow, goldenrod, and smoke—muted, soft-spoken colors she
produced with dyes made from plants. "Indigo," she says, pointing to
the blue wool. "I order the indigo from India." From under one of the

goldenrod piles, a giant tabby stretches awake. Weed apologizes: "We don't let the cat sleep on any wool that's not ours."

Weed tells me she trained as a geologist and met her husband, a civil engineer, in Maine. Neither one of them grew up in a farming family. Yet both of them are drawn to this work, the many steps needing hands: washing, pulling the heavy wool out and loading it in the spinner, drying it, carding it, combing it, spinning, and plying—and that is before it is ever woven or knitted into fabric. And that does not count the sheep! I notice them now, white, black, and ruddy, healthy-looking and grazing in the vividly green fields behind the barn. On her website Weed writes, "We're still learning, but sometimes it seems that our late arrival to agriculture is as much help as hindrance. As a geologist and an engineer, both of us have had professional careers that have given us the chance to see landscape in a context that includes, but is not limited to agriculture. That has made it seem natural to ask hard questions about what the goals of a modern ranch should be." Thirteen Mile Lamb and Wool Company raises their sheep without chemical fertilizers or antibiotic supplements. They practice crop rotation and keep the sheep out of the creeks to protect both the water and local wildlife. The lamb they sell is certified organic.

➤

Lately I have been asking friends if they have a favorite piece of wool clothing. In Montana, no one usually needs more than a second or two to answer. (You can't ask the same question of cotton or polyester; for one thing, they don't last.) For Bryher, it is the pale blue and sand-colored tweed zip-up sweater she bought in Galway on her sixtieth birthday. For Bob, a giant gray cardigan "with two big pockets to keep my cigarettes in." Debra speaks of a plaid woven Pendleton skirt. Terri lists three merino V-necks, which she says she wears at least three hundred days a year, and then she adds her wool long underwear to the list. What comes to mind for me is a charcoal boiled wool, boxy and warm, that I wore until there were holes in the pockets and elbows and the sleeve hems were shredded. Before I leave Thirteen Mile Lamb and Wool Company, I purchase a stocking cap knitted with undyed brown wool trimmed with a darker, chocolate band of spun buffalo hairs from a ranch nearby. It is too warm to wear today, even in this cold spring wind.

Sheep Ecology

In April, a Thursday before Easter, I return to the Hilger Ranch. A flock of western bluebirds, intensely turquoise, are feeding on last year's thistle, and snow dusts the foothills. I am here to join a half dozen students from Carroll College's Intro to Anthrozoology class who are here, like me, to see the new lambs. We load up on hay bales in the back of the ranch's long flatbed. It will take us out to the farthest pasture. Half the students already have their phones out, taking pictures of the lake and mountains but mostly of each other. When we arrive, Denis, the Peruvian shearer, jumps out and sends his border collie into the sagebrush hills where about a hundred sheep are grazing. He whistles, and the dog does not run but lowers itself into its characteristic herding slouch—stalking, seeking eye contact with the sheep, respectful but relentless. In less than ten minutes, the dog has sent every last sheep swirling instinctually into a spiral, each heading for the middle where it is safest, and then the dog herds the spiral to where Denis is standing, a quarter mile away. It is an impressive, choreographed effort, with no loose sheep, the dog running now from the left side to the right to keep the flock contained.

I ask Cathy Campbell what predators the shepherds guard against once they take their charges up into the nearby mountains for the summer. She says coyotes aren't a problem but mountain lions are. Still, she loses fewer than five sheep a year, which is very good on a ranch that raises four hundred. Two shepherds constantly monitor the flocks, each with a dog to herd them. There are also two giant white Pyrenees who function as guard dogs. This time of year, especially, they are important. Campbell and her shepherds know when a ewe has lambed because one of the big dogs will lie right down next to it as protection. A sheep's gestation period is just under five months. They give birth in a fenced field. Immediately, the lambs and their mother are taken inside a small barn, where they can be watched over in the days when they are most vulnerable.

The American sheep industry loses "half a million sheep a year, mainly to coyotes and marauding domestic dogs," according to Stephen Budiansky, author of *The Covenant of the Wild: Why Animals Chose Domestication*. A sheep or goat's predators vary depending on where it lives, but there are always plenty of them: coyotes, bears, mountain lions, birds of prey, snow leopards, Australian dingoes. Nothing, however, rankles American shepherds and nonshepherds alike as much as the American gray wolf. "The evil-ization of the wolf," Perkins, the anthrozoology professor, says, "is fascinating, given that most ranchers—sheep and cattle ranchers alike—hate it for its predation, and yet the dog is one of the most common protectors of sheep. Witness the German Shepherd and border collies." The 2011 federal delisting of the wolf as an endangered species has led to wholesale slaughter, as it is now left to the states to allow or disallow trapping, snaring, baiting, and poisoning. Hatred of them is fierce: in 2013, Montana Fish, Wildlife and Parks issued 24,479 wolf-hunting licenses.

In Australia, a 3,307-mile fence made out of steel mesh and barbed wire protects some 123 million head of sheep—and an export business worth over $5 million—from the wild dingo. *Canis lupus dingo*, cousin to the jackal and coyote, descendant of the Asian wolf, has increased in population a hundredfold since merino sheep were introduced to Australia in 1788. Keeping these wild dogs from the domesticated sheep takes enormous amounts of time and money to repair fence, set traps, lay out poison, and hire "fence riders" who look for holes and shoot dingoes who get within their sights. This constant vigilance has, indeed, saved Australia's sheep industry, but at tremendous cost to taxpayers, ranchers, and the environment. Saving the sheep industry means, of course, more sheep. More sheep means more overgrazing. Interestingly, trying to eliminate the dingo has caused the kangaroo population to explode so that, in 1997, the government was forced to cull three million of an animal that, with their cute pouches and rabbit-like ears, has come to symbolize the Land Down Under.

In the Himalayas of India, China, and Mongolia, where most cashmere is grown, goatherds can lose 100 percent of their annual income in one night of predation by snow leopards. Because of "retaliatory killing," along with poaching for furs and body parts, there are now only 4,500 to 7,500 snow leopards left on earth.

According to the United States Department of Agriculture, predators account for an average loss of 2 to 4 percent of sheep and lambs. When I talked to Weed at Thirteen Mile Lamb and Wool Company about it, she did not deny it is a problem. "Predation," she responded, "is clearly distressing when it happens." Despite the distress, however, she and her husband see a bigger picture. Their farm is one of a growing number of farms and ranches in the United States whose owners have signed an affidavit declaring themselves "Predator Friendly." What, I asked, could being friendly to predators mean?

"Killing a coyote only brings more coyotes," Weed had told me. "They are social creatures. If I shoot one that isn't bothering me, a coyote who doesn't respect my boundaries might take its place." Weed and her husband lamb in secure fenced lots near their house. They also use guard animals, as most sheep ranchers do. Only the biggest flocks can rely on shepherds. "Our guard llamas have developed some kind of an understanding with a local population of a fairly stable coyote pack," Weed says in an interview for the Maine Organic Farmers Association. "They know the ropes and we know the ropes, and I think they understand that we don't bother them. We see them frequently. We like to have them around, because they hunt gophers." Studies have found that the more coyotes are left alone, the less they bother livestock. "In general," Weed writes on her website, "coyote population fluctuations correlate with fluctuations in natural food supplies (mice, gophers, rabbits), not sheep numbers." She points out that even though tens of thousands of predators have been killed, predation of sheep and cattle has not stopped or even diminished.

Predator Friendly took formal shape in 1991 when a "coalition of ranchers, conservationists and clothing manufacturers" worked together to provide guidelines and certification to those woolgrowers who wanted a better way to live with neighboring wildlife. In signing a pledge, owners agree to not use any "lethal control" to protect their livestock, which includes shooting, trapping, or poisoning. The coalition works with ranchers to find ways to coexist with predators, employing strategies such as pens and fencing, careful observation, and guard dogs. Just like the Predator Friendly program, administered now by the organization Wildlife Friendly Enterprise Network, international efforts by a number of conservation organizations are also working to mitigate hostility between shepherds and predators. One, the Snow Leopard Conservancy, led by Rodney Jackson, helps herdsmen in the Himalayans fund and build better predator-proof corrals and initiates environmental education programs that lead to better practices. Wild animals prefer eating wild animals. If herdsmen are paid to be part of wildlife conservation efforts—through ecotourism, as one example—more wild animals will exist and livestock will not be as tempting to predators.

New methods of managing livestock are also offering solutions. "Rangelands have evolved with grazing by large ungulates since the late Mesozoic Era," Matt Barnes writes in "Livestock Management for Coexistence with Large Carnivores, Healthy Land and Productive Ranches." Considering that wild herds have been successful in their response to large predators in their environment, agriculturalists have developed techniques that are patterned off those behaviors, an approach called "ranching in nature's image." The new methods include dense herding and rotational grazing, as well as less invasive ways to move herds across a landscape. More and more, people who understand these entangled ecological issues, ranchers and scientists and shepherds who love sheep *and* coyotes and wolves, who raise live-stock not only for immediate profit but for their help in controlling noxious weeds and improving the soil, are literally changing the field.

Back at the Hilger Ranch, Perkins's class and I are being led into a shed, which has been divided into mesh lambing pens called "jugs." Today they are all full, with each sheep and her lambs, most commonly twins, kept apart from the others. Color does not seem to carry over with these Shetlands: beige mothers nurse black twins, and a black-and-white brindled lamb nuzzles her gray mother. There is perhaps nothing as adorable, or vulnerable, as lambs, with their curls and wide eyes and bandy legs, except maybe kittens. When Campbell gives them to us to hold, they don't struggle. The class, predominantly female, crowds in, oohing and aahing, cradling and petting. The two men in the class stand back, amused and a bit cynical. They don't touch the lambs. One of the class textbooks, by anthrozoologist Hal Herzog, affirms this behavior. Men and women, he writes, have similar atti-tudes about animals, but women are much more likely to take action on behalf of them. "Women dominate nearly every aspect of grass-roots animal protection," he writes. They make up 85 percent of the membership in the American Society for the Prevention of Cruelty to Animals and the Humane Society, and outnumber men eleven to one as dog rescuers. There is evidence that historically it was men who were the shepherds, women who went yearly to the high fields to comb out the locks in order to spin them into cloth. By the time we leave, I have heard almost every woman, including me, say she wants to take a lamb home.

❥

Thirty miles north of the Hilger Ranch and a week later, I am at the Sieban Ranch, a much larger, commercial operation run by the family of Montana's former US senator Max Baucus. Lambing has peaked over the weekend, says his brother John F. Baucus, who greets me near the sheep barns, but there are at least a hundred pregnant ewes still in the field. It is 7 a.m., chilly, and local sheep woman Stephanie Sater, who works the yearly lambing, is late due to an unexpected death in the family. When she finds me, I am watching a bald eagle atop its nest in the faraway cottonwoods who perhaps is watching for afterbirth to eat. Sater, dressed in a ratty wool sweater, a green wool cap, and Carhartt pants, is carrying a shepherd's hook as tall as she is, curved on one end and made of wood, just like Little Bo Peep's. Together with another woman, she raises approximately fifty adult Rambouillets on her own small ranch outside Helena. She arrives sad but not distracted. "My heart's in being a shepherd," she says.

Sater's first task is to move a flock of ewes and yesterday's lambs from the smaller pen where they have been sequestered to a larger one with the others. As I try to stay out of the way—sheep can't be approached head-on or they will scatter—I see how really difficult it is to get them to go in one direction. Sheep are wicked-smart, Sater had told me earlier on the phone. They can remember the face of someone who has treated them poorly or well. Indeed, they don't seem panicked as Sater expertly moves from one side of the flock to the other like a border collie, relying on the outliers' instincts to join the rest, brandishing her stick, while the crowd bleats and trots. "Moving livestock is much more gentle than it used to be," she says. "We don't have a lot of time in a big operation like this, but we don't want to shove them around either. Ranchers are learning that stress is worse in the long run for the wool, the meat, and people." She mentions the teachings of Bud Williams, who has almost single-handedly changed herding methods with his "low-stress handling techniques." Like Temple Grandin before him, who pioneered designs to make the movement and corralling of cattle easier, safer, and more pleasant for the animals and those who handle them, his methods are based on building trust and using the animals' natural actions "and nothing more": no yelling, hitting, shoving, or poking. "He never wanted his critters to look at him as a predator," a testimonial about Williams reads. "He simply wanted to take the stress off of an animal, read the animal, and get the animal to believe what Bud wanted was what she really wanted."

The Sieban Ranch, in operation since 1897, raises Rambouillets—a larger French-bred merino—for the meat and wool market. Unlike the multicolored Shetlands, these Rambouillets all look alike, like the ones you count to put yourself to sleep: stout, monotonous, all the color of cobwebs, with wide-set eyes and docked tails. Rambouillet lamb is said to be one of the most flavorful, and Rambouillet wool is one of the finest, its fibers used to make SmartWool socks and long underwear so soft it can be worn next to the skin. The micron count for these sheep is 19–26 (remember that a micron is one-millionth of a meter), not quite as fine as Australian merino, which can sometimes have a diameter as small as 10, but considered fine nonetheless. This year's shearing produced about nine pounds of wool per ewe. Multiply that by 1,500 sheep and that's 13,500 pounds of top-grade wool that will be sent to an auction where buyers from all over the world will bid on it.

By the time the week's done, over fourteen hundred lambs will have been born at the Sieban Ranch, Sater tells me, all of them in a fenced pasture and without human help. Once these lambs are weaned, most of them will go to a feedlot to be fattened for market. ("Friends of ours think being a shepherd means we are always protecting the life of the flock," Sater says. "But if you breed and it results in a sheep that you don't want, what do you do? If you breed, and you keep getting more animals, what do you do?") Those lambs that are not culled will "mother up" (rejoin their mothers) and begin their lives of constant movement. Through a cold spring and a hot, dry summer, they will graze first at the ranch, then for many miles over the mountains to the west, and then back again before the winter. They will be separated into bands of about a thousand, with one shepherd trying to keep each band safe from mountain lions, wolves, and grizzly bears. "You can have an easy life or an interesting life," Sater says. "These sheep have an interesting life."

The Baucuses, like many ranchers in the West, employ Peruvian families as shepherds, ranch hands, and cooks. Their deep knowledge of shepherding in the Andes and their willingness to work long hours—basically twenty-four hours a day—for less than regular American wages make them an asset for ranchers who must find skilled workers to protect their flocks. "I tried it once," Sater says, "staying in one of those cute little sheep wagons. No one tells you how lonely it will be. There are weeks that go by where you see not one human. You have to be wary and attentive all the time." She introduces me to Roberto—full name: Roberto Enrique Ninahuanca Tocas—who has been working for the ranch for twelve years. A thin, handsome man wearing a red hand-knit wool hat with tassels, he had been a Spanish teacher in his city, but makes much more here. He sends money home to his daughter, he tells me, who is majoring in electrical engineering at the college there.

Tocas watches the birthing pasture like a hawk, by which I mean expertly, scanning the perimeters quickly, silently, out of deep habit. He points out a ewe with her neck stretched out, lying on her side; another pawing the ground, and a urine-colored puddle that has slipped from the uterus of another and is now trembling as if with wind. "We wait for the head to lift," he says. "Then we know it's okay." He watches each ewe lick the yellow placenta away and clear the lamb's nose passages. After a few minutes, he strolls in a wide circle toward them, then narrows in and picks up the lamb by its forelegs. He takes a few steps, and then lays it on the ground. The mother follows, hesitantly, and begins to lick again. I watch him do this a number of times—lift, walk a few feet, lay the lamb down—and each time the sheep follows more determinedly. By the time he is halfway across the barnyard, he can carry the lamb in his arms straight through the gate without looking back, and the mother will follow.

Inside, the lamb's umbilical cord is snipped and iodine swabbed on the wound. Mother and child are placed in a "jug" to ensure they bond and begin nursing. I watch as one ewe, still licking her lamb, gives birth to another in the five-foot-square pen. The newborn is as slick as a plucked chicken, white, and smeared with blood. Tocas uses his hands to wipe away some of the mucus as he lifts it out. "They make it look so quick and painless," I say, "unlike humans." He laughs. "They just can't tell us it's painful. It never looks so easy to me." Sheep often birth twins, depending on how well they are fed, exercised, and kept free from stress. Here at the Sieban Ranch, 60 percent of births are twin births. "You are lucky you came at the tail end this year," Tocas says. "Two days ago, we wouldn't have had time to talk. Every ten minutes, we had to use the cart to pick up five or six sets of twins at a time."

No one, even now, seems to be letting their guard down. Each employee and employer has their own job, from checking on the "singles" (not twins), as Sater is doing, making sure all are healthy and nursing and penned or unpenned, to bringing the new lambs in from the field, as Tocas does, to nursing the "orphan" lambs, whose mothers rejected them, to castrating the older ones, to paint-branding mother and child with the same number and docking their tails. "You can always tell whose lamb is whose anyway," Tocas assures me, as we stand watching two identical ewes who have each just had identical twins. I raise my eyebrows. "Look at them," he says. I watch as the mothers, like human mothers, follow their offspring steadily with their eyes.

I had asked Sater if I could accompany her to the Sieban Ranch this morning because I suspected those working for a huge commercial sheep business would have a far different relationship to the individual animals and workers than the "hobby" or cottage farmers I had visited so far. "The nineteenth century . . . saw the beginning of a process, today being completed by twentieth century corporate capitalism, by which every tradition which has previously mediated between man and nature was broken," writes John Berger in his essay "Why Look at Animals?" It is clear that mass production of fiber worldwide has come at great cost to animals and workers involved with them. It is also sadly true that agricultural skill sets like the ones Tocas and

Denis and Sater and Weed and Campbell have demonstrated are dying out. And yet here they are practicing them, improving them, thinking ahead to a future that is better for both land and animals. Here, at one of the biggest sheep ranches in Montana, abuzz as it is in fostering all this new life—all this *investment*—I see a mutual enterprise. Dogs, ewes, people protecting, moving, feeding, watering, making a living, shepherds on one side and sheep on the other, wool as the medium connecting them. But what cost the breeding itself?

"Breeds are disappearing at an alarming rate because most people are in it for the money, and the money is in the McSheep, what we call the merino or the Rambouillet," says Cindy Kittredge, a small-flock owner I spoke with a few weeks ago. She and her husband raise Icelandic sheep on a ranch about an hour north of this one. Like the Shetlands at Hilger Ranch, the Icelandics developed in isolation and thus have retained a lot of their ancient characteristics. A northern European short-tail, they are known for their double-coated fleece, one soft and bulky and one long and tipped. Kittredge, who also raises Highlands, a primitive breed of cattle, was eager to talk about overbreeding. "Most breeds have been jinxed," she claims. "A lot of their characteristics have been bred out in favor of that one that the industry wants. My husband and I raise these animals because we wanted to see all parts of the animal displayed—its meat and wool and milk, its endurance and its personality." Sheep that are raised commercially and bred for one quality lead a totally different life than primitive breeds, Kittredge explains: "Our relationship with the animal changes. If you breed for one characteristic—say the merino's silky undercoat—you don't care how that sheep mothers her lamb, if she is resistant to disease, if her meat tastes good. Eventually you have an animal that produces beautiful wool but is very difficult to keep alive." The Kittredges aren't in a hurry—with their cattle or their sheep—so their animals can develop slowly. "We don't have to breed yearlings and damage them beyond repair. We don't give them routine antibiotics. It's a totally different way of producing material. A much more holistic one." I think of the

Idaho breed I recently saw in the field guide. Bred for maximum profit in both wool and meat, it is named the Polypay.

New Zealand and Australia have by far the most sheep per human population. China and Australia have the most sheep. (In 2006 China had more than 173 million compared to 9.68 million in the United States.) In addition, China is the main raw wool importer, buying 39 percent of the market. China is now also the world's largest producer of wool textiles. Wool processing, though not as chemically toxic as leather processing, is water-intensive. The lanolin that coats most high-quality wool has to be washed and rewashed out of it. Dyeing, in commercial operations, uses heavy metals and produces intense chemical waste. Most wool processing is now done in China for the same reasons as leather tanning: fewer environmental regulations and cheaper labor. Reviewing the labels on my closetful of lambswool, merino, and cashmere sweaters—Land's End, J. Crew, Banana Republic, as well as numerous lesser-known brands—I noticed that almost all are manufactured in China. One label reads Hong Kong.

The tremendous global demand for cheap wool products has caused more problems than poor labor practices and toxic waste. It has resulted in the tremendous increase in the worldwide number of sheep and goats. If we think of domestication as a form of mutualism where both human and animal don't merely survive but thrive, the growing of wool has been a success story with both good and bad results for both parties. In the past fifty years, the domestic goat population of Inner Mongolia rose from 2.4 million animals to 25.6 million due to worldwide demand for cheap cashmere. This exorbitant growth has led to overgrazing a very dry, fragile landscape and, in some places, to desertification of native grasslands. In Australia, New Zealand, China, and now Mongolia, as has happened in many developed countries, a wild landscape, along with its animals and people, is being transformed into a profit-making machine. China is now the largest producer of cashmere, at a clip of ten thousand metric tons a year. Mongolia is second and sells more than half of its product to China to be processed.

Along with causing desertification, the number of sheep and goats in Mongolia, India, and China's Tibetan Plateau has displaced native wildlife. In a study published in *Conservation Biology*, "Globalization of the Cashmere Market and the Decline of Large Mammals in Central Asia," the authors attribute the reduction to habitat displacement, as well as avoidance of dogs, humans, and domesticated animals. These wild animals, caught in the web of global trade, include such exotic species as saiga, chiru, Bactrian camels, blue sheep, ibexes, and gazelles. In Inner Mongolia alone, the shift to a market economy in 1993 resulted in a fivefold increase in the number of goats. Something similar happened in Ladakh, where wild species account for just 2 to 7 percent of animals. Even in Eastern Mongolia, where there are far fewer livestock and humans, the researchers found that the presence of dogs and herders reduced gazelle density by 76 to 98 percent. Who, one has to ask, is ultimately responsible for this explosive thriving, and in consequence, the diminishing numbers of gazelles?

Don't get me wrong. I love the smoothness, warmth, and rich color of my merino sweaters; I also love that they don't need to be dry-cleaned but can be washed. The cost, usually under forty dollars, is not unimportant to me. Yet in learning about the global and labyrinthine journey these mass-produced garments have traveled to get to me, and the impact on the health of the sheep, the textile workers, and the land, I see that their value is not necessarily accurately reflected in their price. Primitive breeds, predator-friendly protections, low-stress handling techniques, small flock wool ranching—gauged against the worldwide wool industry—don't seem enough. Yet interest is increasing steadily. "It comes down to a choice," says Kittredge. "If you have a monoculture, the whole species could be in danger. Look at what happened with wheat! A fungus hits and the monoculture goes down all at once. You're shot. We have forgotten that it has taken thousands of years to domesticate these animals." She is clearly passionate, as many of these sheep women I have met tend to be when discussing agribusiness versus what they are trying to do with their own flocks.

"It comes around full circle. If pasturing is done correctly, animals are good for the land. If incorrectly—driven by high numbers tangentially tied with government grazing costs—the land suffers, the sheep and cows suffer, and eventually, the consumer suffers. Eventually you end up with cheap but inferior goods."

The Pastoral

In Virgil's *Eclogues*, written around 30 BCE, the carefree, innocent, and rustic shepherd makes one of his early appearances in Western literature as figure for both the poet and for all humans. "O come and live with me in the countryside," a herdsman sings, "Among the humble farms. Together we / Will hunt the deer, and tend the little goats, / Compelling them along with willow wands." Pastoral comes from the Latin word *pastor*, for "shepherd" or "herdsman." What we call the pastoral—the literary representation of a bucolic, agrarian, simpler way of life amid the equally bucolic domesticated animals—is, of course, a romantic construct. In its tendency to idealize the rural, it expresses, as Leo Marx writes in his classic book *The Machine in the Garden: Technology and the Pastoral Ideal in America*, a "yearning for a simpler, more harmonious style of life, an existence 'closer to nature'" in response to increasing urbanization and industrialization. Arcadia, the original pastoral countryside, was, in Greek legend, the home of the god Pan. In contrast to Athens, with its corruption, worry, and struggles for power—including, ultimately, wars—Arcadia represented a more harmonious and peaceful, as well as *independent*, human existence. In this way it is often framed as a kind of lost paradise, a back-to-the-land movement as escape from the front lines and the assembly lines.

Being a shepherd, in reality, is a lot of work—cold, hot, dusty, requiring long hours at low wages—which is why it is often done by the poorest people in the world. Even in ancient Arcadia, the shepherds rarely owned their own property and were constantly beholden to the wealthy who allowed them to graze their sheep and goats there. (In Virgil's *Eclogues*, one of the shepherds laments that he has lost his pasture because it was given away by the government to returning soldiers.) Most of the romantic poets who took on the shepherd's voice, such as William Wordsworth, John Keats, and Percy Bysshe Shelley, or politicians like Thomas Jefferson, who saw an ideal America as a land of small farms and gentleman farmers, had never herded a goat or sheep in their lives. Still, it is the *perception* of the shepherd's love, attention, and protection of animals, his seeming freedom from mass incarceration in a system of employment controlled by others who instrumentalize his human life and work—his *sustainability*, as it were—that still appeals to us.

The ideal of the pastoral life falls in between two opposites: wilderness and civilization. The problem with wilderness is, of course, that it is dangerous. We must always keep it at bay if we don't want to be eaten or have our own food stolen from us. The problem with civilization is that it is prone to corruption. "Getting and spending, we lay waste our powers," as Wordsworth writes. Jefferson initially wanted industry to remain in Europe. He believed the "manufactures" would degrade us. Our goods, our labor, our land would be sold to the highest bidder. The shepherd, however, stands in the middle state, untainted. His is the dream of an *improved* wilderness, as Marx describes it, a "landscape of reconciliation, a mild, agricultural, semi-primitive terrain." But not entirely reconciled; a shepherd's job is to protect his or her employer's property.

Some ecologists, such as Paul Shepard, believe that we have maimed species as well as our own physical and cognitive abilities by domesticating plants and animals. His admittedly radical perspective views modern animal science as "the systematic creation of animal deformities, anomalies, and monsters, and the practice of keeping them alive." As to the life of catastrophe and drudgery that, he says, it has imprisoned *us* in, he believes that it has also influenced our basic attitude toward our place and power on the earth, paving the way toward the practices of colonization, slavery, and eventually war. "As soon as people began to kill wolves to protect sheep and to squash grasshoppers to protect crops," Shepard writes, "nature became an opponent and wild forms became enemies of the tame in a way analogous to a war between human armies." Yet while it is true that the pastoral idea of the carefree shepherd's lot is a romantic fiction, that more and more of us live in cities where we have never encountered a sheep, and that the few shepherds who exist have to negotiate three-month green cards in America, it is still more than a fiction. Sheep and shepherds—and the wool that connects them—draw us back to the yearning we have as humans, even now, to belong to a world in which animals and humans can be beneficial to each other. It affirms, in a larger sense, that we do belong.

⌣

"Draw me a sheep," the Little Prince says to the narrator of *The Little Prince*, by Antoine de Saint-Exupéry. But the narrator doesn't know how to draw a sheep. His first sheep looks sick, the next too old. After many unsatisfactory attempts, the narrator draws a box and asks the Prince to imagine the sheep within it. The Prince does not want to tame the sheep, though taming is one of the important themes of the book. He wants it to eat the sprouts of the baobab trees that keep springing up on his faraway planet. It is the rose, with only four fragile thorns to protect itself from the world, that he wants to protect from the encroaching forest.

The story is less simple than it may initially seem. A fox appears and asks the Little Prince to tame him. What does "tame" mean, the Prince asks.

"It is an act too often neglected," said the fox. "It means to establish ties."

"To establish ties?"

"Just that," said the fox. "To me, you are still nothing more than a little boy who is just like a hundred thousand other little boys. And I have no need of you. And you, on your part, have no need of me. To you, I'm nothing more than a fox like a hundred thousand other foxes. But if you tame me, then we shall need each other. To me, you will be unique in all the world. To you, I shall be unique in all the world."

The fox adds, "Men have forgotten this truth. But you must not forget it. You become responsible, forever, for what you have tamed." Perhaps it is true also for what we have bred.

3 Silk

The Secret

In Nishijin, the historic weaving district of Kyoto, Japan, I select a scarf for my sister, brownish-pink, dyed naturally with cedar bark. It is the color of sand at sunset, the fabric so thin, so light that holding it is as if moving my hand through mist. Silk production has flourished here for over twelve hundred years. Nishijin weavers were famous for *nishijin-ori*, a shimmering fabric woven of scoured silk, which is shiny and smooth, and raw silk, which is muted and coarse, making it appear magically three-dimensional. My companion and I have arrived at the Nishijin Silk Center just in time to see a fashion show: five young women, pale imperial swans, modeling the latest versions of the kimono, the elegantly designed, T-shaped national costume whose name means simply "thing to wear."

Afterward we walk the narrow alleys to the Orinasu-Kan textile museum. A serious young man ushers us briskly into a traditional wood-beamed merchant house, where we sit on large floor pillows at a red lacquer table facing a window that looks out at a Zen garden and are left alone. On the table, a teapot, two cups of green tea already poured, and on a tray, two wrapped bean-paste sweets. We assume that the message is to compose ourselves, to leave the street and the clutter of our minds and prepare ourselves for the lustrous fabrics that await us: a woman's white undergarment patterned with orchids. Heavy black men's robes, lined surreptitiously with crimson or yellow silk. One kimono, silver and sea green, is sewn of a fabric woven to express waves, with sparkling threads that catch the eye like light on water. One is painted with stylized maple leaves, another embroidered with gold to replicate dew atop the peonies.

I can imagine the medieval Europeans, wearing their rough woolens and sackcloth, encountering from the first traders this exquisite star-stuff. They must have gone mad for it. What world, they must have thought, could have produced this? The Romans and Persians believed silk was plucked from *silk trees* (the silver-barked birch? the camphor?) or harvested from webs. Greed for silk spurred the extravagant building of the Silk Road, a system of trade routes four thousand miles long—one-quarter of the earth's circumference at the equator. Braving the marine route or crossing the deserts or following the Great Wall of China to the northwest, taking two years to complete the trip, the caravans, laden with silks and spices, still capture our imaginations. No one could have guessed that silk came from the spit of worms.

Chinese folklore attributes the discovery of silk making, like the origins of much human invention, to a chance encounter. It occurred during the reign of the legendary Yellow Emperor, a semimythical figure who is credited with domesticating plants and animals and inventing the calendar, compass, Chinese characters, and music—in effect, inventing civilization. As one story is told, his preferred wife, Leizu, was sipping hot tea in her courtyard when a cocoon fell into her cup from a white mulberry tree above her and began to unravel. The Empress Leizu immediately made plans to cultivate the *Bombyx mori*, China's native wild moth, employing leagues of her maidens to hand-feed them, devising a method to coax long silk threads from their cocoons, and inventing a loom to weave them, thus transforming the economy of China for millennia to come and becoming known, as she is in China today, as the "Silkworm Mother" (Can Nainai).

According to Dieter Kuhn's essay "Tracing a Chinese Legend," a "cut half cocoon" was excavated in central China in 1992 dating from 2200 to 1700 BCE, and fragments from silk weaving were found in a bamboo basket in Chekiang province dating approximately from 2750 BCE, which is, coincidentally, about the time of the legendary rule of the Yellow Emperor. Although the Chinese were by then raising animals for food and clothing, when the cocoon fell and began unraveling its dramatic series of events, of imperial control and court intrigue, war and trade, the empress, sipping her chrysanthemum tea, was probably wearing robes made of animal or bird skins or some kind of bast fiber: hemp or ramie or mulberry stems, or, as in Japan, a rough material woven from the wild wisteria (*fujigimono*, a kind of work clothing for peasants, meant "wisteria kimono"). Older legends, Kuhn writes, sometimes credit the Yellow Emperor, instead of his wife, as the inventor of all fabrics: "The Yellow Emperor started to discard garments of skin, he made jackets in the image of heaven," says the *I Ching*. Yet the cult of Leizu (which became official in 557 CE), replete with altars and sacrifices, continued in many villages into the twentieth century. One can guess why. Cultivation of silkworms—or *sericulture*, as it is known—was, for most of this time, the responsibility of women.

Clothing made in the image of heaven, understandably, was only for the elite, who wore it, sat on it, and slept covered in it. In silk's beginnings, the imperial family reserved the right to wear it, yet slowly its use was extended to other classes. Craftspeople created a multitude of products from silk: paper, fishing line, musical instruments, furniture, glue. Silk cultivation flourished during the Shang dynasty (1600–1100 BCE). With the establishment of the Silk Road in 130 CE, China began to export silk fabrics to Persia, India, Arabia, and Japan. The Chinese knew what a treasure they possessed. For more than two thousand years, anyone caught trying to smuggle eggs, cocoons, or worms out of the country was tortured and executed.

Despite harsh penalties, the desire to spread silk production beyond China was an enduring temptation. In the second century, according to legend, four Chinese emigrants who reached Japan by way of Korea were the first to breach the secret of silk. In the fourth century, as recorded in the *Great Tang Records on the Western Regions*, the king of Khotan (what is now western China) married a Chinese princess and told her that if she wanted to wear silk, she had better bring its secret with her, which she did, hiding the eggs in an elaborate headpiece. Soon thereafter, the *Bombyx mori* made its way into India and Pakistan. Edward Gibbon, in his *History of the Decline and Fall of the Roman Empire*, records the story of two Byzantine monks who smuggled silkworm eggs out of China in the sixth century, concealing them in their hollowed-out bamboo canes.

Today, in Kyoto, young women from the provinces rent silk kimonos in Gion, the traditional geisha district, and walk the streets during Golden Week, posing as Imperial princesses. I, too, am from the far provinces—from America—yet feel heavy, overheated in my bast fibers, my cotton and linen. A well-dressed older man and woman pass me on the sidewalk. She is erect and delicate, wearing a garden-colored sleeveless silk shift over thin beige pants, sandals on her feet, and a gold silk scarf pinned around her shoulders. Or was it mint green? What I remember is the coolness of the impression, as if she wore shade. The difference between leather or wool and silk is that the former are inherently practical. They were necessary for survival in cold climates, and they were made from materials at hand, whereas silk is labor-intensive, precious. Silk is very absorbent, so it takes dye well, yet it also blocks the day's heat from passing through. Tapestries, saris, the finest glove linings are made with silk, as are parachutes and the very best fly-fishing line. Leather is durable, and wool is graded for its warmth and softness, but silk is pure pleasure. When I tie the scarf I bought in Nishijin around my neck, it is as if a song sparrow's voice had landed there; some silk, like the heavy, black secondhand kimono my companion has bought, is smooth and weighted as a moonless night. One can imagine its hem mopping the glossy floors of a monastery.

China monopolized the silk trade for more than three thousand years and, after a lull of a couple hundred, is doing so again. Yet during much of the twentieth century, Japan was the world's largest exporter of high-quality silk, producing fabric "according to rituals and secrets that had arrived at a state of mystical precision," as Alessandro Baricco writes in his novel *Silk*. Looking into the background of any of Japan's booming companies today—from cars to audio to high tech—one will find its roots in the earlier silk industry. Sanrio, which owns the international, ubiquitous Hello Kitty brand—a franchise based on a cartoon of a small white cat and now worth billions of dollars—originally made its fortunes as the Yamanashi Silk Company. Although all aspects of clothing manufacture, including wool and leather, have moved to more "cost-efficient" regions like China, Brazil, Vietnam, and India, Japan continues to be one of the top ten exporters of silk. It is Japan, even more than China, which has sold the idea of silk as a fabric embodying grace, serenity, refinement. It is in Japan that silk was immortalized via the kimono.

With all this in mind I have come to Japan. I am hoping to see the white mulberry leaves, which feed the worms that spin silk, a material once so valuable it replaced currency, and the *Bombyx mori* moth, which spins thread over a mile long. Who is this creature whose secret was worth torture and death, who miraculously spews liquid silk from glands in its head to form a cocoon in which to give birth to itself, who nods its head as it spins like horses do when they are agitated, giving rise to the Chinese legend of the "animal spirit" of a horse transformed into a worm? *Who is the silkworm?*

The Silkworm

On the first day of my ten-day silk tour, I wake in a traditional *ryokan* outside Annaka, in Gunma prefecture. Pale green tatami mats cover the floors, scenting the room with the fragrance of drying hay. The room is spare and wide, furnished with a low lacquer table and pillows to sit on, and with recesses where one or two art objects are artfully placed: a vase, a print of peonies, a watercolor of a chickadee. At seven last night, while we were having dinner, the staff came in and made up our futons on the mats. The futons are silk-covered, plush. Floor-length windows frame the river below and the scalloped line of jagged, blue mountains. The *yukata* or robes we are provided with are printed with black cutouts of birds in homage to the famous Japanese folktale "The Tongue-Cut Sparrow," a story that is supposed to have originated in Annaka.

In the story, a greedy old wife begrudges the scraps her husband feeds to his pet sparrow. One day, after the sparrow eats some of the wife's starch by mistake, she cuts out its tongue and drives it away. When the husband comes back, he is horrified at what happened and goes to look for the bird. He finds it with its family, who offer him what food they have and let him choose between a heavy or light basket as a gift. Being a humble man, he chooses the light one. Later, at home, he will find that it is filled with marvelous things: gold, silver, and rolls of silk. The greedy wife makes him tell her where the sparrow lives. When she arrives, feigning repentance, the sparrow family feeds her and offers her too a basket. She chooses the heavy one, and, after struggling home over the mountains with it, opens it to discover not treasures but a multitude of demons.

The expansive Kanto Plain of Gunma has been occupied by humans since ancient times. Archaeologists have discovered burial mounds from the fifth and sixth centuries, as well as evidence of preagricultural habitation. Nevertheless, it has always been poor. Because the soil is thin and rocky, peasants in the past couldn't grow rice, so they lived on meager rations of barley, wheat, and millet grown on terraces. Even as late as World War II, as Haru Matsukata Reischauer notes in her family biography *Samurai and Silk*, "the peasants lived hard, frugal lives even compared to ordinary Japanese rice farmers. I would watch men, women, and children trudging each morning and evening through the valley on their way to and from work. Because they were too poor to own horses, and wheeled vehicles could not negotiate the steep hillsides, they walked along with their backs bent double under bamboo baskets loaded with tools, fertilizer, wood, or crops." Mulberry trees, however, could be grown in the borders between fields and on mountainsides. Raising silkworms became a way for people to supplement their incomes.

After Japan closed its ports in 1639—initiating a two-hundred-year period of isolation called *sakoku*—trade with China was halted, and in 1685 even the use of Chinese silk thread was banned, with the result that sericulture grew into a huge industry, and farmers in Gunma prefecture, who had been nurturing mulberry trees for hundreds of years, increased their production. The nearby city of Kiryu became an important weaving center, producing cloth that rivaled the Nishijin silks made in the old imperial capital, Kyoto. The Tomioka Silk Mill, the world's largest filature factory at that time, was established just after Commodore Matthew Perry forced open the port of Yokohama, precipitating the end of Japan's isolation. Soon after that, Japan began to replace China as the world's preeminent exporter of silk.

Our two tour guides, one American, one Japanese, are personally invested in this history. Glennis Dolce grew up in Yokohama, the daughter of an American industrialist who worked in occupied Japan after the war. Fiftyish, with blond hair to the middle of her back, wearing yoga pants, flip-flops, and an indigo-dyed silk shawl of her own design, she had greeted us this morning in the hotel lobby looking fresh and invigorated after having flown from her home in LA only yesterday. Dolce is a *shibori* artist; she works with silk using one of the oldest Japanese techniques of stitch-dyeing. Our Japanese guide, Takuo Hirata, is in his mid-sixties, trim, sharply dressed in khakis and short-sleeved shirt, bespectacled, fluent in English after years working in Seattle; he lives in Kamakura with his wife, Rumiko. His time in the United States instilled in him a love of beef, coffee, and ice cream, though he, like most Japanese people I meet, has a deep interest in and respect for his own country's history and culture. In fact, this is the only tour he does. His curiosity about silk comes from the fact that his great-grandfather owned and operated a silk filature mill in the mid- to late 1800s, whereas his grandfather spent his life in New York, serving his family's thriving silk export business. Dolce had emailed everyone beforehand that she would prefer to be called Glennis and that, as per Japanese custom, we are to address Takuo Hirata as Hirata-san.

Today, as our bus travels through the small cities of Kiryu and Tomioko, toward the hills where our first visit to a sericulture farm awaits, we pass incredibly narrow strips of land planted with corn and squash between the roadway and the urban sprawl. As we approach the outskirts, rolling orchards of mulberry trees come into view. The trees are dark green, oak-leafed, and much shorter than I had imagined, only about five feet high. Before I can ask, Hirata, who rides in the front with a portable microphone in his lap, says they are constantly cropped so that women can pluck the leaves.

Nobue Azuma is a fairly new enterprise run by a young husband and wife team on the grounds of a hundred-year-old farm. Neither speaks English, so Hirata translates. We are, he tells us as we disembark, their first American visitors. Wataru Hiraishi wears hip, dark-rimmed glasses, a striped T-shirt, and, like most men his age, the outline of a cell phone in his jeans pocket. Nobue (Azuma) Hiraishi, his wife, is shy, though not nervous. She smiles and bows to each of us as she waits for Hirata to stop telling them who we are and why we are here. They both look more like modern college students than proprietors of an old-fashioned artisanal enterprise with roots in the preindustrial past. Nobue Hiraishi is dressed simply, an indigo-dyed worker's smock over jeans, her long shiny hair pulled back. She has clearly been working and seems anxious to get back to it. As her husband leads us to the worms, she quickly disappears.

It is a warm late May afternoon, and the delightful Japanese bush warbler, known as the country's nightingale, is singing from the slopes of bamboo, maple, ginkgo, cyperian, and cedar. (Even strangers in the parks in Kyoto would imitate its sound perfectly for me, and then laugh, bemused that they had done so.) We follow Hiraishi to a large series of plastic-covered greenhouses a few hundred feet from the traditional two-story Japanese farmhouse he and his wife live in. In the old days, the worms were raised on wicker trays in the attics of houses like this. They built these greenhouses because, once the worms get bigger, Hiraishi says, the noise would rob them of their sleep. Reischauer speaks of this in her account of her grandfather's life: "No one who has heard the sound will ever forget the low all-night roar created by the munching of thousands of voracious silk worms in a Japanese mountain farm-house."

In the greenhouse, on tables covered with mats of chopped mulberry leaves, we encounter forty-five thousand worms, each the length of my fingernail, each lace-colored, by which I mean white with shadows, with tiny black markings and what I suspect are eyes. Together they form a mass of feeling-life, squirming, twisting, lifting their heads, crawling over each other, and, most of all, chewing. There is the unmistakable odor of animal body. Hiraishi says that in the roughly two weeks before they spin their cocoons, they will go through 300 kilograms (662 pounds) of mulberry leaves—about two pickup loads. The worms will double in size and need for space. Silkworms can be grown only in spring and summer, when the mulberry leaves are growing, because they must be fed constantly. The first leaves are said to be the best. In Japan's climate, that means at most three sets of worms a year. Here, at Nobue Azuma, they settle for two.

The life cycle of a domesticated silkworm is simple and short yet, as cultivated through generations, successful. It occurs in five stages: egg, worm, cocoon, pupa, moth. (The silkworm is, in reality, a caterpillar.) As a worm, it eats its way into bigger and bigger selves, each time shedding its exoskeleton and returning hungrier. Each self, or stage, is called an *instar*. The worm will make its way through five instars before it is ready to create its cocoon. Because the Hiraishis purchase their worms in their third instar, this happens, Hiraishi says, on the ninth or tenth day after they arrive. On this day, the worms eat the most, preparing to spin. They will weigh ten thousand times what they did when they hatched from their eggs. Once the worms start spitting, they will quit eating, and the Hiraishis, alerted, will load them on trays and carry them by hand upstairs into the attic of their house.

Butterflies and moths, we learned in grade school, build cocoons to protect themselves as they metamorphose from lowly worms into the brilliant-winged sky creatures they will become. They are vulnerable as they do so, drifting into what we humans might call an unconscious state, silent, unmoving, while their old skin dries and is pushed back to make room for the plump, yellow body that is the pupa—which will develop legs, scales, wings, the sense organs of its antennae, and compound eyes. Change in the dark. Internal transformation. A complete reimagining of the self. No wonder the Japanese and Chinese thought of Lepidoptera as personifications of a person's spirit; no wonder the Greek word for "butterfly" is *psyche*, the soul. In the case of the silk moth, it is the first creature from which scientists learned of the existence of pheromones, the chemical substances certain animals release in order to elicit desire.

Hiraishi invites us to climb the steep wooden stairs into the attic. It is hot, the dimness slatted with brown light from dust and the open windows. Large cardboard trays, each sectioned into numerous silkworm-size compartments, about an inch square, hang vertically from the rafters. Because worms climb up, never down, the trays will be lowered to the floor and the worms spread out in front of them. As a mass, they will ascend, each choosing its own little room and beginning to attach itself with silk spit to the walls. About 10 percent of them, Hiraishi says, will decide that they don't like the cardboard trays and refuse to climb onto them; these will be offered the upgrade: old-style, and more expensive, lattices woven of dried rice-grass. These *mabushi*, or traditional houses for cocoons, presumably look more natural, and those few worms that, despite centuries of breeding, still retain a memory of what was once a tangle of branches and leaves must find them more attractive. Once the worms select their homes, the trays—and the *mabushi*—are raised off the floor.

It takes each worm approximately four days to make its cocoon. A few, Hiraishi explains, are slower, and they will be given more time. Of the 100,000-plus insects that spin cocoons, only the silkworm spins them out of silk. It does so by spitting, from a spinneret atop its head, a single thread made up of filaments from its two silk glands, stuck together by a sticky substance called *sericin*—which is why silk farming is called sericulture. It does so in a characteristic figure-eight movement. The natural twist, and thus luster, in the resulting silk thread originates in the worm's head movement. Sometime during the process of cocoon building, the worm turns into a pupa. Fourteen days or so after it has begun spinning, the pupa will start chewing its way out of the cocoon and eventually emerge as a moth, which will mate, lay eggs, and, in a short time, die. In order to harvest the silk, the sericulturalist must stop the pupa before it chews its way through the precious thread. Silk farmers keep careful records and careful watch to prevent damage to the cocoons.

Upstairs in the warm loft, Hiraishi slides out four trays loaded with thousands of cocoons. They resemble Styrofoam bullets, the larger ones the size of half a thumb; some have a waist, and some are bright yellow or the palest green, shades better for black or darker dyes, he says. During the Edo period, cocoons were very small; over time, the moths have been bred to spin faster and to create bigger cocoons. In the old days, the finished cocoons were plunged into hot water to cook the pupae alive. Reeling—the process of catching the end of a silk filament and unwinding it from the cocoon, as well as the twisting of a number of filaments together to form a thread—had to be undertaken immediately or the cocoons would rot. Industrial mills now buy live cocoons from larger farms all over the prefecture. These cocoons arrive in canvas bags stamped with their origins; the pupae are quickly killed by being spilled onto conveyor belts that take them through a hot air dryer. This process, developed in 1830, made it possible for women to postpone their silk work until after the agricultural season, when they were needed for planting and harvesting crops. Large landowners bought cocoons and doled them out to their peasant tenants for winter reeling. Here, at Nobue Azuma, all cocoons are flash-frozen to kill the worm. With only two people to do the work, this allows the Hiraishis to retrieve only the number they are able to process at one time.

People who call silk producers "murderers," Dolce interjects, don't understand what would happen if they let the pupae live. "If we allowed all the silkworms we've bred to hatch, breed, lay eggs, and on and on, there would not be enough mulberry leaves on the planet to feed them! Or, more likely, they would all die, having lost their natural ability to feed themselves." The modern *Bombyx mori* is not only blind but also unable to fly. Brown like a paper bag, shaped much like its own cocoon, its wings are now small in proportion to its body; it can only flutter. It couldn't find its way to a mate or to a mulberry tree to lay its eggs. (Most eggs are laid on paper now.) According to Ron Cherry in *Cultural Entomology Digest*, the *Bombyx mori* is the sole living species in its family, Bombycidae; all wild populations are considered extinct. Even in India, where 88 percent of the silkworms are mulberry-eating worms, all silkworms have to be hand-fed. The silkworm is a human invention now.

In India, Hindus and Jains, who don't believe in killing animals, produce a silk, *matka*, out of cocoons from which the moths have been allowed to emerge. The silk threads are broken and so must be spun rather than reeled, resulting in a product nowhere near as smooth but "considered unpolluted and suitable for the garments and ropes" used in religious rituals. Ahimsa silk, marketed as "peace silk," is produced in much the same way. *Ahimsa* is a word with Sanskrit roots that means "nonviolence." It refers to the Buddhist philosophy that people should refrain from causing suffering to others. Most Ahimsa manufacturers use the same moth as traditional silk manufacturers, the *Bombyx mori*. The *Bombyx mori* can lay five hundred or more eggs in four to six days.

From one ounce of eggs come about thirty thousand worms. Unless they are hand-fed, as Dolce pointed out, most of the worms will starve or dry out, complicating the issue of avoiding harm.

While in Kyoto, I had the opportunity to ask a Zen priest what the Buddhists thought of wearing silk, given their vow of nonviolence. Was there something in the sutras that prohibited it? Shaku Yuho, whose Western name is Thomas Kirchner, is a scholar and translator at the International Research Institute for Zen Buddhism, as well as a Zen priest at the Tenryu-ji temple in Arashiyama. Having lived and practiced in Japan for over forty-five years, he is the only *gaikokujin* (foreigner) living as a monk in a temple in Kyoto. "Well, people have to wear something, I suppose!" he responded, caught off guard by my question. The first followers of the Buddha, Yuho says, after a pause, got the material for their robes from the trash, from the roadside, or the cremation grounds. They were beggars and thus had to rely on castoffs for their clothing. Because of the stains and rot, they would have to dye the scraps with plants and vegetables, which turned them saffron. That is why, even today, a Buddhist priest's vestments, called *kesa* in Japan, are made of odd pieces of textile, mostly silk, sewn together. Yuho remarks that Dōgen, a Zen priest writing in the thirteenth century, spoke about northern monks wearing leather robes in winter. "Zen Buddhists are not all vegetarians, you know," Yuho says. "There is nothing that dictates that in the sutras." However, Buddhist monks are not known to hunt animals or raise silkworms themselves.

It is a lot of work to metamorphose from a silkworm egg into a worm, then a pupa, only to be aborted at the last stage, yet it is also true that the moth will die naturally, as soon as it has bred and laid its eggs. It is also a lot of work to raise worms and spin the silk, which is how the Hiraishis themselves survive. Hiraishi says that their forty-five thousand worms will yield 100 kilograms of cocoons, or approximately 220 pounds. Twenty percent of the cocoons will be unusable. Each of the cocoons at Nobue Azuma will produce two thousand to three thousand feet of filament, about half a mile. Four to eighteen strands need to be twisted together to make one silk thread. Because raw, reeled silk is gummy, it must be scoured to remove most of the sericin, leaving a bit for strength. And this is far before the threads are dyed and woven into anything resembling a textile. In the end, all the worms I saw eating their way through the two truckloads of mulberry leaves will have produced enough silk for twenty kimonos. (In preindustrial days, before the availability of electric heat or freezers, single farm households in the region could produce only about four pounds a year, or about a third of one kimono.)

The Hiraishis don't sell their cocoons to area factories. All the silk they produce Nobue Hiraishi hand-reels into thread patiently, methodically, by hand. Their silk is called Gunma 200. She lets us watch as she sits at her wooden reel, one by one coaxing the threads from cocoons floating in a trough of hot water and setting them twisting onto a spindle. The result will be a hank of thread coveted by silk artisans worldwide. Yet I am able to purchase that hank for thirty dollars. A week later, in the Silk Center museum in Yokohama, Mr. Koizumi, the director, will tell us that it takes 9,000 cocoons for one woman's kimono and one undergarment, 110 to make a silk scarf, 140 for a tie. "We get it for sad price," Hirata remarks.

The Cloth

Cloth making—reeling, spinning, weaving, knitting—is historically "night work," usually done by women, most often poor women, then and now, all over the earth. In Japan until the late 1980s, farmers and fishermen in rural areas usually owned only one piece of clothing, made from hemp, passed on and patched from generation to generation, and dyed a deep blue with fermented indigo flowers, a clothing that in the Aomori region was called *boro*. "Dyeing the hemp cloth indigo blue and sewing the cotton threads into the loose texture for heat protection, retaining warmth, and reinforcement were the skills of the women who tried to shine in their life of poverty," explains ethnographic researcher Chuzaburo Tanaka in his work for the Amuse Boro Museum in Tokyo. In the villages a hundred years ago, he says, needle merchants were much-anticipated visitors. In many cases, a poor woman's cries heard in the streets were "simply due to the tragic case of a broken needle." Even in areas where women stayed up winter nights reeling silk, it was too precious a material to waste on clothing because it could be bartered for food.

"Not poor," says Sensei Okonogi, when we visit her at the Koyato family's traditional sericulture farm. "I don't use that word," she says. "I call them regular people. They were farmers and merchants. Farmers raised cocoons, along with rice, cotton, hemp, barley, but they rarely saw what they were made into." The sensei, as I have been instructed to call her, is a tiny, black-haired woman, perhaps in her eighties, a retired university history professor now involved in the Japanese renaissance of artisanal silk-growing. In the Shinto religion, she tells me, silk was dedicated to the gods. The emperor would buy a bolt of white silk and offer it once or twice a year to a Shinto shrine. Silk was also used as a tax, and wealth was measured by it. Even as late as the beginning of the nineteenth century, the use of silk was restricted to samurai (military class) and wealthy merchants, then about 20 percent of the total population.

Yet the silkworm sustained people in other ways. "During the Edo Period [1603–1868], in premodern Japan," Okonogi says, leading me to a small wooden frame set up in the yard, "farmers saved the damaged cocoons and boiled them, making the collection of broken and small strands bind together into a material they could spread over a frame. They used this material as warm padding for clothes or blankets." She sits down at the frame and selects a cocoon soaking in a tub of hot water. With a few deft moves, she has opened it, removed the dried pupa, pinned a corner of the cocoon onto the frame, and stretched it into a large, thin square. It resembles a window streaked with rain. "Silk is a protein fiber, much like our skin," she says, picking up another cocoon. "This method of using it was probably the first, the most primitive, like the making of felt." Making *mawata* is not as easy as it appears, I find, but no matter how clumsily I manipulate it, the silk does not tear. We move next into a barn where a group of four women have already made *mawata* squares and, with one on each side, proceed to stretch them even further into panes four or five times their original size. They layer nineteen, twenty, thirty of them on top of each other until the barely-there material becomes something tangible, as well as something which could be blown away by wind. When the pile is about ten inches high, the women slip it into a printed cloth and sew it shut; it has become a baby blanket, something once passed through generations. "You don't know how valuable this is," the sensei says, "when you have nothing."

It is a long way from the plain *mawata* stuffed into the sleeves of a work jacket to the lavishly dyed, woven, and sometimes embroidered silk we associate with the Japanese kimono. As Hirata suggests to me, it is the beauty of the silk that must have inspired the kimono in the first place. "The Japanese," he says, "did not need to concentrate their fashion efforts on tailoring and design because of the striking material they were working with. This is why the kimono is so simple, as well as elegant."

The kimono evolved from the robe-like clothing of the medieval Chinese, and for centuries it was referred to as a *kosode,* which had smaller sleeve openings and was worn with a lower half-apron over it. Sometimes it was made of hemp, sometimes of silk. By the fourteenth century, it lost the apron and was secured with a sash called an obi. In the seventeenth century, the sleeves grew in length and width, creating the traditional butterfly shape, and the obi became longer, its tying more involved and prescribed, its weaving more decorative and textured. (There are different kinds of obis. For instance, geisha obi are one and a half times longer than traditional *fukuro-obis,* at over twenty feet!) Chinese, Japanese, and Western weaving techniques—chiffon, shot silk, brocade, organza, dupioni, velvet, gauze, figured weave, satin weave, twill, and plain weaves—exploited silk's prismatic quality, how each triangular-shaped thread is able to absorb and reflect dyes. It is the shimmering colors of kimonos that captured the world's attention, transforming a piece of clothing into an art object as well as a symbol of Japan.

Many cultures have colors associated with them; the red, white, and blue of the American flag and the greens of Ireland are obvious examples, but no country, other than China perhaps, has developed such a precise sense of color *in and of itself* as Japan. In fact, the traditional Japanese system referred to in literature or used in crafts, and especially in the design of kimonos, contains 465 colors. The system originated with the Chinese over a thousand years ago and is based on their theory of the five elements of nature: wood, fire, earth, metal, and water. Each color is thus associated with certain natural qualities, and its name is often derived from the plant or animal it resembles. The browns include sparrow brown, boiled red bean brown, the brown of a distant river, or cattail; and the greens, pale green onion, old bamboo, young bamboo, water, and a-thousand-herbs. Animals are another inspiration, and the colors used most often are those of mice: grape mouse (purple-gray), Fuji mouse (light purple-gray), willow mouse (light green-gray), and tea mouse (light brown-gray).

In the Azuka period, 538–710 CE, Prince Shōtoku established a class system that forbade the wearing of certain bright colors by commoners. Like all sumptuary laws—enacted in most cultures worldwide at some time or another—they were meant to distinguish the various classes and to make sure lower ones did not usurp the position of the higher ones. In feudal Japan, that meant, in descending order, the samurai, the farmers who supported them, the artisans, and the merchants who sold their goods. Oranges and reds were restricted to the highest rank, the warlords and samurai, possibly due to the fact that they were the most expensive dyes to produce. Some merchants, out of love for color, their growing wealth, or feelings of defiance, lined their dark kimonos with crimson or lemon where no one could see. But color seems to have meant far more than just social status, given the sensitivity to it I see reflected in the fabrics, gardens, and even the food I encounter in Japan. Although those who produced silk for expensive kimonos, bedclothes, and ceremonies did not use it themselves, it seems that most people understood the symbolic power of color and how its use connects them to the trees, flowers, earth, and sky.

Many Japanese travel within their own country, Dolce says, specifically to celebrate each season. They try seasonal foods and plan excursions around what plants are flowering or changing color in autumn; there is cherry blossom season, hydrangea season, moon-viewing season. A garden pavilion we visit is "known as a place to enjoy the autumn grasses." In traditional haiku, the moon, plum blossom, and maple leaf are *rigos*, or seasonal markers that evoke time spent viewing them with others. "One word can create an environment; one word can create this sense of history and lineage," says Hoshinaga Fumio, a contemporary poet, about why he still writes haiku. I once asked Yae Inoue, a Japanese friend in Tokyo, if the schools teach this affection for nature, whether it is perhaps part of the literary or science curriculum. No, she said, the families teach it. Her family marked each season from the time she was a small child, making time to appreciate its beauty. They brought spring foods for their picnics under cherry blossoms. Certain fountains in Tokyo, she said, are famous for the icicles they form in winter. And, as the Japanese say, the moss in their gardens is never as beautiful as when it is raining.

Kusakizome is the word for the ancient Japanese method of dyeing cloth by using natural and seasonal ingredients like roots, buds, leaves, and bark from plants and trees. The word was coined in 1930 by Akira Yamazaki, a scholar of Japanese literature, who used it to distinguish it from the new synthetic dyeing methods being introduced from Europe. Before that, for a thousand years, there was no need. Each dye was simply named for the plant it came from: *ai* (indigo leaves), *akane* (madder root), *yamamomo* (bayberry bark), *shou-en* (pine soot), *enju*

(Japanese pagoda tree buds). Yamazaki spent thirty years collecting and replicating the village hand-weaves and natural dyeing techniques during a time when they were gradually disappearing. In the preface to his pattern book *Nippon Hand Weaves in "Kusakizome" Dyes*, he writes, "I recall with nostalgia my mother's collection of [striped fabric samples] which seemed to symbolize the deep attachment of the old time weavers to their crafts." With the advent of modern chemical dyes as well as Western looms, in just a few decades "wooden hand-looms became firewood in the hearths, and old craftsmen came to be ashamed of their former profession." Yamazaki's book, published in English in 1959, is for connoisseurs: only two hundred copies exist. Each page includes a swatch of fabric handwoven with naturally dyed silk threads: an almost-black made with Asiatic dayflower, a bright gold glittering tweed, the threads dyed with madder, saffron, and gardenia. A fairly mundane-looking striped swatch comes alive when I read what its colors consist of: mountain peach and plum, fermented indigo balls.

Before coming to Japan, I had run across an article by Martin Fackler in the *New York Times* about a Japanese island, Amami Oshima, where the last practitioners of *dorozome*, or mud-dyeing, were trying to hold on to their craft. Their method involves burying a bundle of cloth "in the island's iron-rich soil to turn the silk the color of the darkest chocolate." But long before this happens, the silk is dyed over thirty times with the pulp of a local plum tree, turning it burgundy. Apparently, the tannins in the tree dye interact with the soil, creating the unique dark brown. But even the dyeing is not the last step. After mud-dyeing, the woven silk is unraveled, revealing white stripes where the threads overlapped, and then it is rewoven into intricate patterns. "In a nation that esteems its traditional form of dress as high art, Amami Oshima's kimonos became some of the most prized of them all, once capable of fetching more than $10,000 apiece," Fackler writes. Yet today the weavers say they "are lucky to get more than $400 for a month's exacting work."

Most of the world's clothing is now dyed with synthetic chemicals, which are cheap and readily available, often produced from petroleum or coal. Indigo, for instance, which dyes our blue jeans, was once made from the indigo flower. Today synthetic indigo is a combination of soda, sodamine, and sodium phenylglycinate. Still, Akira Yamazaki's prediction that the ancient crafts of handloom weaving and natural dyeing would disappear has not come true, at least within his own family. His son, Seiju Yamazaki, was named a Living Prefectural Treasure for his skill in keeping the old knowledge alive. And today we have the good fortune to be visiting the studio of Akira's Yamazaki's grandson, Tatehiko Yamazaki. Kusakizome Studios, located in the countryside near Tomioka, produces silk scarves, clothes, and artworks using the traditional natural dyeing methods documented by Yamazaki's grandfather.

When our bus arrives, the entire Yamazaki family—the father in silk-screened T-shirt, the mother in black pants and blouse, the twenty-one-year-old daughter and the tall, thin, oldest son in jeans—greets us in the driveway and ushers us in. The walls of the large, open studio, which we are told used to be a car repair shop, are hung with elegant images of bamboo, maple, and wisteria painted on silk. A back room holds sinks for dyeing. There are outdoor drying racks as well, and large tables on which Yamazaki produces his traditional designs, some harking back to the Heian era, a thousand years ago. He introduces his wife and children, a son whose name in Japanese means Tree, and a daughter named Twig. The son explains that this is because the family loves the forest.

Yamazaki begins by showing us a length of gray silk on which we see, on close inspection, a bamboo grove floating under clouds. The piece seems almost three-dimensional, the scene emerging as the fabric is held this way and that, as if we had encountered the grove in the flickering light before dawn. *Yūzen*, the ingenious method of painting designs on plain-weave fabric rather than having them woven into it, uses stencils and rice paste that resists the many applications of natural dye. Yamazaki cuts his own stencils by hand, an accomplishment that requires such precision that it alone seems skill enough to be known for: one stencil for the individual bamboo leaves, one for the row of trunks, another that produces the trunks' shadows, one simply of clouds. With each layering of a slightly different shade of gray, the elements arrange themselves, collecting into a full picture, an impression as quiet as a light rain beginning or a mist lifting off the moon.

Yamazaki's son, Tree, invites us into the dyeing room, where he gestures toward a tub of water in which steamed cherry stems are soaking. He demonstrates how to take a length of silk and perform a graduated dipping, one end first in the cherry—so lovely a juice I feel an urge to drink it—then wringing it, rinsing it in a tub of clear water, then wringing and dipping it in a tub of alum to set the dye, over and over, with more fabric being lowered each time into the dyestuff, resulting in a color that deepens from the palest pink at the top to a deep blush at the bottom.

A dark, thin woman arrives in an azure kimono, and Hirata tells us that she is going to perform a tea ceremony for us. She wears this summer-weight, unlined kimono due to the unseasonably hot weather, he says, but because it is May, she has chosen an obi woven with tiny flowers. Each kimono, she tells us, has designs and weaves particular to the season it is worn in. It, like the plum blossom she arranges in a vase on the table, the pottery bowls she has brought for tea, even the bean-paste sweets—molded into shapes of pink azalea, rose, bamboo—expresses the freshness of spring. Yaeko Asami slowly spoons out the matcha powder for the tea and whisks it with the required concentration. It is the bright green of lichen. We learn later that she is an expert rock climber and that she has dyed the silk and made this kimono herself. We are instructed to first eat the treat, which is sweet, and then drink the tea, which is bitter.

The Yamazaki family has arranged for other silk artists from Gunma to have lunch with us and later to share their work. Some are hand-loom weavers, some *yūzen* painters, and some natural dyers, like the Yamazakis. Most of them met at the Japan Silk Center or are members of a local dyeing group. When it is time, each artist stands and unfolds some wonder-inspiring thing that looks as if it took months to make and a lifetime—or generations—to learn how to do. "No, I don't sell," one of the women says when asked by one of my tour-mates. "Only for family and friends," Hirata translates. "They are meant to be gifts." Although the Yamazakis make a living off their products, and a few of the women show in galleries and department stores in Tokyo, the silk industry is not where they make their livings. Eriko Okamato, who has shown us a resplendent *roketsuzome* (wax-dyed) wall hanging of the four seasons, for example, is an English teacher at a community college. One woman is a nurse's aide, another a housewife. Just as in America, being an artist often means having another job to pay the bills.

"Not artists," Dolce corrects me, and I sense she is speaking about herself as much as anyone else. "Artisans. Makers of things ordinary people can use." I have been wondering at the vast amounts of time all these artisans take to learn their crafts and execute them—the island mud-dyers of Amami Oshima who unravel the cloth after burying it and then weave it again, and the Yamazaki family heading out to the groves and forests to collect their twigs and buds. I am wondering at the making of clothing as an art form, something that seems to have been practiced in every culture until recently. This may be the first time in history when, globally, most people clothe themselves in overproduced and inferior factory goods.

"I suppose," I say, "people have always wanted to decorate themselves with beautiful things."

"More than that," Dolce responds. "People need to *make* beautiful things."

In the 1920s and 1930s, Sōetsu Yanagi, in reaction to mechanical mass production, founded a folk arts movement called *mingei*, which means "hand-crafted art of ordinary people." In his influential book *The*

Unknown Craftsman, he writes, "On reflection, one must conclude that in bringing cheap and useful goods to the average household, industrialism has been of service to mankind—but at the cost of the heart, of warmth, friendliness, and beauty." Yanagi, a scholar and collector of ancient Korean and Chinese pottery and a pupil of the great Buddhist writer Daisetsu Suzuki, was interested in answering the questions "How does the individual artist function in a world of machines?" and "Is there still a place for handmade things?" The *mingei* movement promoted a return in contemporary culture to a more traditional form of art making. In direct contrast to the Western adulation of individual artists and their genius, the foundation of *mingei* was that art could be made by hand communally, by anonymous craftspeople; that it would be affordable to the ordinary person; that it would be functional in everyday life, or, in other words, useful; and that it would reflect the traditions of the region from which it came.

Yanagi believed in beauty as a human need, in particular the subdued, restrained kind of beauty Westerners associate with Zen Buddhism, and he thought that the ancient folk arts reflected it. *Shibui*, an adjective, refers to the beauty found in Japanese objects, rooms, gardens, textiles, even literature. Yanagi says that its features are "quietness, depth, simplicity, and purity. The beauty it describes is introversive, the beauty of inner radiance." *Shibui* calms; it does not excite. It is, of course, not the only kind of beauty, but Yanagi says that, in the opinion of the Japanese, it is the most mature. "It is this beauty with inner implications that is referred to as *shibui*," he writes. "It is not a beauty displayed before the viewer by its creator; creation here means, rather, making a piece that will lead the viewer to draw beauty out of it for himself."

The *mingei* movement advocated for traditional crafts made without an artist's signature and communally, in guilds where artisans support and teach each other, using regional designs, much like the artisans I am meeting in Japan. Yanagi believed only these ideas would save folk crafts for the future. His call was motivated by more than mere nostalgia or a desire for historic preservation. He believed that the making of art is good for our humanity, for our souls. His thinking, although utopian, was not unrealistic. He believed that there is a place for our machines, but that that place should not be first. First should be human skill and human design. Responsibility also falls to the consumer. Handmade things, though relatively expensive in comparison with cheap goods from factories, he argues, can be enjoyed by generations if we are willing, instead of thrown away when the new season's fashions arrive. "It is unlikely that the clothes we wear today will ever be displayed in art galleries," he writes. "This is because they are poor in material and design."

Yanagi was not asking us to give up our love of art museums, galleries, or even the paintings, or prints of paintings, on our living room walls. Although he speaks for the utilitarian nature of art, he also founded the Nihon Migei-kan (Japanese Folk Crafts Museum) in Tokyo and for decades was its director. There countless objects sit, unused, except for the modern use we make of things simply by looking at and thinking about them. Yet the fact that *making* has been taken away from the hands of ordinary people everywhere is now, as it was when Yanagi wrote in 1952, "so widespread that a number of awakened people are seeking to counter it by working with their hands."

The Indigo Master: A Microbial Interlude

Anyone who has been fortunate enough to encounter Mount Fuji in person—internationally recognizable because of Hokusai's series of thirty-six woodblock prints, including *The Great Wave of Kanagawa*, *Red Fuji*, and *Rainstorm beneath the Summit*—will understand why the artist was so obsessed with it. Rising as a perfect pyramid far into the sky, seemingly from nothing, it looms volcanic, ancient, godlike. We are lucky, we are told, that Mount Fuji, or Fuji-san, as many Japanese respectfully call it, is not hiding in mists when we encounter it. We are even luckier that this morning the mountain is doubled by its perfect reflection in Lake Kawaguchi, which sits at its base. After breakfast, as we are driven into the foothills, a half hour up a winding, narrow, two-lane road lined with rice paddies and small cottages bordered by blue hydrangeas, Hirata tells us that today we are in for another special treat. We have been invited to the studio of an artist who practices a form of natural dyeing that is different from but every bit as ancient and specialized as *kusakizome*. Today we are to meet an Indigo Master.

When we arrive at her mountain home, Fumiko Satoh comes outside to greet us, bowing, as the Japanese do, and clasping our hands warmly. Satoh is a tiny woman with a shock of thick white hair, like mine. Dressed from head to toe in dusk-blue cloth, she laughs at my hair and touches hers, and tells Hirata I should come to live with her. I will teach her English, and she will teach me Japanese. "Because you like a simple life, too," Hirata remarks. I don't know if it is my hair—few Japanese women let their graying hair go undyed—or because I told him I have no TV, but Hirata has formed a vision of my life in Montana as primitive and ascetic. The Indigo Master's studio, a classically designed wood-frame home with sliding screens and a wraparound veranda, is hardly that, nor is mine. But as with my life in the mountains, which involves a pastoral tension between the forest and the city, the ATVs that invade on weekends and the mine tailings that have entered the stream, her life is not as simple as people who divide the world into rural and urban want to believe. The first thing I noticed when we pulled up to Satoh's home was the tracks for a new high-speed bullet train under construction right across the road.

Satoh's studio is dreamy—two open rooms, one wood-floored with a low table for tea, the walls hung with white banners splashed with inky swirls, and one in which four circular vats are embedded in a concrete floor. She squats over a hole in the center of them and uses an iron hook to pull up a bucket of burning ash. She is around seventy yet has the flexibility of a child. She must weigh all of eighty pounds.

The ashes are to keep the vats warm as the indigo flowers, stirred with a mixture of wood ash lye and bran or sake, ferment for a week. This process is called *sukumo*, or "building indigo." We crowd around as she lifts the lid on one of the vats, revealing a bubbling purple-green soup. She uses a stick taller than she is and vigorously stirs, turning the fermenting indigo a deep, outer-space violet. And then she bends over, sticks her tongue in, and licks it.

Kon-zome is the art of dyeing with the fermented indigo plant. In Japan, it was once the most popular dyeing method, coloring the hemp clothes of farmers and fishermen as well as the silk robes of the samurai. The leaves of Japanese indigo, *Persicaria tinctoria*, were allowed to decay, as Satoh has demonstrated, then compacted and dried into *aidama*, hard, black balls that could be sold to dyers. To learn how to make it, Satoh worked on an indigo farm for five years in her youth, learning to pick and dry the leaves and layer them with water to start the fermentation. "After about a hundred days of fermentation time, the mixture becomes a kind of compost," she says. "This is a difficult job conducted by an indigo master who controls and adjusts the temperature constantly." In Japan, it has always been common practice for indigo farmers to make the dye and for dyeing artists to purchase it. Like much other textile work, it depended on a division of labor. But Satoh wanted to know how it was done.

She says she checks the conditions inside the vats once a day. She smells the brew, looks at it, and listens for the sound it makes when she churns it: "If the sound of the churning stick makes a high-pitch clattering noise when it comes into contact with the vat, I think of it as a sign that the alkaline is in a stable condition." If the levels are low, she hears a muffled sound. Finally, she tastes it. Satoh says that, like people, the bacteria will be happiest when the temperatures are comfortable for it. Like people, she says, it finds itself most comfortable at sixty-eight to seventy-eight degrees. When the dye is overused, the colors become unattractive. "I believe that this is advice from the indigo dye saying, 'You need to take a break.'" When she underuses it, she says it is telling her she might want to start working hard again. "I think indigo dye gives me lessons on how to work in harmony with the flow of nature," she tells us.

Fresh indigo produces the lightest blue. Unlike the powdered, synthetic kind, which wasn't available until 1897, it must be watched over, stirred, and heated to produce the dark blue we associate with denim. Satoh reaches her hand in, brings up the sludge, invites us to feel it. Only one woman does, staining her hand with its ink. An intoxicating, putrid smell of rotting lettuce fills the space, and the rest of us step back. Satoh is talking in Japanese about the alkaline levels, and Hirata has stopped translating, intuiting perhaps that the rest of the group is eager to move on to the silk scarves and clothing Satoh has on display. Something, Satoh seems to be saying, has gone wrong with the process in one of the vats. She gets on her knees, bends over the offending vat, and frowns. Although bacteria are neither plant nor animal, they are living organisms. Satoh is worrying over them as if they were friends.

With indigo dyeing, Satoh explains, soaking the fabric longer doesn't result in a darker color. It is the successive repetitions—soaking, wringing, air-drying, which she does by flapping the fabric in the air—that create the deepest dyes. Satoh also practices a special kind of indigo dyeing called *itajime shibori*, which utilizes a wooden board to prevent parts of the fabric from absorbing the dye, thus creating the white and various blue designs associated with this kind of cloth. The way Satoh speaks of the process of building indigo reminds me of the way Sensei Okonogi spoke of the *mawata* and those who stretched the cocoons, spreading the breath-thin layers into a blanket for the next generation; the way Tatehiko Yamazaki's children are named Twig and Leaf; how for thousands of years, so far under the radar of most of us, millions of people all over the world have been feeding silkworms—how these beings, these delicate beings, are fed with care.

The Rise and Fall of Tomioka

In Gail Tsukiyama's novel *Women of the Silk*, a small group of women sold into servitude to a Chinese filature factory form a sisterhood, vowing to remain unmarried and to devote the rest of their lives to silk work. To go through the "hairdressing ceremony"—hair pinned atop their heads to distinguish them from the other women in the village—was a choice, unlike the vows of marriage, which were arranged, or their servitude, which had brought them there. "It's a choice that cannot be taken lightly. It must be a way of life that you want more than any other, and to wander from it will bring great shame to your family and anger the gods," a character says. The women begin their apprenticeship sorting cocoons, removing the stained or damaged ones, before they are promoted to steamy rooms where they stir the cocoons in boiling water to loosen the web. The most skilled position goes to those who deftly lift the end of the almost invisible filament in each cocoon and reel it together with the others, forming a thread to be spooled onto the mechanical reels. They are responsible for spotting any breaks in the winding filaments and splicing them rapidly by hand.

I am thinking about these women when we visit Tomioka Silk Mill, founded in 1872 and closed in 1987, now a UNESCO World Heritage Site. Along with a hundred or so Japanese tourists, we stroll the cavernous, abandoned warehouses, regimentally lined with long rows of mechanical reels, imagining the heat and the deafening roar such machines must have produced as they reeled lengths of silk from tiny cocoons. As in Tsukiyama's novel, at Tomioka the mill hands were women, over three hundred of them, some as young as fourteen. (From 1894 to 1912, women made up 60 percent of Japan's industrial labor force, most of them working in the textile industry in major centers like Tomioka.) Our tour guide says that in order to lure women employees from the countryside, the first Japanese supervisor, Junchu Odaka, had to hire his own fourteen-year-old daughter as an example. Someone who had seen the French consultants drinking wine had started a rumor, which spread fast across the country, that the French drank blood, so most families were afraid to send their daughters to work there.

The place is bare and boring without the women. On display are photos of the French experts, who came to teach the new techniques, as well as those of the various owners: Mitsui, Hara, Katakura. The reeling machines, built in France and modeled on their industry, were specifically manufactured, a sign reads, "to suit the average size of a female Japanese worker." At one point, our tour guide says, international demand for silk was so great that the owners of the mill distributed silkworm eggs for free to area farmers. The Arafune Cold Storage, a natural cave located in the mountains above the city, was the largest place to store silkworm eggs in Japan. Over a million trays of eggs, which must be kept below 65 degrees to prevent hatching, were stored there until they were needed. Research stations proliferated. Silkworms were bred to be bigger and for their cocoons to reel more easily onto the new industrial machines. In fact, demand for healthy silkworms caused many farmers to abandon traditional crops like rice altogether in favor of mulberry trees. Today the grounds of the former mill are ghostly, the machines dusty, the dorms where the women slept too dilapidated to allow entrance to tourists. The countryside is once again poor. The dramatic rise and fall of the Tomioka Silk Mill took place in a little over a hundred years. One might ask, What in the world happened? Almost everything, it seems.

✦

Silkworms were introduced into Sicily and Spain by Muslim traders in the twelfth century, and sericulture quickly spread across Europe. Because Japan's raw silk was unavailable and Chinese cloth was limited and costly, each region developed its own silkworm strains, bred to thrive in its particular climate. Once reeled, the raw silk could be shipped to distant weaving mills fairly easily. By the fifteenth and sixteenth centuries, Italy was dominating the market for silk textiles;

Venice and Florence, in particular, became renowned for producing a sumptuous brand of velvet that incorporated gold and silver threads. In France, Louis XI ordered mulberry groves planted near Paris, Tours, and Orléans, in order to supply the crown and nobles with less expensive silk than they had previously gotten from the Italians, enlisting and training women reelers and weavers from the ranks of peasantry. The industry subsequently moved to the south, near Lyon, where at one time eleven thousand handlooms were established. More than a third of the population, about fifteen thousand people, were at one time silk workers.

Most of these weavers were Protestants; when the Huguenot persecutions began in 1685, approximately fifty thousand trained weavers abandoned France and fled to England, thus establishing Britain's fledgling silk industry. "Silk brocades and watered tabinets, satins and satinettes, camblets and cheveretts, prunelles, allimancoes and florentines, diamantines and grenadines, blondines, bombazines, belle-isles and martiniques," writes novelist W. G. Sebald in his description of the silks produced in preindustrial Norwich, "were of a truly fabulous variety, and of an iridescent, quite indescribable beauty as if they had been produced by Nature itself, like the plumage of birds."

In 1623, James I, hoping that the New World climate would produce better raw silk than the wet, cold weather of the homeland, demanded that Virginians plant mulberry bushes and practice sericulture. Bounties were decreed and fines levied if farmers didn't obey. Two problems persisted, however. First, sericulture, as it had been practiced from China to Europe to India, was a cottage industry, meaning it was practiced in individual households, often employed the entire family, and sometimes took over the farmhouse with its cocoons. Although it required less acreage than other forms of traditional farming, it was invariably time- and labor-intensive. In the colonies, where land was abundant and where tobacco and cotton growing were more lucrative and much easier, farmers resisted silk. The dramatic seasonal changes were also terrible for mulberries. Frosts regularly decimated groves. Then, in 1844, blight wiped out almost all the trees in the country.

In 1849, the *pébrine* pandemic hit the silkworms of southern France. The disease, which caused black spots to appear on the larvae, made the worms unable to weave their cocoons and eventually killed them. Pébrine sped north to Tours and south to Italy, even threatening the populations in northern Africa. The European climates, with their fluctuating temperatures, could possibly have been a factor, as might have been low-quality mulberry leaves, or unhygienic growing practices. Regardless, worms died by the billions. Fifteen years later, the silk industries in France and Italy were in ruins. In India, where sericulture had been practiced almost as long as in China, silk produced from indigenous moths was traded extensively during the Middle Ages. The *Bombyx mori* was introduced in 1771 and soon became the preferred species, producing a higher-quality silk that weaving centers in England would accept. When the epidemic hit in 1866, the industry in India too collapsed.

Contemporaneous with these disasters, the Taiping Rebellion in China was raging through the sericulture districts of the Yangtze valley, causing great damage to the farms and disrupting the weaving industries in the cities. Lasting from 1850 to 1864, it was one of the bloodiest wars in human history; thirty times more people were killed during the Taiping Rebellion than during the American Civil War. Consequently, Chinese silk production foundered.

It was exactly then, in 1853, amid these auspicious events, that Commodore Perry's black ships forced the opening of Japan's ports. British and European merchants, anxious to protect their crop, rushed to Japan and eagerly bought up all the healthy silkworm eggs and silk they could find. Because of *sakoku*, Japanese silkworms were thriving. While the pébrine pandemic was doing its damage in Europe, writes Junko Thérèse Takeda in "Global Insects: Silkworms, Sericulture, and Statecraft in Napoleonic France and Tokugawa Japan," female sericulturalists in Japan continued their ancient practices: "Respecting the insects with whom they cohabitated, the women gave their caterpillars honorific titles, 'kaiko-sama' (Sir Silkworm) or 'oko-sama' (Madame Silkworm). They fastidiously cleaned their clothes, hands and utensils. At certain stages of rearing, they abstained from sex with their husbands, devoting themselves exclusively to their caterpillars."

Japanese production doubled between 1904 and 1914, mostly to meet American demand. By 1916, the country was supplying the United States with 70 percent of its raw silk. In 1929, the United States imported $396 million worth of raw silk, 95 percent of which came from Japan. It was the age of the silk stocking in America! It was, at the same time, the "apex of kimono production in Japan," as Terry Satsuki Milhaupt writes in her book *Kimono: A Modern History*. Before industrialization, only about 20 percent of the people in Japan—the samurai and wealthy merchants—could afford to wear silk kimonos. The surplus of silk, a consequence of new industrial looms, better genetic strains of silkworms, and increasing demand, made the fabric suddenly affordable to the general public. In a 1925 survey of the Ginza district in Tokyo, most of the women wore silk kimonos.

World War II was the tipping point. In the 1940s, American customers began to boycott Japanese silk in protest over Japan's invasion of China. When Japan entered World War II, all imports of Japanese goods were, of course, cut off in America and Europe. Back in Japan, because of the time-consuming work of weaving, dyeing, and design, silk came to symbolize a decadent way of life in wartime. Eventually the Japanese government banned its manufacture—except for use in the thousands of *yosegaki* flags that Japanese soldiers carried into battle, a red sun printed on white silk, covered with the handwritten signatures and wishes of their families and friends. In Nishijin, power looms were broken apart and repurposed for weapons manufacture. Former silkworm farmers were reduced to boiling and eating the pupae inside the cocoons. The people called it "cheese"; it prevented many farm families from starving.

After the war, petroleum-based synthetic fabrics, which could be manufactured cheaply, further diminished the demand. Rayon (or "artificial silk"), nylon, polyester, Spandex: all these took a big bite out of the textile markets in Europe and America that were earlier dominated by silk. Suddenly, everything about silk began to seem ostentatious and old-fashioned or at least inconvenient. Japanese women were increasingly adopting Western dress in lieu of the kimono. For Westerners, heavily embroidered and woven silk garments were too bulky for streamlined modern tastes and too hard to care for. Milhaupt writes, "By 1920, Nagano prefecture had gained a reputation as a 'silk kingdom' and silk dominated the region's economy....By the late twentieth century, only one silk spinning factory survived in Nagano, and only one household was still engaged in sericulture." In 1987, the Tomioka mill closed after operating continuously for 115 years. (The decline of sericulture was not limited to Japan; it is said that Lady Diana's silk wedding dress was made from cocoons grown at England's last active silkworm farm.)

In *The Silk Weavers of Kyoto: Family and Work in a Changing Traditional Industry*, Tamara K. Hareven writes that even Nishijin, where I bought my sister's silk scarf, is facing "impending doom." I remember walking the side streets of the neighborhood, crowded with wooden cottages where weavers have lived and worked for generations. The houses are called *nagi-no-ne-doko*, "the sleeping place of the eel," because of their narrowness. "Today," says Matsuo Hiroko, one of the elder handloom weavers, "the traditional townhouses of the artisans are being pulled down, creating a desert of vacant lots in which it is now rare to hear a child's voice." Weaving is being outsourced to rural areas, where labor is cheaper. According to Hareven, 40 percent of silk weavers in Japan now either work in the countryside, as is true of fishermen and farmer's wives on the Tango Peninsula islands, or are trained and equipped in China and Korea.

Secondhand kimono shops, as we discover on our tour, are everywhere in Japan, from street stalls in Kyoto and Kamakura to back rooms in souvenir shops located miles from cities along country roads. Usually narrow, with tables and racks crowded with thousands of folded and hung kimonos of every possible hue, as well as stacks of bright, ornately woven obi embroidered with flowers, trees, and birds, they are treasure troves for those kimono connoisseurs who recognize pattern and vintage and a delightful confusion for someone like me. Walking into one of these shops is like walking into a rainbow. One day in Imaizumi, after a lunch of miso soup, braised pork, and plum ice served in the tiniest blue-glazed bowl, the proprietor of the restaurant opened for us the vintage shop she kept next door. The rest of the women on the tour immediately began shopping, somewhat madly, in a way that reminded me of how I have acted when allowed into my friend's raspberry patch.

One woman found a white undergarment splashed with scarlet raindrops, on the right sleeve, something written in kanji. When asked, the proprietor explained to us that once, when she was young, a famous Japanese writer came to dine at her restaurant. That night a geisha happened to be entertaining the clientele. Recognizing the writer, the geisha pulled back her kimono sleeve and asked him to sign his name in order to honor him. Did the geisha trade her undergarment for money owed the restaurant that night, or, coming on hard times later in her life, perhaps during the war, did she come back to the inn of her youth, knowing the garment's value? "Too expensive for someone to buy who doesn't know what it is," Hirata said. During the war, Milhaupt writes, the term *takenoko seikatsu*, "bamboo shoot existence," was used to describe the situation where one "peel[ed] off one's clothing, like the layers of a bamboo shoot, in order to trade these precious commodities for food and other necessities." During the lean years of the US occupation after the war, kimonos were often bartered. Today people who need extra money or extra room often sell or donate the wardrobes their ancestors left them.

If one envisions the Silk Road as a temporal rather than spatial route, one could follow it up and down through thousands of years of global warfare, political alliances, migrations, fluctuations in disease and human rights, economic boons and failures—a trajectory that might also be mirrored in the fluctuating fortunes of the silkworm itself, and those who tend to it. In China, the decline in demand for raw silk in the 1920s and '30s affected thousands of women, like those in Tsukiyama's novel who worked in the modern reeling factories, sending them, as it did the characters in the novel, into domestic service. The women who worked in the Tomioka Reeling Factory: where did they go? Since 1984, an average of fifty manufacturers have shut down each year. Sericulture in Japan has also suffered. According to the Japanese Information Network, in 1975 there were 250,000 farms producing "90,000 tons of cocoons." Today, the site says, that number has diminished to almost nothing.

As we board the bus after visiting the Tomioko factory, the manager of the bus company, who has been accompanying us in his home region of Gunma as a matter of personal pride and goodwill, gives Dolce a large, stuffed plastic bag. Using the microphone to get our attention, she tells us that he was approached by an old samurai family who had heard of our silk tour. Perhaps we would be interested in an antique kimono, which they have been keeping within their family for centuries but for which they now have no room. They would like to give it away to anyone who would appreciate it. Dolce pulls the heavy fabric out of the bag and holds the kimono up for us to see. It is king-sized, a blanket of heavy, hand-loomed white silk, lined with crimson. At the bottom of the bag, she fishes out an emerald obi glittering with gold threads. She decides that the only fair way to do this is to have a drawing. We all put our names in. Then, to my astonishment, I win.

Holding the heavy garment in my lap on the bus, I instantly regret having put my name in the raffle. I feel embarrassed by my greed for something glittering—like the farmer's wife who chose the heavier gift from the family of the Tongue-Cut Sparrow—but even more ashamed by the fact that I don't want it. Thick padding weights the hem, made to drape as the samurai's wife glided across clean floors, floors cleaned by someone who was most likely prohibited from wearing silk. But some woman—many women—made it by hand. Someone grew the caterpillars that wove the cocoons, while someone else reeled the silk, and someone, or probably many, wove the stylized chrysanthemum designs into it. Someone dyed the cloth, perhaps with cochineal. Yet I have no place for it, just as there was no place in the family home of those who inherited it. I was offered the kimono, and then I, too, passed it on.

Later, when I return to America, I will find an image of a startlingly similar kimono in Milhaupt's book, in a reproduction of a painting by James Tissot titled *La Japonaise au bain*. In this painting a European woman stands in a doorway wearing a kimono with the same bright lining and weighted trim, only she wears it open so we can see a glimpse of her naked body underneath. What I had been offered, the text says, is an "outer robe," called an *uchikake*. It was a formal garment, something to be worn on state occasions, by a wealthy woman of the military class. In Milhaupt's book, I also read of the tradition of "preserving clothing as family heirlooms," which I witnessed in many homes in Japan. One afternoon, Hirata's wife, Rumiko, had shown us drawers filled with the kimonos her mother wore, each carefully wrapped in rice paper.

◥◣

In Japan, silk production has dropped from over twenty thousand tons to fewer than two thousand in the past forty years; however, it is still the number-one consumer of raw silk in the world, most of it imported from China. According to *Trade Forum Magazine*, 50 percent of it is used to make kimonos. The kimono, in fact, is enjoying a resurgence. Milhaupt writes that, since 2000, men and women wearing kimonos have "strolled the Ginza" on Saturday afternoons when Tokyo's shopping streets are traditionally blocked off. People purchase kimonos for their weddings and wear them for special family occasions. In Kyoto, buses sometimes offer free rides to those wearing kimonos, and kimono fashion shows, as I experienced, are well-attended. Worldwide, silk production hasn't slowed; it actually has doubled during the past thirty years. Though silk accounts for only 2 percent of the global textile market, it is a multibillion-dollar industry. India, the second-largest producer in the world, can't keep up with its own demand. For China, history has come full circle. After 4,700 years, it is again the source for most of the world's raw silk, producing 80 percent of it.

There are about ten million silkworm growers in China. Seven hundred thousand households in India rely on sericulture, as do hundreds of thousands more in Thailand, Brazil, and Vietnam. There are many reasons for this. Silkworms can be grown on very little land, require inexpensive equipment, and result in a high return—silk sells for roughly twenty times what cotton does. It has been, and is, a way for many rural people to move out of poverty. Sericulture is also environmentally friendly, using little energy and a fraction of the water needed to grow cotton. (Cotton accounts for 3 percent of global water consumption and 7 percent of US use of pesticides.) The growing of mulberry trees contributes oxygen to the air and nutrients to the soil. On the other hand, no one would argue that silk isn't labor-intensive. There is the growing of worms, the filature reeling, the weaving (whether on a handloom or a power one), the dyeing, the sewing and embroidery. It is said that women working in the large filature factories in today's China often toss the pupae into the boiling water and eat them, since they have few breaks to sit down for lunch. Given all this, silk is relatively cheap to buy. Whether or not we "get it for a sad price," as Hirata says, depends on a depth and wealth of factors, as well as our awareness. It depends on the health of the silkworm and that of its caretakers, one could say its kin.

4 Feathers

Symbol

To catch the eye of potential mates, to claim authority over others, to distinguish oneself as a member of a clan, a tribe, a religion: these are traditional functions of clothing, in addition to what is the most obvious—to protect us from the elements, to provide shelter. Earrings carved of ivory, necklaces strung with the claws and teeth of bears, bright feathers threaded into the weave of a grass skirt—some historians believe that the first clothing was not for a physical purpose at all: "The fact [is], in more temperate regions, hunting peoples are adorned rather than clothed," states François Boucher in *20,000 Years of Fashion*. If one distinguishes, as Boucher does, between *clothing*, which is what one wears to keep oneself warm or dry, and *costume*, which reflects one's belief system—religious, aesthetic, political—we can say that clothing often depends on climate and resource availability, whereas costume is culturally determined, whether one is dancing in an eagle feather headdress on the Pine Ridge Reservation or in ostrich feather boas on stage in Las Vegas.

Feathers, in particular, have played a role in our costumes. It makes sense that they would: in preindustrial landscapes around the world, bird feathers were often the brightest and most durable sources of color. In addition, birds themselves, perhaps more than any other animal, have captured our imaginations. As Thor Hanson, author of *Feathers: The Evolution of a Natural Miracle*, writes, "Unlike paints or dyes, feathers bring more than just color to a composition. They come imbued with all the characteristics, symbolism, and mythologies associated with their species." Depending on the bird, feathers can represent peace, war, fragility, strength, courage, joy, and even humor. Birds soar high in the sky, which in many cultures is the upper world, the realm of the gods. The Latin word for "bird," *ave*, originally meant both "bird" and "spirit." We earth-bound creatures are in awe of them.

Think of the pure turquoise of the mountain bluebird's wing or the yellow warbler, a gold spark in the willow. Nothing else but the green of plants, which is perishable, and the blue sky, which is unattainable, is more saturated. Bird feathers gain their colors in two ways. The first is through pigmentation, which they make inside their cells—the pine siskin's brown, the raven's utter black—or ingest through their food. The cardinal has to eat the redness in berries to be red, the flamingo the pinkness in crustaceans. As Hanson explains, "When light hits a pigment-bearing feather, part of the spectrum is absorbed, and the rest is reflected back to our eyes as color." The second way is caused by the structure of the feather itself, which splinters light in different directions. One sees reflection in the purple sheen off the black raven's wing, the green iridescence off the magpie's. Blue feathers are almost always produced by light-scattering air pockets in the barbs, which is why jays don't appear blue in shadow.

The number of bird species in the world is around 9,672, and the number of birds close to 400 billion. Each bird comes equipped with feathers: in the case of a hummingbird, a thousand; in the case of a swan, twenty-five times more. Feathers are considered part of the "integumentary" system that protects an animal's body: skin, hair, scales, hooves, fingernails, toenails, feathers. For humans, clothing is an imitation, and extension, of this system. Feathers, like our skin and hair, are made of the protein keratin. Like hair, they grow out of the bird's skin from follicles that are surrounded by sensitive muscles and nerves. The bird uses these to control the movement of each feather as it flies, lands, preens. Many kinds and colors of feather can grow from the same follicle during the lifetime of the bird, replacing ones that molt or are damaged. Once feathers reach their optimum size, the blood flow, and thus the growth, stops.

We are also attracted by feathers' plumed shape. Like the leaves on deciduous trees, feathers vary in color, size, and to some degree shape, but they all follow the same basic design. Each feather begins as a hollow tube, called the quill or *calamus*, which grows out of the follicle and extends into the *rachis*, the feather's central shaft. Growing from the rachis, as from a tree's trunk, are slender branches called *barbs* that are, in turn, branched, forming what we identify as the feathery part of the feather. These *barbicels* have tiny hooks that enable them to attach to one another, which is what we observe when we find a disheveled feather and are able to smooth it back into shape. Together, rachis, barbs, and barbicels form the feather's *vane*. Each bird has different kinds of feathers. *Contour feathers* are the most numerous; they overlap like the shingles on a house and protect a bird's body from the elements. *Flight feathers*, found on the wing and tail, are recognizable because one side of the vane will be noticeably thinner. *Down*, as most of us know, is light and fluffy and provides insulation under the other feathers. Down feathers are short and grow without any barbs to knit them together. *Semiplumes* and *filoplumes* are extralong plumes that may fine-tune flight, and *bristles* function as protection and as sensors on the bird's head, neck, and eyes.

Paleontologists have been arguing for centuries about whether bird feathers developed for flight, which has been popularly assumed, or for something else—mating, protection, species identification. But, if flight, why do birds that can't fly have them? If something else, how did feathers contribute to flight? These are some of the questions that initially led Hanson to write his book, and such questions have led me to a seaside cafe in Friday Harbor, San Juan Island, one of the many islands in the San Juan archipelago that lies between the US mainland and Vancouver Island. I have made this extended pilgrimage from Montana to interview him because as far as I can tell, *Feathers: The Evolution of a Natural Miracle* is currently the only comprehensive book on feathers—their origins, structure, symbolism, and use across cultures.

Trained in botany and resource conservation, Hanson grew up on nearby Lopez Island. He is a small, thin man in his early forties, professorial, his blond hair in a ponytail, his glasses wire-rimmed, wearing a well-worn wool sweater ragged at the cuffs. "I couldn't believe that no one had written a book about feathers before—not an identification guide but one that explained what a feather is and does," he says. "It started with my fascination with vultures and the lack of feathers on their heads. I started thinking about the evolutionary pressures that would cause that, and that got me thinking about the evolution of feathers in general."

In Hanson's book, those who believe feathers evolved for flight debate whether the impetus was from the ground up—dinosaurs flapping their arms to gain momentum to scale the trunk of a tree— or from the tree down—dinosaurs needing help to drift back to the ground. Some argue that the seemingly unnecessary patterning and color in feathers point to a desire for sexual display. Others speculate that they were primarily for cooling—or for warming when the climate cooled. "What about down?" I ask him. "Not every bird produces it, right?"

"All birds have feathers with down, even if they don't have a layer of full downy feathers like a tundra swan," Hanson says as we watch three ravens perched on a post at the ferry dock below, the wind ruffling their glossy feathers. There must be some down to them, or they wouldn't seem so comfortable in this mid-February damp chill. "Even birds in hot places need some insulation," he says. "No matter where you are, it still cools off at night. But you're going to get a lot more from geese or swans who have evolved sitting in cold water all day."

I am thinking about my friends who, when I tell them I am writing about feathers and our clothing, immediately picture ornament—a pheasant's plume on a fedora—but seldom the down stuffed into the "featherweight" North Face puffer jacket they are wearing. In one of his chapters, Hanson describes the down supply chain in China as a pastoral of merchants bicycling from rural farm to farm with their carts, collecting the duck and geese feathers the peasants have been saving all year from their dinner tables, a symbol of sustainability that I find rather romantic, given the popularity and ubiquity of down jackets, vests, and parkas one sees everywhere on the streets today.

"It's really hard to imagine, I know," Hanson says. "But here's a statistic I find helpful. The last time I checked, China's population was 1.2 billion, plus or minus 3 percent. If we're talking about something as common in a people's diet like duck or goose...well, you can see how that is possible."

In his book, Hanson writes that birds use their own plucked feathers to line their nests, softening and warming them as we do when we cover our beds with down comforters. At least a quarter of bird species do so. Symbol, sex, status, shelter—could there be any other use for this material that already seems so multifaceted in its usefulness?

Hanson ponders a second and then smiles. "It's lovely to watch swallows passing feathers to each other in the air, I suppose as a kind of play. Certain grebes take feathers out of the water and eat them, which is thought to be protection against the sharp bones of the fish they swallow whole. They feed feathers to their chicks so they can make pellets to throw up the bones. Mice and other rodents also line their nests with feathers. But, as far as we know, they don't collect them like I do for, say, their beauty."

"Is there anything about feathers you didn't cover in your book, anything that remains to be said?" I ask, laughing.

"Feathers are one of the only materials that are not processed before we use them. They don't have to be spun or woven or dyed or tanned or cultured. They are gathered and washed with simple soap and water, whereas if you're going to make something out of wool, there is a lot of processing. Or silk. Or leather. We haven't changed a thing. We use feathers for the exact same purpose that they evolved—except, of course, for flight. And I think that's extremely interesting."

Sex

The ostrich (*Struthio camelus*) can't fly, although it can run up to forty-three miles an hour, using its wings to turn. Contrary to popular belief, it does not stick its head in the sand. Rather, when frightened, it has a habit of lying flat on the ground, its dirt-colored head blending in with the dirt, and thus disappearing as if down a hole. It is the world's largest bird, yet ballerina-like, with overlong, almost featherless legs and neck and enormous, unblinking eyes. Until 1863, when they were first domesticated, ostriches lived wild in small herds in southern Africa and the deserts of the Sahara and the Sahel. Domesticating them was not that easy. In the wild, ostriches exhibit elaborate patterns of dominance that affect breeding; these did not transfer well to being caged. Often, farmers had to hire native girls to sit on the eggs, a scene incredible to imagine considering each egg weighs as much as two dozen chicken eggs. An ostrich egg incubator, invented in 1864, solved the problem and eliminated many of the girls' jobs.

"Ostrich feathers were valuable commodities at the beginning of the twentieth century, their value per pound almost equal to that of diamonds," writes Sarah Abrevaya Stein in her fascinating book *Plumes: Ostrich Feathers, Jews, and a Lost World of Global Commerce*. In the 1850s, feathers decorated hats in Europe and America, but most were "fancy feathers," those that came from wild songbirds, turkeys, herons, and egrets. The popularity of the extravagant ostrich feather, which took the fashion world by storm, was fueled in part by the colonization of Africa, where it was, as Stein says, seen as exotic "colonial booty." Napoleon's wife, the Empress Eugenie, favored a small hat worn tilted over one eye, decorated with a large ostrich plume, and soon fashionable women across Europe were wearing the "empress hat." One can see why the ostrich feather caught everyone's attention: huge, buoyant with fluff, easily dyed, it resembles nothing so much as a flamboyant tail. Flamboyant, from *flambe*, French for "flame." At the market's height, in the 1890s, South Africa fed and plucked a million ostriches a year. England, center of the millinery trade, became the biggest purchaser. When the *Titanic* sank in 1912, bound for New York, twenty thousand pounds of ostrich plumes sank with it.

Prior to the farms, ostriches were hunted by nomads who, after killing and plucking the birds, transported the feathers by camel caravan to ports on the Mediterranean: Tripoli, Tunis, Cairo, Mogador. It took six months to a year for the caravans to complete the round trip and return with trade goods: spices, teas, sugar, perfumes, mirrors. As demand for ostrich feathers increased in Europe, the wild flocks were quickly decimated. One of the most coveted feathers came from the so-called Barbary ostrich in Sudan, which produced a lofty "double fluff." (Regular feathers often had to be augmented by sewing a number of trimmed feathers together so that they looked like a gigantic one, a highly skilled process called "willowing.") In a story worthy of a crime novel, Dutch farmers stole into French Sudan in 1912 and kidnapped 156 Barbary ostriches. These they successfully bred with the Cape ostrich, turning Oudtshoorn, in the eastern part of South Africa, into the home of the world's largest ostrich population.

According to Stein, Jewish emigrants controlled the feather industry of the late nineteenth century for many reasons: they were often fluent in many languages; they had a wide network of family and trading partners around the world because of the various diasporas; they were fleeing pogroms in Russia; and they were already experienced artisans, working as tanners, tailors, weavers, and dealers of hides, furs, and guano for generations. "In the Cape, over 90 percent of feather merchants—numbering roughly five hundred at their peak— were Yiddish-speaking immigrants from Lithuania in the Russian Empire," says Stein. In Africa, Jewish men were the middlemen between the farmers and the clients. (The Dutch owned the farms, and native Africans did the dirty work, usually for poor wages, tending to the birds, plucking them, and sorting the feathers.) In London, New York, and Paris, the centers of feather-related manufacturing, Jewish women and girls filled most of the skilled and unskilled positions, such as cleaning, trimming, willowing, and dyeing. Twenty-two thousand people worked in the feather industry in London at its peak, most of them immigrant females. Then, just as suddenly as the feather market exploded, it collapsed. By 1915, Stein writes, ostrich feathers, which had been thought to be classic like diamonds, were "viewed as fragile, dated, and tawdry." What happened?

Biomimicry, Hanson told me in our interview, is behind much of our human attraction to feathers. The showgirls in Las Vegas and the Moulin Rouge or the revelers in Mardi Gras parades in New Orleans and Brazil are, if one is willing to shift one's perspective, displaying breeding plumage and breeding behavior, albeit with a switch in genders, for in the bird world it is the males who most often grow the showy feathers that are variously called *breeding, nuptial, spring,* or *alternate* plumage. Hanson explains that this insight came to him suddenly while watching the feather-adorned showgirls in the Jubilee! stage show in Las Vegas. As he tells it, his jaw dropped open: "My amazement stemmed from more than just the show's over-the-top production: I had expected bright lights and loud music, I knew there would be showgirls, and I knew they would be wearing feathers. What left me stunned was how much they looked like birds displaying at a lek."

Birders know that during the breeding season the appearance of birds can change dramatically; the male indigo bunting, for instance, is a dull brown when he is not trying to seduce a mate. Many species, when the time comes, replace their workaday attire with scarlet and saffron or with long tail feathers, as the quetzal does; some sing, some dance, and some strut like, well, peacocks, vying for female attention in competitive displays called *leks*. As David S. Scott and Casey

McFarland write in *Bird Feathers: A Guide to North American Species*, "Birds wouldn't have developed beautiful feathers and songs if the female bird didn't appreciate them."

Darwin, in a view that was unpopular for many years, accounted for the brilliant hues and shapes of bird feathers by proposing the idea of sexual selection. Not every trait evolved in order to promote survival, he argued. Certain traits like the lemon hue of the yellow warbler must have evolved in order to improve a bird's chances of mating. Male birds, we now know, gain access to females by fighting over them or displaying qualities that females like. Geoffrey E. Hill, author of *National Geographic Bird Coloration*, writes, "When an ornithologist is asked why birds are so beautifully colored, the simple answer must be 'because of female mate choice.'" In one study of house finches, he notes, females who were given a choice between males with drab but large patches of color on their breasts and those with small, saturated patches consistently chose the smaller but deeper reds. In another, mountain bluebirds engaged more often in "extra-pair copulations" (i.e., affairs) with males who displayed the most brilliant blues.

Although most peoples have killed birds to use their feathers and skins for personal adornment, in America after the Civil War the practice accelerated, influenced by fashion trends in Europe. "Market shooting for the table and to supply the millinery trade, which used bird skins and feathers as hat decorations, was exploding in the late nineteenth century," writes Scott Weidensaul in *Of a Feather: A Brief History of American Birding*. Songbirds, owls, waterfowl, flickers, and especially herons and egrets, whose breeding plumes, called *aigrettes*, were especially sought after, were killed indiscriminately by hunters selling to the industry. Weidensaul states that in the late 1890s, in the Everglades, hundreds of thousands of egrets were shot and plucked on their breeding grounds, their chicks left to die. In nine months, the London market was said to have imported feathers from 130,000 birds. If one included all species, the American feather market in the late nineteenth century was consuming the lives of over 200 million birds a year.

Naturalists at the time blamed women. George Bird Grinnell, founder of the original Audubon Society, saw the slaughter as a product of female vanity, especially that of upper-class women who could afford the expensively trimmed hats. In 1886, he developed a plan to go to the source, pitting women's sense of moral outrage at violence against their desire to look attractive, recruiting them to sign pledges "to refrain from using bird skins or feathers as decoration or on clothing." Grinnell had some luck, but when he tried to get Congress to pass legislation restricting the hunting of birds for clothing, the time was not right; he failed, and the Audubon Society disbanded.

But ten years later, longtime birdwatcher and Boston socialite Harriet Lawrence Hemenway read a "bloodcurdling account of the killing of herons and egrets in Florida for the millinery trade" and decided to do something about it. She urged all of her rich acquaintances to instead buy "Audubonnets"—featherless hats. Suddenly, it was more attractive to *not* wear feathers. The Audubon Society was thus brought back to life. The movement Hemenway reinvigorated was instrumental in the later passage of three antiplumage bills designed to stop trade in feathers: the Lacey Act (1900), which made it a crime to trade in illegally killed birds; the Migratory Bird Act (1913), which outlawed market hunting; and the Tariff Act (1913). In England, activists helped pass the English Plumage Bill in 1921.

The final piece of the story is that, although ostriches were no longer wild or endangered and were not killed but rather plucked, most consumers in America and Europe didn't understand the difference. Men and women who shamed those who wore feathers in their hats could not tell ostrich from egret, and most did not know that ostriches were raised on farms. Ironically, the collapse of the market for feathers saved the egret in Florida but was a catastrophe for ostrich farmers— and often the ostrich—in Africa. By the 1920s, merchants were going bankrupt, and feather workers were laid off in New York and London. Hundreds of the birds were slaughtered when farmers couldn't afford their keep. At the market's peak, South African farmers had fed and plucked a million birds a year. By the time World War I began, flocks had dwindled to twenty thousand. Some blamed Henry Ford and the automobile, which made it impossible for women to ride in open cars with such plumy hats. Some blamed the approach of war and a consequent demand for austerity. But what really seems to have happened, according to Hanson, is that women, who were blamed for the feather hat craze to begin with—for wanting to mimic the brightness and beauty of birds—were instrumental in causing its demise.

Status

In Christopher Howell's poem "King of the Butterflies," the king of Poland demands a tribute of two million butterflies that will be caught in "the most delicate snares so that each lovely animal could be brought perfect and alive to the grace of sacrifice." Peasants constructed nets, prisoners were released to join the hunt, and those "who brought moths by mistake were impaled." The "fluttering magnificence" that accumulated was contained in a conservatory built especially for them in the king's garden. Many people were killed and tortured because they didn't meet their quotas. And when finally the "last painted lady was tipped into the enclosure" and the king ordered his underlings to torch them, no one had the heart to do it. Exasperated with them all, the king approached the "immense cauldron of wheeling color," torch in hand, but even he was "unable to take so much beauty from the world," so he cut the netting, releasing "an explosion of confetti, like all the world's flowers flung into the arms of God."

In many societies, kings, chiefs, emperors, and warlords have demanded tribute from the people they rule. Whether it came in the form of grain, fruits, gold, precious stones, textiles, feathers, or butterflies, the tribute usually involved something rare, luxurious, and difficult to obtain. Five thousand years ago, the dried skins of birds of paradise, a member of the bird family Paradisaeidae native to New Guinea, surfaced in the regalia of royalty as far away as Thailand and Nepal. Because they arrived without heads or feet but with spectacularly colored feathers, people thought they were a gift from the gods, hence their name. The world's famous feather cultures—Mayan, Incan, Aztec, Hawaiian, Polynesian—had access, albeit difficult access, to many tropical birds. The expense of procuring these feathers would reflect one's status in the society. Wearing them invoked awe or inspired fear or imposed authority. For a commoner, daring to wear any of them often meant death.

Bird catchers in the Hawaiian Islands, called *kia manu*, lived high in the mountains where the birds lived, and they developed elaborate hunting techniques over generations. They sewed fine nets to snare birds as they flew through the forests. One technique, *kahekahe*, was to shave the branches from flowering trees so that only a few remained at the top. Climbers then spread a sticky sap near the blossoms so when the birds came to feed they would become stuck. After plucking the feathers they wanted, they often let the birds go, first applying an herbal salve to help the bird heal. It is said that Kamehameha I, one of the most famous kings, declared that anyone caught purposely killing a bird for its feathers would be executed, although more common birds were sometimes killed, plucked, and eaten.

Feather regalia was considered sacred, so its manufacture was relegated mostly to male priests. The garments were, according to the Bishop Museum of Honolulu, constructed by "tying bundles of small feathers, usually 6–10 per bundle, to a foundation of netting. This netting was made from an endemic plant that produced one of the strongest fibers in the world, the olonā." So much time and expertise were demanded in their making that the garments were sometimes named as if they were important personages. One of the more spectacular garments is an *'ahu'ula* or feather cloak originally made for Kalaniopuu, a high chief in the eighteenth century. It was gifted to Captain James

Cook when he landed on the island of Hawaii in 1779. Woven in patterns of gold and red, it required over twenty thousand feathers. (It has recently returned to Hawaii after 237 years, on loan from a museum in New Zealand where it traveled after being sold from one European collector to the next, a trajectory that in itself maps ongoing lines of power and tribute.) The feather cloak of King Kamehameha I is even more extravagant: it is woven from approximately 450,000 rare yellow feathers plucked from an estimated 80,000 birds!

Most of the feathers for the royal capes, cloaks, and helmets came from the finch-like Hawaiian honeycreepers—the shiny red from the more abundant species, *Vestiaria coccinea* and *Himatione sanguinea*, and the precious yellow from the mamo honeycreeper, *Drepanis pacifica*. Honeycreepers are small, colorful birds with black wings. At one time, it is estimated, there were 5.7 million of them. Today, according to George H. Fenwick of the American Bird Conservatory, two-thirds of them have gone extinct. The yellowish-orange feather used in many of these cloaks came from a honeycreeper that disappeared as early as 1898. Coveted yellow feathers were also obtained from the Hawaiian honey*eater*—as opposed to honeycreeper—the *Moho apicalis*, a soot-black bird with a small number of brilliant feathers in its armpit and tail. Honeyeaters are estimated to have evolved in Hawaii fourteen million years ago, writes Fenwick. The last one was seen in 1934, the first instance in modern times of an entire family being wiped out.

The cloaks are resplendent, which I sense even in looking at just the plates in *Royal Hawaiian Featherwork: Na Hulu Ali'i*, the catalog of a recent exhibition at the DeYoung Museum in San Francisco. Worn in war, the clothing must have shone in the distance as the armies advanced, the large blocks of bold red and gold set alive and ruffling by even the slightest wind. Despite the unbelievable numbers of feathers used in these costumes, Fenwick claims that the *kia manu* are not to blame for the birds' disappearance. Like many indigenous cultures, the Hawaiians were well aware of how many birds they could harvest and of the balance in nature they were trying to sustain. It was not until the 1800s, he says, soon after European contact, that the honey-creepers and honeyeaters of Hawaii began to disappear, probably due to newly introduced disease, rats, cats, and mosquitoes. Habitat loss, as well, hastened their decline.

✧

"The bright blue feathers come from the lovely cotinga," writes art historian Claudia Brittenham about the "penacho de Moctezuma" or headdress that legend says the Aztec emperor Montezuma gave to Hernán Cortés, "while the dark red plumes of the roseate spoonbill are barely visible above the blue." But what makes this headdress, now in a museum in Vienna, even more splendid are the 450 blue-green, shimmering quetzal tail feathers. In photographs, they form a fan that most resembles a tropical forest after rain: vividly green, shimmering as if with water and light. The headdress is also trimmed with pearls.

The quetzal, *Pharomachrus mocinno*, is surely one of the most spectacular birds in the world. Turquoise, emerald, and ruby, its hues resemble semiprecious stones. During breeding season, the male grows two long tail feathers, sometimes up to three feet in length. (In Nahuatl, *quetzalli* means "precious tail feather.") Aztecs, Maya, and Incas kept aviaries where they bred particularly vivid species for use in their feather garments: parrots, macaws, egrets, thrushes, flycatchers. But the quetzal can't survive in captivity. It lived in the undisturbed canopies of cloud forests of Central America and Mexico, far from the flatlands of the Aztec empire. Thus, all of the feathers that came to the kingdom had to be procured from distant lands.

Tribute in raw feathers was often measured in handfuls. According to the organization Birdlife International, the Aztec emperor once demanded of his subjects in five distant provinces 2,480 handfuls of quetzal feathers: "If it is assumed that each 'handful' contained ten to fifty such feathers (four from each bird), this would have meant a harvest of 6,200–31,000 Resplendent Quetzals per year." Frances Berdan, in "Circulation of Feathers in Mesoamerica," states that feather tributes were solicited by rulers from conquered territories throughout Mexico and Central America. They were used for royal and religious ceremonies, in soldiers' uniforms, and as gifts to allies to buy favor or to enemies to demonstrate the ruler's prestige. "It is notable," Berdan says, "that more feathers were paid in the form of manufactured objects such as warriors' costumes, mosaic shields, and feather adornments than were delivered as raw feathers alone." Aztec feather workers, called *amanteca*, had their own guilds and were highly respected. Almost everyone in the culture—as feather hunters, merchants, artisans, soldiers, or rulers—eventually participated in this circulating economy.

Although tribute in many indigenous cultures was required, it was also quickly redistributed in what Berdan calls the "hierarchical movements of goods." The Hawaiian ruler who gave the feather cape to Captain Cook was demonstrating his wealth as well as his generosity. He was rich enough to give something so precious away. The headdress Montezuma gave to Cortés was not only meant to honor him; it was also an emblem of the vast riches of the Aztec kingdom. In Mesoamerica, feathers and feather work were often set on fire as public sacrifices to the gods of fertility, both human and vegetable. Tribute was thus framed as a cultural obligation and as an offering to ensure the community's future health, both spiritual and physical. The feathers were regarded as sacred offerings from the forest to the people. In returning them to the earth, the priests honored the gods from which they came.

In Lewis Hyde's classic study *The Gift*, he describes this kind of exchange as a "gift economy," one that is fundamentally opposed to commerce: "A market exchange has an equilibrium or stasis: you pay to balance the scale. But when you give a gift there is momentum, and the weight shifts from body to body." To be considered a gift, Hyde says, a gift must *move*. From the scarlet macaw who provided the feathers to the Aztec *amanteca* to the artisan making the headdress to the king and then to the priests: it was a circulation not only of goods but also of art and of spirit that, Hyde says, left "a series of interconnected relationships in its wake." Passing the feathers on—regifting them—united the participating individuals in the name of something larger: a culture, a country, a common enterprise. The modern science of ecology is based on similar principles. "When we see that we are actors in natural cycles," Hyde writes, "we understand that what nature gives to us is influenced by what we give to nature."

For hundreds of years the Aztec, Maya, and Inca used countless feathers for headdresses, shields, capes, fans, and sandals and wove them into textiles for clothes and house furnishings, gifts that circulated in an ever-widening arc. (Archaeological evidence of scarlet macaw feathers traded four hundred years before the Aztecs has been discovered in Chaco Canyon in the US Southwest.) In the precontact jungles and forests of Mexico and Central and South America, there must have been billions of birds, thousands of species. They would have seemed common, as if they would propagate forever. Given their numbers and their beauty, it would be surprising if humans hadn't used bird feathers. Today, however, like many other birds, especially in the tropical regions of the world, the quetzal is listed as Near Threatened. Partners in Flight, a network of organizations that works to conserve bird species, estimates the quetzal population to number fewer than fifty thousand individuals. In Guatemala, although the quetzal is the national bird and supplies the name of its currency, it is possible that it is already extinct. As with the honeycreepers and honeyeaters of Hawaii, however, indigenous harvesting of quetzal feathers does not seem to be responsible for the decline. In Mexico, Guatemala, Honduras, El Salvador, Nicaragua, and Costa Rica, the birds' native homes, the number-one reason for their depopulation is widespread rapid deforestation.

One could think of this overreach as a form of tribute demanded by the new emperors, namely multinational corporations (mining, logging, oil, and agricultural interests)—a tribute to the conquering hero, Capital. Instead of precious and rare goods, what is demanded now is the land itself. According to the Environmental Literacy Council, Mesoamerica's rainforests are being logged faster than almost any other place on earth. As of 2005, 80 percent of the forests have been "cleared or significantly altered," mostly for lumber extraction and livestock expansion. Quetzal feather headdresses, of course, are not worn by heads of state or CEOs of extractive industries, who rarely redistribute their spoils. But perhaps they should be.

When Cortés first led his army into Tenochtitlan in 1519, his men were dazzled by the Aztec aviaries and overwhelmed by the natural beauty of the city itself—the orchards, the stone patios, the roses. "These great towns and temples and buildings rising from the water, all made of stone, seemed like an enchanted vision from the tale of Amadis. Indeed, some of our soldiers asked whether it was not all a dream," wrote Bernal Díaz del Castillo about his entrance into the Aztec capital. When Cortés returned to the city a year later, in 1520, he ordered his soldiers to set the aviaries on fire. "The image of Cortés burning the aviaries," Barry Lopez writes in his powerful essay "The Passing Wisdom of Birds," "is not simply for me an image of a kind of destructive madness that lies at the heart of imperialist conquest; it is also a symbol of a long-term failure of Western civilization to recognize the intrinsic worth of the American landscape." Cortés ordered the destruction of the birds as an act not of sacrifice but of war. For the Aztecs who believed the macaws, parrots, flycatchers, and egrets were an expression of the sacredness at the heart of their relationship with the animals and plants around them, it was an act designed to destroy their souls.

Shelter

After my maternal grandmother slaughtered the hens on her farm, she scalded and plucked them and stuffed the feathers into pillows. *Featherpillows*, she called them. I hated them. I can still feel the prick of the quills on my childhood cheek as they poked through the ticking, and the sour animal smell, reminiscent of the scald and the barn— very different from this lightweight down jacket that can fold so smoothly into my purse. Is its down plucked from Canadian geese? Or ducks? Or even swans? The label doesn't say. It lists only "bird feathers and down," its provenance obscured just as feathers are under the nylon shell of my jacket. As unheralded and mysterious as the down and feather industry is, the outdoor garment manufacturer Patagonia earned over $575 million in 2013, much of it from feather products. A larger company, North Face, made $2 billion. Relatively, both are small actors—apparel accounts for about 1 percent of total down sales— when compared with manufacturers of down pillows, mattresses, and comforters. In 2000, in the latest count I can find, over 55,000 tons of feathers were commercially harvested worldwide.

Today I have flown to Montebello, California, eight miles south of Los Angeles, and driven my rental car to a warehouse district of noodle factories, box companies, and makers of pumps, dollies, and drains to learn about down production from an expert. Allied Feather & Down is the world's largest supplier of high-quality down to the apparel industry. Daniel Uretsky, president of this family business, greets me in the lobby of a block-long, windowless building. He has a bad cold, he explains, which he contracted in his most recent global search for the best feathers. "Largest supplier?" Uretsky repeats, skeptically. "It depends on which market you're talking about. We supply to the Gap, as well as to the higher ends, but then all those mass-market cheap jackets? Other people supply for them." Allied was founded thirty years ago by Uretsky's father, Steve, and is now managed by himself and his brother Jon. I tell him that I was taken aback, when I first made contact with Allied through their web email, that he had personally phoned me back. "It's in our best interest," he admits. "There's so little information. We still get questions like 'So you guys have the farms and you kill the birds for the down'? Positive and informed stories are always welcome."

It is a slow time on the factory floor, he says. Because most clothing manufacturers are readying their cold-weather lines in the spring, they need the down by January to begin their sewing. Still, this August the warehouse is stacked to the ceiling with huge red, green, gray, pink, and sky-blue plastic-wrapped bundles on pallets, each about four feet long, each heavy enough that I would have difficulty lifting it. Considering how light feathers are, each bundle must contain a massive number of them. Large steel piping runs the length of the ceiling, dipping in and out of machines in a closed system where the down is washed, dried, and passed through a magnet that removes any heavy metals picked up from the farmyard or the initial processing. Sometimes this process is repeated over and over. The raw down often comes already separated from the larger feathers, but the factory does have a machine—one the size of a small building—that spins the raw material so that the lighter down rises and is trapped in an upper chamber, and the rest is divided further as it falls into coarser and heavier lots.

"For every shipment," Uretsky says, "we draw a sample. Then we dissect the composition." He gestures at a man holding tweezers, bent over a pile of down. He laughs. "This is absolutely not automated. He's separating the dust and broken fibers from a cluster and recording the percentage. You want the cluster unbroken. Unbroken clusters should make up the majority of the shipment, not a bunch of shreds. Another thing, if you're seeing a lot of dark spots, that's really weird. It's a different species, perhaps. Different species of duck or whatever. We need a microscopic analysis. Species analysis. Cleanliness test. Rinse the down and strain it and analyze the water." I am clearly in the arcane reaches of the passions of the feather merchants.

Until he joined the company six and a half years ago, Uretsky was an attorney. His father, a biochemist who started the company in 1987, chose Montebello because it is close to a port, making it easy to ship and receive materials, and because, at the time it was founded, it had abundant and available water, which is necessary for processing feathers. "In places like China," he says, "you'd have to treat the water before using it. Here it's clean, although, because of the drought in California, it's not as easy or cheap to come by." Allied now recycles almost all of the water it uses, over 65 million gallons annually. In addition, the company uses biodegradable detergents. In 1987, Uretsky says, the company processed 100,000 kilograms (220,462 pounds) of down, enough to fill the Statue of Liberty twice. Today they are processing seven million kilograms (15,432,358 pounds), which would stuff the Empire State Building five times.

Down used in clothing as well as bedding comes from domesticated waterfowl, specifically geese and ducks that grow the small feathery clusters without quills on their chests and bellies to insulate themselves from cold water. Domesticated ducks were probably originally bred from an Asian bird. No one knows for sure what they are descended from, but most likely the wild mallard (*Anas platyrhyncos*) in China, which is why it is called the Peking, or Pekin, duck. The indigenous Muscovy duck (*Cairina moschata*) from South America is also an ancestor. Geese are believed to be one of the very first birds to be domesticated; there is evidence that humans were farming them four thousand to six thousand years ago. The greylag goose (*Anser anser*) has its origins in Europe, and the swan goose (*Anser cygnoides*), the stocky white goose associated with city ponds, in Asia. The latter is often called simply the Chinese goose. In China there are over twenty different breeds of the Chinese goose.

Feathers and down are by-products of the meat industry. "If you want to develop a supply chain, you have to look at who is eating the most ducks and geese," Uretsky says. According to an estimate published in *Poultry News*, China produces 80 to 85 percent of the world's supply of down and feathers, and 90 percent of it comes from ducks. The Peking duck, though it has lost favor in America's kitchens, is a centerpiece of Beijing cuisine and a staple for every rural family. In 2013, a study calculated that the Chinese consume four million tons of duck meat and two and a half million tons of goose a year. China produces three times more geese than Europe, although Europe is also a major supplier of Allied's goose down, specifically from farms in Hungary, Ukraine, Poland, and Romania, where geese are still eaten and exported.

"No one's wearing down from migrating geese," Uretsky says as we enter a nearby office. "It's all farmed, but farmed elsewhere. There is no production to speak of here in the States."

"I love duck. I eat duck everywhere I go," says a young man whose beige, untidy office we have just entered. "Around here, we joke that we're going to start a campaign in America like Chick-fil-A did: 'Eat more duck!'"

Uretsky introduces me to Matthew Betcher. Athletic, sunburnt, shaggy-haired, he reminds me of young backpackers who hang out in Western coffee shops waiting for their next climb. Betcher is Allied's creative and marketing director. Uretsky excuses himself for a meeting, and Betcher pulls up a diagram on his laptop, picking up where his boss left off. The diagram shows a goose, its body divided into percentages. "There's very little down on an individual bird to begin with," Betcher explains. "It only grows on the bird's chest and belly under the contour feathers. The total plumage for an average-size goose is about three hundred grams. Ninety grams of that amount consists of large, unusable, heavy feathers; 150 grams consists of medium-sized feathers that can be used to stuff furniture, cushions, that sort of thing. Less than sixty grams is usable for clothing." A medium-weight goose-down jacket uses about 250 grams, or the down from approximately five to seven birds. The goose is raised, watered, fed, then killed and plucked at the slaughterhouse. Those feathers are sent to a raw processor who cleans them and separates them down the line, sometimes as many as four or five times. Consequently, Betcher states, it doesn't make economic sense that birds would be raised only for their feathers.

"Volume-wise, more of our product comes from China, but value-wise, I'd say Europe and China are closer to equal," he adds.

"Why?" I ask. "Is goose down, for instance Hungarian goose down, that much better than a duck's?"

Betcher sighs. "That's a difficult question, one for which you have to know something about down itself." What most people know is that down insulates better than any other material on earth. It does so, he explains, because, instead of growing from a quill or rachis, like regular feathers, down grows as a cluster; thousands of filaments emanate from a central point. Each of these filaments has tiny nodes that attach to other nodes. Together these clusters create pockets that trap static air. The trapped air acts like a barrier, keeping the cold out and the warmth in. "Goose has always been regarded as qualitatively better," he continues, "but when you look at how down insulates, you can see that it's not an easy answer. The quality of down isn't measured in size or weight but by the strength of those interlocking clusters."

He asks me to stand up, hold my hands out, and close my eyes. I do as I am told, waiting for him to place what I imagine to be the feather of a duck in one hand and that of a goose in the other. I wait and wait. When he tells me to open my eyes, I see that my left palm is balancing an eight-inch pile of lovely brown-and-cream speckled feathers. I hadn't felt a thing when he placed them in it.

"Can you feel your hand heating up?" he asks. I do. Slowly, almost imperceptibly, as sun might warm the treetops, the warmth deepens. It is an extraordinary feeling. Betcher explains that these are down clusters from the common eider (*Somateria mollissima*), a wild duck that breeds on the Arctic coasts of Canada, Scandinavia, and Siberia. The largest duck in the Northern Hemisphere, the mother lines her nests with her own feathers, which she plucks from her breast before laying her eggs. In Scandinavia, raiding the nests of these migrating birds for their feathers was ancient practice; in Norway, archaeologists have found evidence that Vikings took blankets stuffed with eiderdown on their ships, and in Finland it was gathered for clothing.

"An experienced collector will harvest about 100 nests per hour on fairly regular terrain and between 50 and 75 nests per hour on steep terrain or in thick forest undercover," writes Jon Sveinsson in a manual called "Real Eiderdown." Because the birds flock in thousands and nest together in one place, this is not impossible. In case anyone would want to pursue this vocation, Sveinsson offers advice: "Members of harvesting teams must be disciplined, wear dark clothes, move about smoothly and avoid yelling or erratic movements. Obviously, under no circumstances should domestic animals be brought to eider colonies. To reduce the harvest time and keep disturbance to a minimum, pickers must forgo lengthy discussions about procedures, lunch breaks and rest periods until after leaving the island." In some places today, such as Iceland, eiderdown is harvested from "farms," where humans encourage the wild birds to nest by building up sheltered areas and protecting them from development; from predators such as gulls, ravens, and mink; and from illegal hunting.

Despite these precautions, the yields are never extensive. As Sveinsson notes, "The total worldwide annual harvest of eiderdown could be carried by one small truck, while the total annual worldwide goose-down production is counted in tens of thousands of tons or ship loads." Over sixty nests might be harvested for the eiderdown contained in one comforter. Consequently, products made with eiderdown are extremely expensive. One standard-size pillow stuffed with it could cost over three thousand dollars. I try to imagine the life of an eiderdown harvester, roaming rocky seashores and islets in the northern spring, searching for the nests of migrating birds, trying to pinch every airy, wayward cluster into a closed basket. With a single exhale, one could lose a month's wages!

The strength, and therefore the warmth, of down clusters is measured in terms of what the industry calls "fill power." Fill power is calculated by placing thirty grams of down (.105 of an ounce) inside a graduated cylinder, allowing it to loft, and then measuring the space it fills. For instance, one ounce of 800-fill power goose down will loft to 800 cubic inches. The higher the loft, the greater the fill power. The higher the fill power, the more air is trapped and, thus, the better insulating quality.

Down creates warmth by the size of the cluster because the larger it is, the more air it will trap. "Goose nodes are bigger and stronger," Betcher explains, "so the clusters are generally stronger. But honestly, only nominally. Hungary is colder, so the down is more durable. Down quality increases also with the age of the bird. Ducks are harvested at about eight weeks in China. People like them young and tender. In Hungary, geese are consumed in about eleven to twelve weeks, so goose is often seen as better because the animal is older and bigger, and so the feathers are stronger." When killed for meat, only about 55 percent of geese and ducks are mature.

I finger the pile of eiderdown in my hand. It feels sticky, like Velcro. Fill power, Betcher adds, is tricky. Eiderdown has strength but it doesn't have much loft. An equivalent amount of goose down in my palm would have been blown into the corners of the room by just my breath. And if you're going to stuff the down into tiny compartments, such as in a super-lightweight quilted jacket, he says, it's a waste to have a high fill power, as the down has no room to expand anyway. "'Everest suits' designed for expedition climbing often measure only 450-fill power because they stuff lots of down into them. Nevertheless, people are impressed by fill power numbers. The highest fill power recorded at the International Feather and Down Laboratory in Salt Lake is 927. We regularly supply fill powers over 1,000. It's a small niche, though."

"What is the niche?"

"It is the best, most technical, lightest-weight, warmest material around," Betcher says. "It's for professional mountaineers."

I had read in Hanson's book that one would need eleven pairs of polypropylene long johns to match the warmth of one down expedition jacket. Natural down is more than twice as efficient as any other synthetic. Thinsulate, Polarguard, and other materials are also less compressible. In addition, like all plastics, they are made from petroleum. I didn't know, however, that they were less durable. Betcher explains: "It's not only the petroleum base that is the environmental problem, but you look at the life cycle of, say, an outdoor jacket: synthetics break down faster. And what they're seeing now is these microfibers entering the waterways. You wash a fleece and billions of microfibers enter the water. They go through the filters because they are so minuscule. Down is like your hair. It's a keratin. When it's treated properly, like your hair, you have a product that is environmentally friendly and lasts a long time."

"I suppose some people are against it because it involves the killing of animals," I say, "and, in large operations, perhaps not in a humane way." (In most slaughterhouses, geese are killed in a "killing funnel," which keeps their wings from flapping. Then their necks are cut. Usually they are anesthetized first by some form of electrocution.)

Betcher pauses to consider. "It's true that down is a by-product of meat. It's also efficient, and it can be processed in such a way that there is no harm to the environment. Cotton uses a tremendous amount of water, and it destroys the field. It's sneaky taxing on the environment. Down has the lowest carbon footprint. But we're the first ones to say that if you're a vegan and you don't wear leather, then you probably shouldn't wear down."

"So," I say, "I guess I'll bring up an even thornier subject: live-plucking."

What I have read about live-plucking—yanking the down from the breasts and bellies of geese and ducks while they are still alive—is that it occurs in a very small percentage of down purchased worldwide. "Live-plucking is only [involved in] 1 to 3 percent of the goose down products for expensive Japanese bedding and outerwear products. That means a maximum of 0.3 percent of the total supply," writes Yao Xiaoman, vice chairman of the China Feather and Down Industrial Association. Yet anyone who follows animal rights issues on the internet has seen the photographs, supposedly from Hungary and China, of flocks of white geese, their chests plucked bare, bleeding profusely. Are the photographs staged? And if live-plucking isn't a significant problem, why have companies like Patagonia instituted programs such as their "Traceable Down Standard," or why has Allied worked with manufacturers such as North Face, Eddie Bauer, and Lands' End to implement the industry-wide Responsible Down Standard (RDS), a third-party certification standard that, it says, "can be applied to any waterfowl-based supply chain to help ensure humane treatment of animals from gosling to end product"?

Betcher doesn't flinch. In fact, he seems to welcome the question. "We never say it doesn't happen. There are a lot of questionable sources," he admits. "We hate that material as much as anyone. That's why we've worked so hard to develop these standards. We were the first suppliers to certify across our entire supply chain that there is no live-plucked material."

In May 2016, People for the Ethical Treatment of Animals (PETA) released yet another video (there have been many) of live-plucking on farms in China that they claim was shot between 2012 and 2015. In this one, they accused Allied—a major RDS supplier—of buying from some of these farms, in an attempt to challenge the viability of traceable standards and to show that it is impossible for companies to know what is going on at every link of the supply chain. "It started the whole shitstorm again," Betcher says. "But it disappeared fast because it took us less than half an hour to show that they were wrong. The video wasn't shot anywhere near where we get our down. We could prove it."

He lowers his voice, as if PETA had placed surveillance devices in the desk drawers. "Look, no one wants to appear anti-PETA. But they use old clips and paste them together. They try to buy live-plucked down under false pretenses. We heard of one Chinese farmer who they cajoled until he said, yes, he could get them some but not to say whom it was from. If people heard, no one would want to buy his feathers, you see. That fact, that farmers know that live-plucked feathers are something to be ashamed of, is a testimony that the RDS works." Although Allied doesn't partner with PETA—PETA is against any commercial exploitation of animals—they work with animal rights groups, including Four Paws, an international animal welfare organization, to develop, revise, and monitor the program. Four Paws recently released a statement condemning the recent PETA attack.

Live-plucking happens most often when geese are kept alive longer than usual for purposes other than meat production, usually on "parent farms" where they are being raised to produce eggs for other growers, or because they are being fattened for use in foie gras, says Betcher. Made from the fatty liver of ducks or geese, foie gras often requires force-feeding through tubes inserted into the animals' throats in a practice known as *gavage*. The livers grow up to ten times their regular size before the animal is harvested. Whether or not one is repulsed by this process—some people have written that, despite its apparent cruelty, because of flexible esophagi, geese and ducks don't suffer from it—the truth is that the birds are kept alive not for their feathers but for their eggs or livers. Because older birds produce the best down, birds that are living on parent farms or places where foie gras is being produced might be plucked during their annual or semi-annual molt, when the feathers are looser. Because of their higher fill power—usually 800–900—these feathers command prices up to 40 percent higher.

During the Middle Ages, live-plucking was widespread; those who performed it were called "plumers." In the wild, birds molt—shed their feathers—once a year; domesticated birds might do so three or four times. When I wrote to Thor Hanson about it, he replied, "Biologically, it is conceivable that some feathers can be taken from a molting bird without pain at just the right moment. Even in a bird bred for such purpose, however, it's hard to conceive how every plume in one area—the breast, for example—would reach that perfect moment at the same time." Today live-plucking is illegal in the European Union, except in the country of Hungary, where regulations allow live harvesting of mature feathers only at the time of molt. Since 1999, force-feeding has been prohibited by law in Poland. As of 2012, China has no laws prohibiting cruelty to animals.

Betcher pulls up a photo on his laptop of an industrial goose farm in China. Interestingly, unlike in the United States, where chickens are fed in cages so small they can't stand up, in this scene thousands of birds graze a spacious green field. "This is the way geese and ducks are raised everywhere." He pulls up another chart. "I want to show you how convoluted traceability can be. These are micro farms on the far left. A micro farm can be one family, a village, or a collective. Someone goes around collecting the feathers and then sells them to a processor. That processor sells to a bigger processor. One thing we're doing is teaching these collectors to read and write so they can do the paperwork that certifies where things come from. Over here on the right side is industrial slaughterhouses. Much of what we do is identify sources. With the micro farms, traceability is hard because we source globally, but animal welfare concerns are rare. We have farms sign certificates. We have local veterinarians check the feathers. With the slaughterhouses, traceability is easier and our impact greater. In 2016, all our RDS down was 100 percent certified by third parties."

The connoisseur in Japan who sleeps in a nest softer than the eider duckling's or the American mountain climber who must have a 1,000-fill power parka—these are not the average consumers of down feathers. Most people in cold countries buy their down, if they buy it at all, from untraceable sources. Yet even though cheap down coats or pillows from Target, say, or Macy's, aren't the coats or pillows to worry about—their down won't be from live-plucked geese because those feathers would be prohibitively expensive—there is also the question of animal welfare and care, of workers' rights, and of chemicals and water wasted in processing. "It is expensive to have all these monitors," Betcher says. "When you look at those really cheap down products, you do have to question where they came from. So these standards are meant to protect animals from all kinds of things. For example, we've gone into slaughterhouses and helped, for instance, build partitions between the livestock and where they will be killed, to 'help update their facilities' so they can be certified. Maybe it's one minor concern. You know, reorganize their facility to resolve *that welfare concern.*" Betcher has designed a label with a barcode which, when affixed to a product using Allied down, can be scanned to reveal the garment's entire supply chain, whether a small village north of Beijing or an industrial goose farm in Hungary. Even in the store, you can use your phone to see exactly what your jacket contains and where it was made before you buy it. It is called "Trace-your-down."

Although more and more of us want to know where our clothing, as well as our food, comes from, right now only a small percentage of people can afford to care—in other words, can afford winter jackets that cost over $300, made by the exclusive labels one friend of mine calls *Patagucci*. And, of course, companies use traceability to compete with each other: witness Patagonia's Traceable Down campaign versus North Face's RDS. "This is all really good," I say to Betcher, "but what if most people ask, you know, who cares?"

He smiles. "My response is it doesn't matter. If just one person cares, that changes things. We're doing it anyway. And then, eventually, everybody cares."

Spirit

We arrive at Crow Fair with plenty of time before the grand entry. Promoted as the "Teepee Capital of the World," Crow Fair, held on the Apsáalooke, or Crow, reservation in southeastern Montana, is the largest powwow in North America, annually attracting thousands of people of all races and from many countries, especially Native Americans, who come to visit with old friends and family and to compete for prize money in traditional dances: Fancy Dance, Grass Dance, Jingle Dance, Shawl Dance, Traditional Women's, and Traditional Men's. Right now the dance pavilion is almost empty. People are at their campsites or straggling home from the parade, a spectacular affair where fine horses, which the Crow are known for, and pickups alike are adorned with Pendleton honor blankets, beaded saddles, and antlers of animals killed in the last hunt. It is only eighty degrees, unusually cool for an

August day on the plains. My friend Jo, who spent twenty-five years working to protect the Medicine Wheel, an ancient spiritual site high in the nearby Bighorn Mountains, sits on a bench while I go to one of the many concession stands to get us a Navajo taco to share. Jo is eighty-eight. I am so grateful that she felt strong enough to join me.

I bring back fry bread smothered with onions, chili, and cheese, and we eat with our hands. A drum circle wanders in, five or six men of varying ages, one or two carrying a large round wooden drum stretched with elk or buffalo hide. The hide needs to be strong as the men—and sometimes, though rarely, women—will be pounding hard on it with sticks as they sing the hypnotic, powerful songs that sound like eagles crying.

The dancing here, as at many other traditional powwows in the northern states, takes place in a circle surrounded by the audience and drum circles, who are in turn encircled by concession stands, and ultimately the encampment itself. The circle, for many indigenous people, symbolizes the unity of all life. (As a friend of mine quips, "We Indian people have the Round Dance. White people have the Square Dance.") Perhaps a thousand perfectly erected canvas tipis are pitched in rows on both sides of the Bighorn River, on hilltops and in nearby draws, the crisscrossed tops of their peeled lodgepoles visible in every direction. (The *lodgepole pine*, which grows thick on the slopes nearby, was named for its value as a tipi pole.)

Apsáalooke does not mean "crow." The misnomer may have come from French traders, who might have heard it from a neighboring tribe. Plenty Coups, the last hereditary Crow chief, told Frank B. Linderman that Absanokee means "descendants of the Raven" or "children of the Raven." Born in 1848, Plenty Coups recalled his childhood roaming the plains of what is now Montana before his people were forced onto reservations: "We followed the buffalo herds over our beautiful plains, fighting a battle one day and sending out a war-party against the enemy the next. My heart was afire. I wished so to help my people, to distinguish myself, so that I might wear an eagle's feather in my hair."

An eagle feather was a symbol of bravery and strength, the mark of a warrior. A person had to earn the right to wear one by performing some courageous act: stealing enemy horses, striking the first blow in a battle, or "counting coup," which meant getting near enough in battle to touch an opponent and then escape unharmed. In some of the Crow war bonnets, fifty to a hundred feathers trail magnificently to the ground. According to Plenty Coups, the style was given to the people in a vision; the tail of the bonnet was understood to represent the back of a buffalo.

At Crow Fair, grand entry occurs about 1 p.m. and again at 6. It is when all the dancers—four hundred, five hundred of them—enter the arena one by one, one division after another—veterans, visiting dignitaries, men, women, adolescents, "tiny tots"—and begin to dance, the first ones making room for the new by spiraling in until the arena is a festive gyre of color, music, and movement, especially of the feathers. Feathers loft and cascade down the backs of the warriors acting out hunting or war stories. Eagle feather fans are raised into the air by women who step like deer through the forest, solemnly, their backs straight as the lodgepole pine's. The fancy dancers, wearing fantastical pink-, aqua-, and orange-dyed turkey-feather bustles, twirl like break dancers, creating their own breezes. One man wears a bustle of eagle feathers that looks as if it had been dipped in blood, signifying that he is a veteran who has been wounded in battle. One man, who wears over his head a fur with ears, holds a coup stick topped by the ferocious-looking head of a golden eagle, its beak open.

"Everything in their dress is an expression of their history," my friend Jo says, "both tribal and personal. Some are wearing their grandmother's dress, carrying their great-grandmother's fan. Almost all is handmade. The clothing is cared for, kept in trunks, often smudged with sweetgrass or sage and prayed over before using. The eagle feather, of course, is primary. It is always respected." If an eagle feather falls to the ground during a powwow, shaken free from someone's regalia, everyone must stop until a veteran or spiritual leader retrieves it. Or one of them will stand next to it until the song ends, guarding it against being stepped on.

Aren't those two teenage girls something, napping in a golf cart with their eagle-feather fans over their faces? I am sure they know we are all staring at them and their beauty, daring us to take their picture while they pretend-sleep. I watch the young men with their roach headdresses, so called because they resemble the clipping or roaching of a horse's mane so that it stands erect. Made of animal hair, usually deer tail or porcupine guard hairs, the roaches are usually topped with one or two spotted eagle feathers, which bob, cross, and crisscross wildly as the dancers step. (A good dancer is one who keeps his feathers in constant motion.) The grass dancers, long-legged thin boys stomping the ground with their feather crests and tails, resemble sandhill cranes. Many of the dances are patterned after animals and birds, like the grouse and prairie chicken; others may imitate a hunter tracking them. Though the dances and regalia one sees at a powwow may differ according to tribe, sometimes significantly, the dancers seem always to proceed sunwise.

Between the 1880s and 1930s, Native American celebrations like this were prohibited first by missionaries and eventually by the federal government in an attempt at forced assimilation. In 1882, the US Indian Office stipulated that those who were found guilty of participating in the Scalp Dance, Sun Dance, or War Dance were to be imprisoned for thirty days. In 1921 and 1923, a decree was issued urging stricter regulations: officials were advised to punish offenders by withholding food and clothing rations. Government agents claimed the dances "distracted [the Indians] from agricultural pursuits." However, like stripping children from their families, sending them to boarding schools, and forbidding the use of native languages, the bans were a calculated strategy meant to weaken Native resistance to white takeover—that is, when war, disease, starvation, and broken treaties didn't work. The federal ban on Sun Dance participation wasn't lifted until 1951 in Canada and 1978 in the United States, the latter as a consequence of the American Indian Religious Freedoms Act. That is one reason coming to a powwow like Crow Fair is so exciting. The culture—vital, gorgeous, proud—has not only survived but is thriving.

Feathers, as symbols of Native American cultural and spiritual identification with nature, continue to play a part in indigenous struggles for tribal sovereignty. As of 2007, the bald eagle is no longer on the endangered species list, yet it is still protected under the Bald and Golden Eagle Protection Act and the Migratory Bird Treaty Act. These laws make it illegal to kill eagles or to possess or trade in their feathers, body parts, nests, or eggs. Violation of the former act can result in a fine of up to $100,000. Until fairly recently, these prohibitions pertained to everyone, including indigenous people whose traditional ceremonies include the wearing and use of feathers. The irony of appointing the eagle as our country's national symbol yet prohibiting its use by Native peoples was lost on all but the American Indians. In growing acknowledgment, perhaps, of this irony, in 1975 US Secretary of the Interior C. B. Morton announced that tribal members would not be prosecuted for possessing feathers, at least by his agency. In 1994 President Clinton extended the policy to all federal agencies. Still, it wasn't until October 2012 that US Attorney General Eric Holder signed a Justice Department policy that grants tribal members the right to possess, wear, travel with, collect, and trade in eagle feathers and those of other migratory birds, although they, like everyone else, are forbidden to buy or sell them.

"While the right to possess eagle parts is fairly clearly protected, the process for obtaining eagle parts legally, using them to create ceremonial regalia and objects, and transporting them to where they will be used is still unclear," writes the Friends Committee on National Legislation in response to the new policy. Many tribal members across the United States no longer have access to eagle nests or sites where they might find feathers. If someone wants to make a prayer feather, for instance, and hasn't had one handed down or gifted to them, and doesn't know someone with whom to trade, they have few choices.

One option tribal members have is to fill out an extensive federal permit (C22.22), which allows for the killing of eagles for religious purposes. The process is lengthy and must be renewed every year. Another option is applying to the National Eagle Repository, north of Denver, and filling out a request. Run by the Fish and Wildlife Service, the repository collects dead eagles found on the road or in the wild. In 2013–14, Native Americans requested 1,176 bald eagles and 1,795 golden eagles. But only 2,309 eagles were received—77 percent of those requested. Typically there is such a long waiting list that most people give up. In 2016, a Crow man pleaded guilty to killing an eagle, though he said it was for "cultural uses." He said he wanted a fan for his daughter and to make arrows. A federal judge sentenced him to five years probation and ordered him to pay $5,000 (of a maximum possible $250,000). In 2012, a Blackfoot woman, Rachel CrowSpreadingWings, was arrested in Alberta for exchanging tobacco and $250 for an eagle wing, which she was going to use to make powwow regalia for her family.

✦

"Wearing feathers is deeper than just a part of the outfit," Mike Jetty, Indian Education Specialist at the Montana Office of Public Instruction in Helena, tells me when I meet with him a week after the powwow. "It always has a spiritual component. What feather depends on which tribe: hawk, owl, eagle. I know an Arapaho man who asked me to save any magpie tail feathers I found. The magpie has some significance in the stories of his people. I'm a member of the Spirit Lake band of the Dakota. For us, it is the spotted eagle." (The characteristic black-tipped white feather used in Plains war bonnets is from the tail feathers of the immature golden, or "spotted eagle," whose feathers darken after its first five years.) Jetty tells me that when a mutual friend told him I was coming in to discuss the wearing of feathers in American Indian culture, the first thing that happened was that an Eagle Song popped into his head:

A Spotted Eagle
you said, was coming.
He is coming now. He is coming now.

A Spotted Eagle
you said, was coming.
He is coming now. He is coming now.

The song is a Sun Dance song, Jetty says, sung when the dancers enter the sacred dance grounds. Translated into English many years ago by John Around Him, a Lakota who lived at Pine Ridge, it calls on the courageous and strong spirit of the eagle to help the people who are sacrificing at the ceremony.

"Indian people usually have a strong connection with birds," Jetty continues. "You've heard of the four-legged people, like the deer and the elk. Well, birds and people are the same because we are both two-legged people. Wearing the feather of a certain bird is like calling it to you."

Plenty Coups, Jetty reminds me, carried the stuffed skin of a chickadee after his vision as a boy atop a peak in the Crazy Mountains, near present-day Livingston. In the vision, a tremendous storm struck a forest, leaving only one tree standing. A voice told him it was the lodge of the chickadee, "least in strength but strongest of mind among his kind. He is willing to work for wisdom." The voice told him that what he needed to be a great leader was not fierceness or strength but to listen the way the chickadee listened. In battle, he tied the chickadee beneath his left braid. "It was so small," he recounted, "that it could not be seen, even by Big-shoulder, whose medicine was the fantail of a blue grouse, with eagle breath-feathers [eagle-down]. He tied his likewise beneath his braid, and I could see the breath-feathers blowing in the wind. Nothing can strike a breath-feather."

Jetty says he was recently gifted a feather from a red-tailed hawk, a bird powerful to the Lakota. Eagle feathers are given to people partici-pating in the Sun Dance. Jetty tells me that he has just returned from

Heart Butte, on the Blackfeet reservation, where he attended a high school graduation ceremony. This year each of the seniors received an eagle feather. "You have to think in tribally specific ways," he says. "Not everyone's the same. For instance, some tribes will wear owl feathers because they think they are healing. Some think they represent death and won't get near them. There is so much diversity. It depends on a certain context and the historical relationship with the bird. Some people receive an eagle feather when they are given a name."

I appreciate the subtle difference between the meanings of *gifted* and *given*, especially in the way Jetty uses it here. Being "gifted" something implies an act, a ceremony, an exchange. There is a sense of respect for both giver and recipient, and, of course, for the gift itself. Recently I read an award-winning essay by a young Cheyenne River Sioux student, Tristan Picotte, who wrote about the sacredness of earning eagle feathers: "Eagle feathers pushed our culture forward to better the people, not just the individual. A feather is not simply a thing to be owned, it is an honor to be earned and displayed."

Symbol. Status. Sex. Shelter. Spirit. With feathers, the distinctions between the functions of clothing blur. Native Americans didn't, and don't, eat the eagle, but anyone who has been around eagles knows how they inspire awe: with their cries, their wingspan, their soaring. The eagle feathers in the hair of a Crow warrior signified status, which in turn let women know he was brave and a good provider. They protected him spiritually and perhaps physically, creating confusion and provoking terror in his enemies as he sped toward them.

"Any fool can see that feathers are beautiful and enhance the beauty of the wearer," a member of the indigenous Cashinahua people in Peru told anthropologist Kenneth Kensinger, in response to his questions about the bright feathers in their hair and clothes. At the same time, the Cashinahuas said, they knew the feathers were not theirs—to sell, to trade, to waste—for that would undermine the harmony they had achieved with the natural world. The spirits, they told Kensinger, might retaliate by leading birds and animals deeper in the forest. The feathers had to be given. The dancers at Crow Fair are resplendent as well as symbolic: the light and flight of their dancing, their stunning ornithological costumes. Seeing them, one could believe that we share one soul with all the animals, putting on and taking off these particular bodies almost like clothing. The Prairie Chicken Dance. The Deer Dance. The Eagle Dance. At Crow Fair, the eagles seemed to be everywhere.

5 Pearls

The Pearl Myth

I try to imagine the first human prying open a shellfish for dinner and finding a luminous pearl inside. What must he or she have thought? Because of their opalescent whiteness, in Persia pearls were called *murwari*, meaning "child of light." In China, people believed they fell from clouds when the dragons were fighting. Pliny the Elder, writing in the first century, thought they were formed from dew, while others speculated that lightning had somehow struck the shell. Clearly they were magical. When Europeans first saw them, they called them "tears of the moon." The pearl is the only gemstone not mined in the earth but produced by a living animal. Unlike other gems, it requires no faceting or polishing in order to fluoresce. (Faceting, in fact, wasn't invented until the late seventeenth century, while the oldest pearl necklace was made in Persia 2,400 years ago.) Shell itself is perhaps the oldest form of jewelry; some shell beads are 100,000 years old. But the pearl is far more rare than shell. Out of ten thousand wild oysters, only one might contain a high-quality pearl.

The first pearl beds were discovered at least four thousand years ago in the Persian Gulf, the Red Sea, and the Gulf of Mannar, which lies between Sri Lanka and India. (The Hindu god Krishna is said to have plucked the first one from the sea to give his daughter on her wedding day.) Gulf pearls are large and white, with a characteristic glow. It didn't take long for them to become the basis of an extensive global trade route that stretched from Basra to China and for the pearl beds of the Persian Gulf to become famous. They were also extremely costly. During the wars of the Roman Empire, it is said, General Vitellius "financed an entire military campaign by selling just one of his mother's pearl earrings." Two pearls approximated the worth of 1,875,000 ounces—117,187 *pounds*—of silver! As the legend goes, Cleopatra convinced Mark Antony that Egypt was richer than Rome by blithely crushing one of her pearl earrings in a glass of wine vinegar and drinking it down with dinner.

For centuries, the Persian Gulf was filled with dhows, the Arabic word for the traditional sailing vessels with one or two masts, which employed hundreds of pearl divers and their assistants, including those who sang special songs for their safety, called the *nahham*. Beatriz Chadour-Sampson, in her history *Pearls*, says, "The diver's only equipment was a nose-clip, usually made of tortoiseshell, and leather sheaths worn on the fingers of one hand to let him gather the oysters without cutting himself." Using two ropes—one around his waist and a weighted tie around his feet—the diver would plunge to two hundred feet or more, holding his breath for up to two minutes, while he pried out as many oysters as he could. Pearl-diving was highly skilled and highly dangerous. Divers were often on the ships for months at a time, causing malnutrition and dehydration; they suffered headaches and burst eardrums from the sudden, drastic changes in pressure the dives induced. There were storms as well, and many drowned after tangling in their own ropes or from blacking out. Sharks, barracudas, and sea snakes also took their toll.

Although the principal oyster beds were in the Persian Gulf, there is written evidence that the Chinese were harvesting freshwater pearls from their rivers and ponds in 2300 BCE, while two thousand years ago the Japanese were diving for saltwater pearls growing in oysters near their coasts. For millennia, nearly all of the pearls in circulation world-wide came from these three sources. (The pearl trade in the Philippines, Indonesia, and Malaysia began relatively late, in the twelfth century. The Bajau, or Badjao, people, Malay nomads who even today spend most of their lives in boats on the ocean, were the original harvesters, diving for fish and sea cucumbers, a delicacy, as well as South Sea and black pearls. In "Last of the Sea Nomads," *Guardian* reporter Johnny Langenheim learned that the Bajau purposely rupture their eardrums in order to dive without pain. "You bleed from your ears and nose and you have to spend a week lying down because of the dizziness," says Imran Lahassan, a Bajau fisherman about his own experience under-going such an ordeal.)

One of the more astonishing examples in this history is that of the Japanese *ama* or "women of the sea," who, legend has it, have been practicing their trade in the frigid, dangerous waters of the Pacific coast and the Sea of Japan for over two thousand years. (On the Izu peninsula, they are called *kaito*; in Okinawa, *umi-n-chu*.) Descendants of seafaring nomads, *ama* were originally not hunting pearls but sea-food: abalone, lobster, sea urchin, octopus, sea cucumber (*namako*), and seaweed. Finding a pearl, of course, was a bonus. It was a stren-uous livelihood, handed down from mother to daughter, with girls learning the techniques from the time they were five or six years old—increasing lung capacity, reading currents, memorizing the locations of the best beds. Some of these expert divers were said to be capable of holding their breath for over four minutes and descending to depths of thirty-five to forty-five feet. Women were thought to make bet-ter divers because they could naturally hold their breath longer and because women usually have more body fat to insulate them from the cold water. Diving supplemented a family's income; the husbands of most *ama* were fishermen, out all day on the water themselves.

In 1956, there were 17,611 *ama* still diving in Japan, but as of 2010 only 2,174 remained. Most of the traditional *ama* are now past middle age: among an estimated 1,300 of them living in remote villages near

Toba and Shima, the average age is seventy-two. Young women are no longer interested in staying in the fishing villages, it is said, nor in learning a trade that is so physically demanding and financially precarious. As in places all across the globe, ancient trades like those the *ama* practice are being lost forever, sometimes in a generation. Other, more disturbing reasons contribute to the decline. In a 2010 video made by Anne McDonald and Kaori Brand, titled *Japan's "Ama" Free Divers Keep Their Traditions,* an elderly *ama* remembers seawater so cold just a few feet down from the surface that as a child diver she would shiver for hours after emerging from it; now the water is much warmer, and there is no seaweed for the shellfish to eat. With sea temperatures having risen 1.68 degrees, abalone—an *ama's* cash crop—is threatened.

If you search for *ama* on the internet, you will encounter many erotic images of young, sometimes topless, sexy "mermaids" holding pearls. The *ama* became associated exclusively with pearl oysters, rather than the shellfish they hunted for subsistence, due to the businessman Kokichi Mikimoto, who invented the procedure of culturing pearls in the early 1900s. Employing former divers to find donor oysters for his operation, he introduced the semitransparent white bathing clothes now associated with the *ama,* hence the image. (The labia-like organs of the oyster, as well as the association with prostitution—which in Japan was known as "the water trade"—perpetuated the stereotype.) When he opened Mikimoto Pearl Museum on Mikimoto Island in the Bay of Toba, he began hiring *ama* to perform for tourists. Although some traditional *ama* still "claim their hereditary rights to dive for abalone" around Hegura Island, as McDonald and Brand say, most *ama* now are retired or pearl-diving for tourists off Mikimoto Island.

↘↗

If you closely at any medieval or Renaissance painting of a European queen, you most likely will see pearls accumulating like snowflakes on her silk gown; *collars* of pearls resting directly on her throat; *matinees* of pearls falling just above her breasts; an *opera,* long enough to reach her breastbone; or, longer still, a *pearl rope*. Rosaries were made of pearls, as were bracelets, belts, bodices, and crowns. Tiny princes sported pearl-beaded slippers. Gigantic pearls dangled from British, French, Spanish, Indian, Egyptian, and Italian queens' ears. Pearls were lavishly embroidered on the robes of clergy. In Russian Orthodox paintings, pearls were sewn directly onto the canvas, adorning the Virgin's robe and hair. The famous Pearl Carpet of Baroda, initially created to cover the tomb of the Holy Prophet in Medina, was densely covered with natural Gulf pearls, more than a million of them. According to Steve King, for centuries the demand for pearls resulted in mounds of rotting, cracked-open oyster shells covering the beaches of Sri Lanka: in "Naked Lustre" King writes, "The finest [pearls] would be immediately secured for the Indian Courts, and the inferior kinds as well as the seed pearls transported to Europe to be used in the *aljofar* work of the Moors, which bedecked the court dresses of the Iberian beauties." Desire for them was insatiable.

One of those "Iberian beauties" was Queen Isabella of Spain. When she and her husband, King Ferdinand, sponsored Christopher Columbus's first voyage to discover an alternate route to India, lust for pearls was one of their motivations, along with the gold, silver, and other booty they hoped would support their growing empire and, consequently, their wars. The Pearl Myth, a belief that there existed undiscovered pearl beds that would make everyone rich if only they could be found, was a factor in all of the first expeditions to the New World. The Spanish were not to be disappointed. In 1498, on Columbus's third voyage, he landed on a large Caribbean island off the coast of Venezuela. There he encountered Guaiqueri Indians, who decorated themselves and their clothing with enormous quantities of pearls. (Isla de Margarita, or Margarita Island as it came to be called, was named after the Latinate word for pearl.) An extensive oyster bed lay under the waters between Margarita Island and nearby Cubagua Island, producing pearls of incredible luster and with a unique yellowish cast. By 1525, Margarita Island had become a Spanish colony, indigenous people had been enslaved to serve as divers, and full-scale looting of pearls was in process.

"The image of a landscape strewn with putrefying oysters ripped greedily from the bottom of the ocean provides a sobering counterpoint to the millions of luminescent pearls depicted in portraits of the period," says Molly A. Warsh in her article "Enslaved Pearl Divers in the Sixteenth Century Caribbean." Her research shows not only that were Indians enslaved in the pearl fisheries off the coast of Central America, but also that Africans, who were often excellent swimmers of their native rivers, lakes, and coastlines, were brought in when the Indian slaves began to die from overwork and disease. African slaves, who had originally been imported to work in the gold mines, began diving for pearls off Margarita Island around 1526. For the next century, Indians and Africans often worked side by side in the fisheries and endured the same grueling conditions and brutality. Slaves were locked in their huts at night to prevent any clandestine pearl swapping, as well as sex-swapping, which the slave owners believed would impair their workers' strength for the next day's work.

Diving here, as anywhere, was life-threatening. The water was cold, and divers worked at astonishing depths, sometimes diving up to ninety feet. The air in divers' lungs could become so compressed that their lungs collapsed and eardrums burst. They bled and blacked out or rose to the surface to collapse in their boats and die. They were also attacked by sharks, manta rays, and other predators that had come to feed on the wasted oyster meat the pearl owners would throw back into the water. So many African slaves were eaten by sharks that the Spanish Crown proposed a law to prohibit oysters—and dead slaves—from being thrown overboard.

From 1513 to 1540, approximately 120 million pearls were harvested from the waters of the Caribbean to line the coffers of Spain. The Indian and African slaves diving for pearls off the coast of Venezuela produced more wealth than anywhere else in the Americas until the Europeans began to mine the famous silver deposits in Bolivia and

Peru. A third of all New World spoils came from pearls. One of the world's most famous pearls, named La Peregrina, was found at this time by an enslaved African. Pear-shaped, the size of "a dove's egg," the pearl bought the pearl diver's freedom and soon took its place among Isabella's crown jewels. One can see it hanging from the necks of royalty in paintings for the next five hundred years, passed from queen to queen, country to country—*la peregrina* means "wanderer"—until Richard Burton bought it at auction in 1969 for $37,000 as a Valentine's gift for Elizabeth Taylor. In 2011 it sold for $11 million.

Inspired by the pearl beds in the Caribbean as well as the popular *cantares de gesta*, which described questing knights and imaginary, undiscovered lands full of riches, the Spanish Crown financed Cortés and Pizarro to lead even more extensive and expensive expeditions to Mexico and Central America. Hernán Cortés landed near Veracruz, Mexico, on April 22, 1519, and immediately began violently pillaging his way through central Mexico, eventually defeating the Aztec Empire— or Triple Alliance, as historians call it now—in Tenochtitlan. When the Spanish landed in the Americas, Central Mexico was the most densely populated place on earth. Some estimates are as high as 25.5 million people, "twice as many people per square mile than China or India," as Charles C. Mann claims in *1491: New Revelations of the Americas before Columbus*. Tenochtitlan was bigger than Paris. Historians believe that if it weren't for Cortés's horses, guns, and, most devastatingly, the disease his men brought with them, it is doubtful the city would have fallen. "Absent smallpox [which wiped out at least a third of the population before the final conquest of the city], it seems likely that Cortés would have lost," writes Mann.

In 1533, sailors returning to Tenochtitlan told Cortés that their ship had run aground on what they thought was an island off the continent's west coast and which later was discovered to be the peninsula of Baja. There, as environmental historians Mario Monteforte and Micheline Cariño write, they encountered Indians "wearing long hair braided with beautiful pearls and large, startlingly bright nacre [mother-of-pearl] shells adorning their bodies." Cortés immediately began making plans for a northern excursion. He landed at La Paz in May 1535 with three galleons and six hundred settlers. When word arrived that new pearl beds had been found, Spanish treasure hunters on the east coast greedily packed up, taking many of their enslaved African divers with them. For the next five hundred years, thousands of people combed the waters of the Gulf of California, also called the Sea of Cortés, which led to the colonization of the Baja Peninsula and to La Paz becoming as important a pearling center as the Persian Gulf.

Pearl harvesting carried dire consequences for the natives of both Venezuela and Mexico, as John Steinbeck depicts in his novel *The Pearl*, set in the village of Loreto, north of La Paz on the Gulf of California. "Light filtered down through the water to the bed where the frilly pearl oysters lay fastened to the rubblely bottom, a bottom strewn with shells of broken, opened oysters. This was the bed that had raised the King of Spain to be a great power in Europe in past years, had helped to pay for his wars, and had decorated the churches for his soul's sake," Steinbeck wrote. The Indians of Baja (Guaycuras, Pericúes, Cochimíes), who numbered between forty thousand and fifty thousand when Cortés arrived, were soon decimated by European diseases as well as brutal treatment by the pearl hunters, who made them work long hours diving for pearls, either through forced trade or by directly enslaving them. If they were paid, they were paid little, and they often starved. Monteforte and Cariño say that the Jesuits, who established their first mission in Loreto in 1697, tried to ban the collection of pearls in an attempt to "eliminate overexploitation in the isolated peninsular territories and avoid the abuse of the Indians." Their efforts failed. In the 1740s, after finding hundreds of oysters swept by a storm onto the beach at La Paz, Manuel de Ocio, a soldier at the San Ignacio Mission, enlisted scores of Indians to rake the bottom "so intensively that the wild stocks were depleted within eight years."

Before the Spanish came, the Natives had practiced good steward-ship of the sea; shell deposits from ancient times show that the Natives harvested only the larger oysters, which were older, thus helping to conserve the species. After the Spanish conquest, so many oysters were pulled from the seafloor that entire beaches stank with the meat of thousands of oysters, pried open with steel knives and left to rot. There were far too many to be eaten. As early as the late sixteenth century, most of the pearl fisheries in the Caribbean were fished out. "A description of competing boats 'ripping to pieces' newly discovered oyster beds," Warsh writes, "conveys the greed and desperation that prevailed in the fisheries by the end of the century."

The Persian Gulf, the Sea of Japan, Indonesia, the South Pacific, the Caribbean: by the beginning of the twentieth century, most of the world's saltwater oyster beds were exhausted. Modernized diving equipment caused even more damage by allowing pearl divers to stay underwater longer, gathering more oysters than previously possible. La Paz, Mulege, and the other pearling villages on the coast of Baja California were the last places to experience this wholesale slaughter. By the early 1900s, in the Sea of Cortés, it was almost impossible to find a single natural pearl.

The Pearl Farm

My hotel, a sprawling, elegant imitation of a Spanish colonial estate, sits on a hill above the Sea of Cortés, outside the city of Guaymas, in the mainland state of Sonora, Mexico. It is eight in the evening by the time I check in; the waves are splashing below my balcony, azure in the dimming light. Built in 1935 by an American businessman with ties to the copper mines of nearby Nacozari, the rooms have red tile floors, dark furniture, and dark wooden beams, and the courtyards, clearly designed for large fiestas, are lined with palms. (At the hotel's inauguration, the band was asked to dress like *charros*, originating the now-traditional mariachi costume of cowboy hats, silver buckles, and suits with embroidered trim.) Across the bay, the dramatic ridgeline of Cerro Tetakawi rises, treeless and jagged, into the sunset. Within walking distance, though it is too dark right now to see it, is Perlas del Mar de Cortéz, the only operating pearl farm left in the Americas.

I learned about Perlas del Mar de Cortéz through the website of an organization called the Sustainable Pearls project, an association of researchers and farmers studying how cultured pearl farms in the Pacific regions might preserve and improve marine environments. While perusing the site's "Pearl Farming World Map," I noticed, far from the giant pearl clusters that mark sites in Vietnam, Myanmar, China, and Japan, one lone violet pearl sitting in what looked like the Gulf of California. Through Laurent E. Cartier, the project's founder, I managed to contact one of the owners, Douglas McLaurin-Moreno, who was happy to invite me to see his farm's operations firsthand.

The morning after I arrive in Guaymas, at exactly 8:30 a.m. as arranged, McLaurin-Moreno strolls into the hotel lobby. Tall, handsome, of Scottish and Spanish heritage, he resembles photographs of a forty-year-old Pablo Neruda and is dressed a bit like him, cosmopolitan and a bit old-fashioned: tweed sports jacket, wool sweater, button-down shirt, jeans—clothes Neruda might wear on a November morning in Paris, though certainly not here, where it is already seventy degrees. McLaurin-Moreno is gracious, formal, and, I will discover, wickedly funny. Before taking me to the pearl farm, he says that he wants to introduce me to the bay and the nearby towns, and, for nearly an hour, he does. We drive first to the wealthy *tourista* marina of San Carlos, with its gated condos and quaint shopping malls, and then to the poor fishing village of La Manga, where the unpaved main street is lined with stalls selling ropes of seashells the people have found onshore. The day is warm, the bay glorious with sun. Yet in La Manga, ours is the only car moving. McLaurin-Moreno is expounding: "The media have frightened away all the tourists! Look at all these abandoned restaurants and empty storefronts! Look at these unfinished buildings! No one wants to visit Mexico. It is too violent. You might get killed." A dead raccoon lies roadside. He points to it. "Mexican violence!" he exclaims.

We stop for coffee at a roadside bakery owned by friends of his. It is empty. "Mexican people," he says, turning serious, "they have no hope. There are no jobs. Everyone says education is the answer. But you can get an education and still there will be no jobs. If you ask me, the worst kind of violence is poverty. Why doesn't the news talk about that?"

McLaurin-Moreno was a graduate student in biology at the Tec de Monterrey Research Institute in 1991 when he began to experiment with pearl culturing, along with two of his friends, Enrique Arizmendi and Manuel Nava, and a mentor, Sergio Farrell. Their aim was to find a way to grow pearls in the Sea of Cortés while following a vision of low or no impact on the sea. Their experiment grew into a project, Perlas de Guaymas, which was funded by the school, and in 2000 they succeeded with their first commercial harvest. Five years later, when the university closed, Arizmendi, Nava, and McLaurin-Moreno formed a partnership and took over the operation. We pull into a parking lot, and soon I am standing on steps above the tranquil waters of Bacochibampo Bay. I can see my hotel in the distance.

The grounds of the pearl farm consist of three tiers. At the top, on a hill, the university building, with full-length two-story windows overlooking the water, serves as offices and a showroom for pearl jewelry. Halfway down the slope, on an even patch of ground, is the "lab," a small, corrugated shed I am told I probably won't be able to go into. It is where the secret work is done, McLaurin-Moreno says, winking. At the shore, just above the waves, five Yaqui men work under the *palapa*, a picturesque open-sided hut with a thatched roof. McLaurin-Moreno greets everyone by name, laughs, makes jokes, strides into the middle of the action. At a wet rough-hewn table, the workers deftly use machetes to slice apart hanks of oysters and to knock off barnacles and other parasites. Five times a year they must raise the nets, remove each oyster from its pocket, and clean the shells. The nets, or "cages," protect the oysters from predators while still allowing them to feed on algae.

"What would they attach to if there were no nets?" I ask.

"Rocks and each other," McLaurin-Moreno answers. Pearl oysters are members of the family Pteriidae (feathered oysters), which includes clams. They attach themselves to reefs and rocks with threads, called byssus, instead of cementing themselves like true oysters do. Although they can more easily be dislodged during storms, they also require wilder, more oceanic conditions.

All mollusks are capable of producing pearls, including mussels and abalone, though not all of very good quality. Pearl oyster pearls are the most consistent and the most valued. There are four basic kinds of pearl oysters in the world's saltwater oceans and seas. *Pinctada fucata martensii*, typically found in the colder waters off the coasts of Asia, produce Akoya pearls, which are small, classic white, and round. About 18 percent of the world's cultured pearls are Akoya pearls. The *Pinctada maxima* oyster produces the large South Seas pearl, which comes in shades ranging from optic white to soft cream, champagne, and an almost metallic gold. They now account for 47 percent of the world's harvest and are grown mostly in Australia, as well as Indonesia, the Philippines, and Myanmar. Indigenous to the Cook Islands, Fiji, French Polynesia, and the Sea of Cortés, the black-lipped oyster (*Pinctada mazatlanica*) grows dark, almost black pearls that often flash within a spectrum of gray, green, blue, peacock, and purple. "Tahitian" or "black" pearls are of this type. A strand of Tahitian pearls, varied but sea-colored, mirrors the shadows and shallows of a tropical shore. The American Museum of Natural History states that "before Black-lipped Pearl Oysters were first cultured for pearls in French Polynesia in the last century, most of the black pearls seen in Western countries—including many of the larger pearls worn during the European Renaissance—came from La Paz Pearl Oysters in Panama or Baja California."

The fourth type of pearl oyster is the rainbow-lipped oyster (*Pteria sterna*), which is what McLaurin-Moreno and his partners grow. As its name implies, the shell and pearls range in shades from an opalescent purple to green, blue, gray, pink, and gold. The color difference in pearls is due to the natural pigments already present in the shell. Whatever the hue of the inside lip of an oyster's shell, McLaurin-Moreno says, the pearl inside will match it. Rainbow-lipped and black-lipped oysters are both indigenous to the Americas, but the rainbow-lipped is found nowhere else in the world. These two oysters share the same waters here and have cohabited for thousands, perhaps millions, of years.

"These are black-lips," McLaurin-Moreno says, holding up a crusty, brownish shellfish the size of my hand. "*Pinctada mazatlanica*. You can see how big they are. These are older. These are about six years old. They produce dark-colored pearls."

"Six years old? So these are going to be harvested soon?"

"No, these are never to be harvested!" When he sees my puzzlement, he adds, "The black-lips, we don't seed them because their pearls are very much like Tahitian or Australian pearls. And not really well worth it, for us."

"Then why are you growing them?"

"Breeding. We allow them to breed. And that way we have more pearl oysters in the environment. That's the only reason."

I still don't understand. "So you scrape them off by hand five times a year just like you do the others, and you grow them in these nets, just so that they live?"

"It costs us money. It doesn't give us any money. But it's the right thing to do." He isn't sure I am getting it. He tries again. "Everything is connected. The black-lipped, it needs our help."

Perlas del Mar de Cortéz is the only operating pearl farm in the Americas, but it was not the first. In 1903, Gastón J. Vives constructed a pearl farm in La Paz, collecting spat (baby oysters) from Panamire black-lipped oysters and growing them in nets, much as the partners do here in Guaymas. The Baja California Pearl and Shell Breeding Company, or CCCP, was the first successful attempt at massive cultivation of pearl oysters—as opposed to culturing of pearls—in the world. The company harvested its oysters for their nacre, or inner shell, which it then sold to Europe to be used in the making of jewelry, buttons, weaponry, temples, and thrones. Opening the oysters, the

CCCP sometimes found many high-quality pearls. Within nine years the company had become the world's largest producer of nacre and natural pearls. Vive's success was short-lived. In 1914, the Mexican Revolution led to the plundering and complete destruction of the pearl farm. The new government, in dire financial need, lifted restrictions on pearl fisheries. In fifteen years the oysters were depleted, and in 1939 the Mexican government banned pearl diving altogether. Black-lipped and rainbow-lipped oysters are still categorized as "under special protection."

Today the bay is loud, with big swells sloshing over the seawall onto the floor of the shed. McLaurin-Moreno turns toward a rowboat tied off a pier and motions for me to get in. "It's a rough day," he laughs, exhilarated. "A rough day at the farm. It's going to get worse later. So if we want to go out there, we have to go now."

We sit in the stern of the little boat. Jesús, the pearl farm's foreman, operates the motor while McLaurin-Moreno stands in the middle holding tightly to a tow rope, leaning back as if he were waterskiing. We head out into the waves. "Below us is a giant floating reef that the oysters like to live in," he shouts over the wind. "It attracts a lot of fishes in the area. We don't allow fishing here. So since there is no fishing here, there are a lot more fish here than anywhere else. Scientists from the university in Guaymas came and inspected the farm. They said the biodiversity in the surrounding areas is far, far less than here."

"How do you keep people from fishing?" I shout back.

"Jesús here is our guard. He's fearsome. You see him. He's almost seven feet tall." They both laugh at his joke.

We row out to one of the long lines of buoys; the oyster cages hang from ropes strung between them. I ask how many nets are down there. "I don't know. It shifts. It's very dynamic. We just harvested; we have less. Perhaps we have about two thousand pearl nets." Jesús reaches down into the water and hauls up one of the nets, about six by four feet, divided into little compartments, each just large enough for one oyster to fit cozily. There are probably a hundred or so oysters in each cage. Jesús stands there steadily, holding the cage so we can examine it.

Oysters are filter feeders; they use their gills to extract bacteria and algae from the water washing through them. In the wild, only about ten out of a million oysters would survive into adulthood, McLaurin-Moreno tells me. "In the cages, 80 percent survive and go on to breed. There are now approximately two hundred thousand native oysters in Bacochibampo Bay." There are more oysters here than there have been for hundreds of years because it is a protected environment. In addition to being a business, Perlas del Mar de Cortéz functions as a breeding station.

When we return to the *palapa*, an older man is repairing a net that will be used for spat collection. In spring or fall, the mature oysters in the bay spawn and release millions of fertilized eggs into the water. These larvae swim around for a couple of weeks, then settle on something, usually rock or their preferred perch, coral. It is then that the farm lowers hundreds of spat collectors, which stay down for about two months, collecting baby oysters. "They are basically nets made to resemble fan corals," McLaurin-Moreno says, picking one up. "They measure up to twenty meters in length. And we have thousands of these guys." Each net can catch between one thousand and eight thousand spat. When the spat become big enough to be visible, they are brought in, hand-picked off the nets, and then placed inside larger and larger cages. "It's a passive means of collecting," McLaurin-Moreno explains. "We put the nets in the sea and the baby oysters—only those that want to!—attach themselves. We like to think they make a choice to come to us." Some years they collect tens of thousands; some years there are none. "The environment changes," he says. "All animals respond to changes in their environment."

The Cultured Pearl

Natural, uncultured pearls form inside the soft body of a mollusk (oyster or mussel or abalone) because, as water filters through, a tiny parasite, such as the larvae of a worm or crab, gets lodged inside. The oyster feels it and starts to cover it with layers of nacre—the same substance with which it makes its shell—in order to reduce the irritation. As the nacre builds, the pearl takes shape, and because the nacre is applied *around* the irritant, that shape is often round. Those marvelous gems hanging from the necks of royalty for thousands of years? They are basically cysts that grow in the reproductive folds of the oyster—simply a hard nucleus covered with shell. Culturing—or farming pearls—is the process of artificially initiating that process. A cultured pearl is literally made by the human hand. The technique was first developed, as far as we know, in eleventh- to twelfth-century China, though, as Kiyohito Nagai says in "A History of the Cultured Pearl Industry," "the results were far removed from the pearls we have today." To wit, the Chinese induced Buddha-shaped blisters in freshwater mussels by implanting tiny lead or stone or marble figurines. The result was nacre-covered, mother-of-pearl facsimiles of the prophet, thousands of which were sold as talismans, often with the shell attached.

Japanese businessman Kokichi Mikimoto was the first to experiment with culturing natural-looking pearls, beginning in 1905. Employing Kakichi Mitsukuria, a research professor from Tokyo Imperial University, he wanted to produce round Akoya pearls from the *Pictada fucata martensii* oysters of Japan. Naturally occurring pearls had been already depleted by overfishing and devastated by a red tide. Mikimoto's secret method, which he immediately patented (Japan patent office #2670, "Method of Pearl Formation"), involved making a small cut in the oyster's sex organs and placing a shell bead within. Mikimoto pearls began to appear in the gem markets of Europe in the late 1920s. "Jewelers were aghast," Nagai writes, and they demanded a public trial, hoping that scientists would condemn these new pearls as fake. Much to their dismay, the trial, held in Paris, upheld the pearls' authenticity, and Mikimoto became famous—and rich. Most of his process was perfected by the 1930s. In 1952 he patented the special instruments pearl farmers would need to use in the surgical operation. A former dentist, Otokichi Kuwabara, designed them for him, modifying the fine, precise tools he used for teeth.

I ask McLaurin-Moreno if he and his partners have a patent on their seeding procedure.

"We don't have a patent, because with a patent, you have to describe the process. Then everybody knows it." He is leading me up a steep series of rock steps to the windowless prefab shed he had previously said I wouldn't be allowed to enter. "This is the lab," he says, opening the tentlike inner flaps that allow the sea air in. "This is where the magic happens."

After a year and a half or so, the spat, which have now grown to be adult oysters, are ready to be "seeded." It is a surgical operation done by specialists; at Perlas del Mar de Cortéz, the specialists are Arizmendi, Nava, and McLaurin-Moreno. When we enter the lab, Nava, who is deep into his seeding quota for the day, frowns. McLaurin-Moreno had told me beforehand that Nava is suspicious that I will reveal his techniques, but soon he relaxes. I am sure that he can see, by my questions, that I lack a deep understanding of biology and pose no threat. About two dozen rainbow-lipped oysters sit in a bin of cold water on the floor. McLaurin-Moreno picks up a steel forceps. "This is called a spreader. Millions of oysters did not survive operations of this kind because of tools like these! These spreaders sometimes caused up to 100 percent mortality because oysters fight when pried open. In cold water, like this, they just relax. They're lethargic. They open up. We use a little wedge so they don't close."

On the operating table in front of Nava are trays of different-sized beads, various tweezers, clamps, and the device that holds the oyster open at eye level so the surgeon, wearing gloves and a headlamp, can work. McLaurin-Moreno selects an oyster out of the bin and holds it up to our eyes. It has opened its shell a few inches. He shines a light inside. "See, this is the mantle. It is the inner tissue next to the shell. If I lift it up like this, you can see her reproductive organs." He uses a slender tool to delicately separate the skin. The inside of an oyster does look strikingly like female genitalia. "See, she's flashing us!" McLaurin-Moreno jokes.

Mabe, or blister, pearls are seeded by exposing the shell found under the mantle tissue and simply planting a bead there. The mantle, or inner tissue, finding a foreign object, will be stimulated to secrete nacre and grow a shell over it. When they are ready, mabes must be cut from the shell with a tile cutter; they are half-pearls in the sense that they grow flush with the shell and are thus not freestanding. Less expensive than "loose" pearls, they can be set in jewelry, but they can't be strung. At Perlas del Mar de Cortéz, which grows both mabes and the more traditional, spherical pearls, they usually plant up to three mabes per oyster. The growing of traditional pearls requires a far more complicated operation.

On the pearl farm's website, McLaurin-Moreno describes traditional pearl-seeding for a layperson like me. The pearl surgeon begins by making an incision in the oyster's reproductive organ and very carefully inserts a probe until he or she locates a small organ called the pearl sac: "You have to be very careful to avoid every one of the oyster's delicate organs: heart, kidney, pancreas and liver, stomach and gut," he writes. The pearl sac is made up of connective tissue; it has no real function for the oyster, but is perfect for growing pearls. A small bead made out of the shell of the Mississippi mussel is inserted in the sac. "Is it all over now?" McLaurin-Moreno writes. "Not yet. You still need an extra ingredient: mantle tissue cells." The mantle comes from donor oysters—oysters that have been killed to supply this necessary grafting ingredient. The mantle is cut into grafts according to the size of each "seed" and then placed on top or below it. The mantle supplies the cells that initiate the nacre-making. If everything goes according to plan, the oyster will heal and a tiny pearl will begin to grow.

"We have to do the operation really fast so it doesn't bleed to death," McLaurin-Moreno explains.

"How do you close the wound?" I ask.

"It's a hand trick. We each have our tool." He points to a ribbon of brownish skin on the table by Nava. "The donor mantle can influence what the pearl looks like even more than the oyster itself. We believe if we start with a perfect donor, we will get better pearls. The donors are chosen from the same group brought in to seed. They are sacrificed, in other words." One oyster can provide ten to fifteen pieces of mantle. I find myself staring blankly at the mantle, so he begins again. "The mantle is a tissue. It has several functions. One of them is to breathe. These animals can actually breathe through their skin. And the other one is to produce the shell, probably its most important function. It is also where the sense organs are. See that protrusion? There? Those are thousands of microscopic eyes."

Nava calls us over. One of the pearls being operated on already has two natural pearls growing in it. I peer into the mystery of the oyster, behind the curtain. There they are, two pearls so tiny I might be imagining them, glowing like stars in a faraway galaxy. They are so small that McLaurin-Moreno takes the oyster outside so we can see better. "If we used a microscope, we could probably see little holes made in the outside shell by the parasite," he says, excited. "Something got inside, damaged the mantle, and started making the little pearls. Sometimes if we find a big one growing, we will separate it and not seed it and leave it to its own devices. Then we have a natural pearl."

"How many natural pearls do you find?" I ask.

"It depends. There are years when we have none and some years where we have maybe sixty. And from those, we might obtain a harvest of seventeen usable pearls!" He gives the oyster back to Nava. "In this case, the pearls are too small. We will go ahead and seed this one. We usually seed one pearl, but if the oyster is large, sometimes two."

Although it takes experts like Nava less than a minute to seed an oyster, the cultured pearls this farm cultivates require almost four years of exacting manual labor: collecting the spat, separating them into net baskets to grow for two years, and bringing them in and cleaning them five times a year. After seeding, the oysters are set back in the sea, where they will grow the loose pearls and mabes for at least another two years. Each of these steps demands expertise. If hurricanes come, which happens increasingly—McLaurin-Moreno says global warming is causing not only more storms but also acidification of the water, which can harm shells—the entire farm can be wiped out. "You never know what will happen," he says. "The resulting pearls might be misshapen or they may stop growing. Of a hundred seeded oysters, we might get thirty quality pearls. The rest we destroy."

Adding to the risk, for now the bottom has dropped out of the pearl market. One reason is that cultured *freshwater* pearls, mostly from China, have flooded the market. Worldwide, eighteen hundred tons of pearls are marketed each year: twelve tons of Tahitian blacks, eleven tons of white, McLaurin-Moreno states. "And Cortéz pearls? We produce .0004 tons of pearls a year. That comes to about four thousand pearls. We grow the rarest cultured pearls on the face of the earth." He pauses. "I think we are crazy. But if we close, what will happen to these workers? What will happen to the oysters? I'm just hoping that we can turn the tide."

Sustainable Pearls

Sustainability is defined by the World Commission of Environment and Development as "development that meets the needs of the present without compromising the ability of future generations to meet their own needs." In ecology, it is the ability for an ecosystem, including present and future generations of animals and plants, to remain biologically diverse and to be able to continue. Ecologists judge the sustainability of a process or habitat in terms that are not limited to the financial profits. "The Triple Bottom Line," a way of thinking first introduced by John Elkington in 1994, argues that businesses should evaluate the costs of any enterprise by examining "The Three P's": people, profit, and the planet. "Profit" is, obviously, the bottom line. It is the balance of monetary expenses versus gain. Throughout modern industrial history, this has often been the sole criterion in determining success. By "people," Elkington means that we measure how socially responsible a company is to its employees and community. Are they paid adequately? Are they safe and healthy? Can they count on having a job in the future? And as for "the planet," it is the measure human beings have often ignored, to our increasing peril. The Triple Bottom Line takes into account the *actual price* paid for cheap goods and services, not the price subsidized by freely taken lives of the animals and plants, and the health of people.

What makes a pearl farm sustainable? The answer to that question is one that Laurent E. Cartier and his fellow researchers at the Sustainable Pearls project have devoted a great number of years to: "protection of the biosphere; sustainable use of natural resources; production transparency and product disclosure; operation of farms in a socially and culturally responsible manner; and management commitment and local law compliance." Cartier says that unless marine pearl farms are overstocked, there are few environmental impacts. Most farms are low-tech and nonpolluting. The oysters themselves are indigenous and inhabit the same ocean, lakes, and rivers where their wild cousins thrive. Employees at sustainable pearl farms like McLaurin-Moreno's clean the oysters manually rather than using the high-pressure hoses that nonsustainable farms do, which waste water and often kill smaller oysters. Nets are hauled up by hand and lowered into the ocean, where the oysters are allowed to grow in their natural habitat. Natural pearls are not dyed, polished, or bleached, so their processing does not add toxins to the environment.

Pearl oysters, in fact, do their part in cleaning up pollutants. As animals that filter great quantities of water through their gills, they remove toxins from marine environments. Cartier and Saleem Ali report that one oyster "can filter between 11.5 and 25.9 liters per hour per gram of tissue dry weight." Scientists in Australia are experimenting with the oyster's ability to filter heavy metals from the water. In addition, because of their locations pearl farms usually contain high levels of carbon. Conserving these areas—which is what owners of pearl farms have a financial incentive to do—mitigates the effects of global warming, protects coral reefs and marine species, and improves water quality. Because pearl oysters are extremely sensitive to their environment, they are negatively impacted by pollution, viruses, increased temperatures, and overcrowding. "Cultured pearl farming is one of the few economic activities in which sound management and conservation are a prerequisite to economic success," write Cartier and Ali. Many pearl farmers have been able to ban fishing in their areas, thus preventing overfishing and increasing biodiversity. In places like the Sea of Cortés, where pearl oyster populations were exhausted, native oysters are coming back. When Perlas del Mar de Cortéz began, spat collection averaged only thirty oysters per net; by 2010, a decade later, it averaged eight thousand. Wild oyster populations in Bacochibampo Bay have also increased significantly.

And what about people? According to the UN Environmental Programme, "There is a clear link between poverty eradication and better protection and restoration of habitat, marine fishery resources and biodiversity." Pearl farms like Perlas del Mar de Cortéz offer employment in isolated places where fishing is one of the only options. Eliminating overfishing requires the cooperation of local communities. If the fathers, mothers, brothers, and sisters in that community are making a good living at a pearl farm, they will be invested in enforcing fishing bans, as well as in lobbying to keep the waters clean. "The most effective forms of conservation will be those that engage local stakeholders," says Joe Roman, a conservation biologist. As Cartier and Ali write in a 2012 article for *Solutions*, for these communities a clean environment and financial sustainability go hand in hand.

As in most agricultural trades, industrial mass production threatens the skills and knowledge of pearl cultivation and culturing. The Japanese, for instance, know that tranquil water is better for the oysters, so they work to prevent disruptions. The Australians rotate their oysters because they know rotation will give the pearl a better shape. As small pearl farms go under, drowned by huge conglomerates like those in China, these particular skills go underground too. In Japan, the elders who know how to graft the oysters are dying. In "A Brief

Analysis of the Global Seawater Cultured Pearl Industry," a talk he gave at the 2013 Hong Kong Jewelry and Gem Fair, Andy Müller said, "Pearl farming is an extremely tough job that doesn't pay well. There are hardly any newcomers to replace the old guard." Sustainable pearl farms are keeping these very human skills alive and at the same time offering employment to local, often indigenous, communities. One can hope that more and more people find their way back to work that is satisfying *and sustainable,* work that is in close relationship to both the animals and environment in which they live. Although consumers still want their food, their clothes, their goods cheap and disposable and their jobs less strenuous, more and more people also know this kind of consumerism comes at a price we may not be able to afford.

➤

"In the case of China, every year they make available eight to ten pearls for every person on the face of the earth!" McLaurin-Moreno is exclaiming. On my third day in Guaymas, I have met him in his second-story office, where his shelves are cluttered with boxes of seashells, arcane culturing tools, and his childhood collection of Star Wars figures. The view is marvelous—the glittering Bacochibampo Bay, the *palapa,* the Yaqui workers with their machetes, the brightly colored buoys marking the oyster nets. I have had to catch McLaurin-Moreno at the pearl farm before late afternoon, when he leaves for his second job selling water purification systems.

"This is why the price of pearls has dropped," he says as he lays a black square of velvet on his desk. "Pearls are gemstones. Did you know that gemstones fluoresce? A diamond usually glows blue. Rubies? Maybe green. Pearls also glow blue. That is why I have this lamp." He shows me an ultraviolet jeweler's light, which resembles a small flashlight. Cupping a handful of pearls, he slides them under the velvet, and lifting a corner, shines the light inside. I peek in. One tiny freshwater pearl turns turquoise, and so does the black South Pacific pearl. "See," he says, picking one out, "this one doesn't glow at all. That is because it is fake. There are many different tests you can do. A water test. A fire test—fake pearls will burn because they are plastic. Real pearls don't catch fire. They might incinerate, but they're not flammable." He places one more pearl under the velvet and aims the jeweler's light. The pearl glows a soft pink. "This is one of ours, a Cortéz pearl. Why pink? It has a different protein. It is because of the cells and their crystalline structure."

McLaurin-Moreno picks up the freshwater pearl. "Every pearl should look like the shell of its oyster. This looks glassy. Why? Because it has been polished. So all cultured pearls in China have been polished. Why do they do that? When they aren't polished, they are dull and unappealing. This," he says, holding the pearl high in the air, "is fake beauty!"

A freshwater pearl is a pearl grown inside a mussel. Unlike oysters, mussels can be seeded to produce thirty to fifty smallish pearls each. The pearls are of lesser quality than a marine pearl, meaning they have less sheen and are often misshapen. In the 1980s China became the world's biggest producer of freshwater cultured pearls; by 2010 it was harvesting an astonishing 1,500 tonnes of them. (A tonne is a metric ton; it is equivalent to approximately 2,205 pounds.) In "Naked Lustre," Steve King tells the story of Pierre Cartier, who in 1917 traded $100 and a pearl necklace for a townhouse on Fifth Avenue. Today the Chinese are culturing pearls that look exactly like Japanese Akoya pearls for one-tenth the cost.

The handful of Cortéz pearls McLaurin-Moreno spreads before me each display a very subtle individual shape. They aren't imperfect, exactly, but they seem *shaped by someone*, whether animal or vegetable. It is hard to describe this quality, but we know it when we see it in a petal, a shell, a stone. "Why do I have different sizes, and why don't I make them all look alike?" McLaurin-Moreno asks, then answers himself. "Because these pearls are not processed. They come out this way. I select them according to their traits."

He hands over a large oval Sea of Cortés pearl, and I take it to the window to see it better. In my palm, it is a stormy purple gray. In natural light, it flashes lavender, blue, green, pink—like sea-light, like the colors of the sea. Turning it over, I say, "I think this is the most beautiful thing I have ever seen."

Pearls have a fingerprint pattern on their surface, McLaurin-Moreno says, which is destroyed when they are polished in gigantic tumblers, as the Chinese do with their freshwater pearls. A pearl can break. It can scratch. They are some of the softest gems. "Pearls have texture," he says. "That's what makes them pearls. See these ripples? We call that hammering. It's an optical effect. It's not really there. The hammering brings out the opalescence of the pearl."

Freshwater pearls from China are also dyed: black, red, blue. They use regular hair dyes for it, McLaurin-Moreno says, which contain heavy metals, which chip and fade and eventually peel off with part of the shell. "When the Chinese dye the pearls, the first thing they do is drill the pearl. Then they steep them in the paint, and the pearl absorbs it. The paints eventually become dirty and are just thrown into the rivers, where they kill everything. And then the heavy metals end up in your food source. That is why we are so adamant against treatments; bleaching, dyeing, these are things that should not be done to pearls because the pearl dies. And not only that, it pollutes," he adds.

In my research, I found that China has its own problems at the pearl farms. Off the coast of Guangdong, where most of the marine farms are located, chemical pollution from factories creates terrible water conditions, and this water pollution has harmed oysters and other marine animals. Many of the farmers are relocating or closing altogether. Freshwater pearls, on the other hand, are grown in lakes, streams, and rivers, but mostly in rice paddies that have been converted by excavating them and flooding them. In large commercial operations, overstocking can consume nutrients in the soil and water and cause an accumulation of oyster feces, which poisons the watershed. Manure and fertilizer are often added in order to produce the algae the mussels need to feed on. These, in turn, end up in drinking water.

"Most of us want to know where our things come from, that a village was not razed to get them. That is important to us, and to our customers as well. Maybe you don't want to have a tainted gem?" McLaurin-Moreno asks.

I take out of my pocket a white, perfectly round object I found on the hotel beach. "Douglas, this is shell, right?"

"People are always bringing me things," he chuckles. He holds it up to the light, makes a serious face, and then laughs. "This," he says, pausing for effect, "it is a marble." He scrutinizes it. "It is a marble that has polished itself."

"Okay," I say. "This multifaceted endeavor—making sure that humans are taken care of, that the Yaqui you hire keep their jobs, that what you do improves the community and at the same time the ecology of the place where you live—did you know all this ahead of time? I mean, were these your goals when you started?"

He doesn't need to consider the question. "I think all humans know this. We knew it when we were born, and then later we are shaped to become monsters. We grow up and are separated from nature. I grew up in a little town with my grandmother. Fruit trees of all sorts, and we had chickens running around the area. And now I see kids in junior high school, and they say, 'Wait a minute, beef comes from cattle?' We are being detached from the system. From my point of view, we should be able to feel this connection again."

Yesterday, when I had asked McLaurin-Moreno how he felt about the oyster as a living being, he had told me that he loved them. "If you like plants, you will like oysters. They are hardy. They don't move much. They're not very talkative, a little problem they have. But I can pick one up, and I know if it's healthy or not—by its smell, by the color of its shell, its weight, whether it is drooling with mucus. There's no talk, but when I touch them—and this is much more intimate—it's telling me a lot of things." He paused. "I've worked with these animals for years and years, and they continue to amaze me. You see one of these little critters and think, 'It's so weak, it's so unhealthy,' and then you open it up, and there is an amazing pearl. The oyster amazes me."

Beatriz Chadour-Sampson notes that Pliny the Elder spoke against the wearing of pearls in ancient Rome *because* of the danger risked by the fishermen who dove for them. What would he have said about all the slaves in the Americas, indigenous and African, whose eardrums burst, who starved or were beaten? What of the soldiers who were forced to wage war over pearls, the merchants who wanted more and more, who leased ships and raked the ocean floor, shelling and wasting so that entire beaches were piled with the stinking carcasses of oysters, too many to eat, split open for the chance a cyst might have formed in the genitals of a living animal? Six hundred pearls strung in one necklace. Some queens had up to thirty-three necklaces, each at least a foot long. I ask McLaurin-Moreno, "When you see those European portraits of royalty wearing gowns embroidered with thousands of pearls, what do you see?"

"I see a walking genocide," he says. He then picks up the little Chinese freshwater cultured pearl, which has been polished and perhaps bleached. "People need to educate themselves. Why do they go for the mass-produced pearl from China? Millions, exactly the same. Because they are in love with *the idea* of the pearl, not the pearl itself. The pearl is white and uniform and kind of boring, but it speaks for classic elegance and prestige. It makes them think of Jackie Kennedy and Coco Chanel. It speaks of aristocracy."

Most Americans don't know, I tell him, that Kennedy's signature three-strand pearl necklace, which can be seen in hundreds of photographs, and seemed to signify her class and elegance, was in fact fake. Crafted out of 139 European glass faux pearls, it nonetheless sold at a Sotheby's auction in 1996 for $211,000. The buyer, Lynda Resnick, writes that when they were delivered, "the pearls were still in their original silk-lined box from Bergdorf's. As I opened it, I caught a faint scent of Jackie's perfume. It was chilling." (Fake pearls, unlike real pearls, are known to retain the scent of their wearers, a quality that has driven many vintage buyers to get rid of them.) Resnick went on to sell 130,000 facsimiles of Kennedy's necklace for two hundred dollars each. Coco Chanel, who is quoted as saying, "A woman needs ropes and ropes of pearls," apparently meant costume pearls, which she promoted in her fashions. "I only like fake jewelry," she said.

McLauren-Moreno grows quiet. He has shifted his gaze out the window, one of the few times I have seen him unanimated. Pensive, he shakes his head. "If one really looks at the object one is buying, thinks about where it comes from, the skills it took to grow it, to make it, the many *who*'s—who processed it, who harvested it, including who the animal is itself—black- or rainbow-lipped—how long it has grown, let alone its individual features reflected in the pearl—one would come to a different kind of valuing, perhaps a more real, sustainable one."

6 Fur

The Controversy

In 1996, an activist, in protest against *Vogue*'s promotion of fur fashion, spoiled editor-in-chief Anna Wintour's lunch at the Four Seasons by throwing a dead raccoon on her plate. On a freezing February day in 2016, three models dressed only in gas masks, panties, and duct tape on their nipples disrupted Fashion Week in London. Their message: "Fur is Toxic." In between are twenty years of spectacle: naked women, and sometimes men, wrapped in plastic smeared with ketchup, sprawled on the sidewalk as if dead, or crouching in small cages in the city centers of Madrid, London, Copenhagen, Hong Kong, Oslo, and New York. In a 2009 article in the *Guardian*, Elizabeth Day writes, "They have thrown buckets of money soaked in fake blood on audiences at the International Fur Fair. They have stormed the offices of French *Vogue* wearing leg traps around their feet."

Worldwide, fur provokes perhaps the most controversy of any human commodity. Protesters shame the women wearing it, indirectly by posting photographs of them—Beyoncé, Lady Gaga, Rhianna, and Jennifer Lopez—on Pinterest, Facebook, and antifur sites, or more directly by accosting them on the street, shouting, as Ingrid Newkirk, founder of PETA, advises: "That's a beautiful fur. You'd look so much better without it. It makes you look coldhearted." A famous 1984 ad by photographer David Bailey depicts a catwalk model dragging behind her a fur coat that oozes a trail of blood. The caption states, "It takes up to 40 dumb animals to make a fur coat. But only one to wear one." At trade shows, fashion runways, and shops, furs have been slashed, ruined with gum, and splashed with paint. The violence has often escalated. Mink farms especially have been targeted. Activists have broken into farms across the United States, England, Denmark, and Canada, releasing tens of thousands of animals from their pens into the wild. The Animal Liberation Front claimed responsibility for burning a California furrier to the ground. In England, four department stores were firebombed in protest against their sale of furs.

Yet the controversy, like the wearing of expensive furs, seems to be played out on the periphery of the ordinary person's life. Most of us are neither mink farmers nor radical animal rights activists, neither furriers nor antifur celebrities, neither trappers nor vegans. Should we care? "Even I draw the line at fur," a friend says. "Though," she adds, "I would never give up my leather shoes or handbags!" As the fur industry likes to point out, however, leather is just fur without the hair.

The fact is that most of us couldn't afford mink even if we wanted to wear it. So is it fur's luxuriousness that people object to—or the nature of luxury itself? (What, then, of rabbit, coyote, or wolf trim, which is actually affordable?) Or is it, as some say, the fact that we don't eat mink? (But indigenous people in Canada, who make up 40 percent of the trappers there, do eat beaver, rabbit, mink, and sometimes lynx.) Why would it seem inhumane, brutal, and vain to wear an animal's fur but not its silk, feathers, skin, wool, or pearls? Why is it morally acceptable to kill animals if we eat them but not if we use them to clothe ourselves? Why, since we do indeed have to clothe ourselves? These are just some of the questions I am pondering as I head to Denmark to attend the largest fur auction in the world.

The Farm

It's mid-April. Denmark is leafless, rain-swept, bitterly cold. Perhaps because of my jetlag, the whole country, too, appears to be waking slowly after its long, focused winter nap, its black fields not yet planted, my fellow passengers sipping coffee, half-asleep. Twenty hours ago I arrived in Copenhagen, and now I am on a train bound as far west as it can go, speeding across the islands of Zealand, Funen, and the large peninsula of Jutland to Esbjerb, a small town on the coast of the North Sea. Today I meet the minks, creatures surely out of a dream, or at least out of a Hans Christian Andersen fairy tale: sharp-toothed and velvety, elusive like the fox, taking shape in my mind, like this spring, rather warily. Furbearing creatures live where one needs to wear fur—in the far North. Mink, fox, beaver, ermine, sable, seal, bobcat, squirrel, rabbit, raccoon, coyote, wolf: edge creatures, they steal in for eggs or chicks or greens, but mostly they live their lives out of human sight.

Fur clothing comes to us in two ways: by trapping and by animals bred and raised domestically. Furs produced at family-owned farms make up 85 percent of the trade. According to a Canadian government report, in 2000, when thirty million pelts were sold, 90 percent of those furs were mink and 10 percent fox. Most of the world's mink and fox is produced by European farmers, mostly from Scandinavia, though fur farms are located across the Northern Hemisphere, in the United States, Canada, Russia, and China. (They are banned in Austria, Croatia, and the UK.) There are approximately six thousand fur farms in the EU, accounting for 63 percent of global production of mink and 70 percent of fox. Denmark is the leading producer of mink: its roughly 1,500 farmers exported $2.4 billion in mink products in 2013. (By contrast, during the same year in the United States, 275 mink farms across twenty-three states generated about $300 million.)

I had not initially expected to be able to visit a mink farm. After hundreds of break-ins, countless clandestine videos, the scandals, and the increasing public disdain, farmers are understandably suspicious. In fact, when I wrote Kopenhagen Fur to ask if I could attend one of their four yearly international auctions, Søren Jessing Jespersen, the company's "media manager," answered with clear skepticism: "You say that you are not writing an antifur book. I have been told similar stories in the past from journalists and documentarians, but at the end of the day that was exactly what they were doing. People can believe in animal rights and live as vegans; it's for the individual human being to decide. But I do get tired with people having that belief and then trying to lie their way into a fur farm or the auction house in order to do what they see as an exposé." Like most Danes, Jespersen was, however, nothing if not polite: "I'm sorry if this sounds harsh; that is not the intention." He suggested I send him what I had written about leather, and then he would decide. I thought that was fair. A couple of months later, I received my invitation. Along with it, Jespersen asked if I would like to stay three days with the Kvist Jensen family at their mink farm on the Jutland coast.

What might a mink farmer look like? I wonder as the three-hour train ride is reaching its end. I grew up with grandparents who planted soybeans and corn. My grandfather wore tattered, dirty overalls and worn-out boots six out of the seven days of the week. He drove a beat-up Rambler when he went to town. I had been told that Hanne, the wife and mother, would be picking me up and driving me the hour or so north to Hvide Sande, which in Danish means White Sands. But when I step off the train, a blond, rosy-cheeked giant of a young man in overalls is there, holding a cardboard sign with my name.

Jesper Kvist Jensen introduces himself as, at thirty-three, Hanne and Anders's youngest son. I try to conceal my surprise at the flip-flops he is wearing in this cold, and even more so at the brand-new BMW SUV that he leads me to. The car's interior reeks of mammal, a pungent, almost nauseating smell, and it is littered with hay. Jesper's overalls, I now notice, are covered with it, as is his hair. When I tell him I am a writer, he unapologetically declares that he doesn't like to read or write. At all. He just doesn't do it. Along the way, I learn what Jesper does do. Though I am beginning to see that he is an odd character—the flip-flops, the slow, incredibly methodical way he answers any question I pose—I am also realizing that Jesper is a mink savant.

Jesper tells me his father started the mink farm the year he was born. Mink, contrary to my romanticized notions, are not indigenous to Denmark. (In other words, Hans Christian Andersen would not have written about them.) They have never roamed wild. Anders will joke with me later that they came over on a ferry, but the truth is that they were imported from the United States in the early 1930s at a particularly bad period in the Danish economy. By that time, mink had already been farmed in the United States for 130 years. The animals were well suited to Denmark for several reasons, Jesper tells me. It was already an agricultural nation of small family farms with the skills that go with them. The weather is cold, which mink prefer, and there is a steady fresh food supply from all the fisheries. We pass a large warehouse. "That's the factory that makes our food. They deliver it every day fresh."

"Every day?"

"Ja, every day. Except in the winter, when it will keep. Then we get it every other day." Jesper speaks English in the same singsong cadence of his native Jutland dialect. He uses his iPhone when he needs to find a word. The factory, he says, produces mink food—a blend of fish waste from the local fishermen, chicken, corn, blood from cows and pigs, garlic, ginseng, and many vitamins—for the numerous mink farms we pass along the way. Jesper points them out—low, extralong, metal-sided barns set off far from houses and the road. "The mink have to be away from where people live. There are strict regulations," he says. "Because of the smell."

"Ginseng? Really?" I tease, picturing the mink naturopath who mixes it. "For what?"

"I can't remember. I suppose to make them healthy." Jesper says this with complete lack of irony. I am already growing quite fond of

this young farmer, his singular focus, the patience and utter seriousness with which he regards his livelihood. I also notice I am talking
slower and more melodically to match his speech.

Driving the hour it takes between Esbjerb and Hvide Sande, through
small communities of mink, dairy, and pig farms, new and old brick
farmhouses, some with traditional thatched roofs, Jesper gives me a
crash course in mink farming. His family usually raises five colors of
fur: white, pearl, brown, gray, and palomino, the latter pinkish, like the
horse. It is very popular, Jesper says, though the most popular color
is always white. Right now his family is only raising pearl, white, and
black, which, he says, isn't really black but deep chocolate, with under-
tones of orange and gold. The busiest time at the farm is November
at "harvest time," when the animals are killed and skinned, and late
April and early May, when the minks give birth. It takes them three
weeks to kill, skin, and process the skins. Last year they had to kill all
of their mink, even the breeding females, he tells me, because they had
contracted "the virus."

The virus is plasmacytosis, a disease particular to mink, causing
weight loss, renal failure, and eventual death. Twenty percent of
mink farms in Denmark contracted the disease last year. No one
knows where it comes from, and there is no vaccination or effective
treatment. The Kvist Jensens even had to kill their dog, not because
he would spread the disease—many farmers killed their pets for just
that reason—but because he was so traumatized by the mass disappearance of his friends, the mink, that he never recovered. "The dog
started losing her hair when all the minks were killed," Jesper says.
"She became more and more nervous." The virus, he says, cost the
farm the US equivalent of $75,000.

Right now is the quietest time on the farm, Jesper says. Everyone
is waiting. Mink can only breed once a year. They have a thirty-two-
day gestation period: "The egg sits inside the mother until she feels it
is right to be fertilized." This year they have 4,100 pregnant females,
bought from a neighbor whose farm was unaffected by the virus, all of

them less than three years old. In a lucky year, each mink will have six to eight "puppies." In two weeks, there might be thirty-two thousand. "You have to get rid of everything when you see the disease, disinfect everything," Jesper says. "The government tells you how to do it. Here in Denmark, we must follow animal welfare regulations. For instance, an empty space must be obtained between the cages when mink are pregnant, so they aren't upset by their neighbors. We have a rule book this thick."

"Does the government investigate?"

"Oh, yes. They come three, four times a year. You never know when."

As we approach the coast, the rain falls more heavily. The waters of the Ringkøbing Fjord on our right are whitecapped. The roadside fields are flooded. Before a sluice was built in 1931 to regulate overflow of sea-water, this land was all underwater, Jesper says. "Dig a few feet, and it is all shell." The surrounding landscape is heath—flat, treeless, green-gold from low-growing bush-blueberries and beach roses. He points out the many new "summer homes" built in clusters on the sandy soil, by which he means homes people build and then rent out to tourists, more and more each year. Hvide Sande's winter population of three thousand fishermen and farmers explodes to seventy thousand in the summer, when Germans move up for vacation. "It's like a national park here," Jesper says. "Our business can't expand. The land is preserved on either side of us, and there are laws protecting the settlements from the smell of mink. Here, a conservation area for birds; there, the fjord enlarged. Fishing overregulated because of overfishing." Jesper, like people everywhere, complains about his government, but I can see that he's also proud of Danish environmental requirements, of their reputation for being green, how they see the value of it.

Jesper pulls into a cul-de-sac of tidy brick houses built on sand, and, as we enter his parents' mudroom, slides off his flip-flops and goes barefoot, which, again, surprises me, because the Kvist Jensen house is elegant—light-filled, wood-floored, spare in the modern Danish way. A wall of floor-length windows offer a view of the fjord and Hanne's daffodils and tulips, now bent to the earth in what looks and sounds like a gale. Hanne turns from the stove, where she is filleting a fish, smiling. She's short for a Dane, with a blond pageboy, sparkling blue eyes, and a youthful, open face. Anders, the father, is my age—early sixties—wiry, handsome, blue-eyed, too. He doesn't speak English, but he talks to me animatedly as if he does, looking directly at me, letting his wife or sons interpret for him. Jakob, Jesper's older brother, is fluent, though. He tells me he has just moved back to this tiny seaside village after years of working for Hugo Boss in Copenhagen. He's lithe, excitable, expensively dressed in a fine wool sweater and designer jeans. He tells me, as Hanne and Anders stand together somewhat nervously, that the family would like me to know that I am their first visitor from America.

Hanne and Anders have recently remodeled the house, adding more windows and a new room where we dine at a long wooden table for twelve, perhaps a result of the high prices mink farmers enjoyed just three years ago. Hanne pours everyone a lovely rosé, except for Jesper, who doesn't drink. He reaches for a large glass of milk his mother has poured for him. A former commercial fisherman, Jesper also doesn't eat fish. While the rest of us praise the sole Anders purchased this evening from the dock, Jesper cuts the steak his mother has fried for him. They are a jolly family, toasting the two sons, who have just recently taken over the business from their parents. Anders is retiring, though he can't stay away from the mink and still rises early to feed them. He doesn't, he says to me in Danish, want to worry about the profits anymore. Jakob shares with me that he is married to a man from Thailand, who at the moment is visiting his family there. Jakob would have gone, too, but the baby mink are almost due.

I ask them how the auction in Copenhagen is doing, if they keep track of it. Jesper looks up from his iPad. Jakob says, "We have been live-streaming it all week!"

"Six and a half million pelts sold this week already," Jesper says. Right now, he tells me, the prices aren't what everyone would wish for, yet the family has hope. They're better than last year, and the prices might rise. It is only Thursday, and the auction goes on for another week. At its height, in 2013, mink were fetching around 740 kroner per skin (about $112), but recently the price has dropped to 220 kroner ($32). I listen as numbers fly around the table. Eighteen million skins sold at auction in 2015 in Denmark, mostly to Chinese buyers. Even more were sold the year before, but bad prices caused by too much supply, as well as the virus, decreased the number of mink that farmers were willing to breed. The Kvist Jensen family sent 4,800 pelts to auction just last week, less than half what they would have sent two years ago.

"Prices depend on what is fashionable," Jakob explains. "One time a cinnamon tip we bred was popular. Gucci came and bought out the whole lot. You never know what's going to happen." China buys the most pelts, he says, both unfinished in order to finish them and ship them around the world, and finished, for their own people. "It's cold in Beijing. But also the new oligarchs, in Shanghai, for instance, wear furs because it signifies wealth. More and more, Burma, Cambodia, even Thailand are where they are processed and sewn. They have their own fur farms, but they also recognize our quality. The tag Kopenhagen Fur is a status symbol."

Jesper says something in Danish to his mother, she nods, and he leaves the room. When he returns, he has three furs draped over his arm. The first, a midlength cape, is movie-star glamorous, a thick, rich brown with red glints you can run your hands through. It looks old-fashioned, though I can't say why. Jesper holds it up next to a glossy black jacket. "In the old days, minks were bred for long fur, whereas people want short fur like this now. See? This looks more modern." On close inspection, the fur appears shorn, resembling less an animal than a fabric, perhaps even a Polartec fleece. "American short-hair," Jesper says. "We got them from your country." Today 85 percent of minks sold at auction are short-hairs. I pick up a stole made of a striking white-and-black-spotted fur and begin to pet it. There is possibly nothing softer in the world than fine mink; if I close my eyes, it would almost be like touching a cloud. "This color, like a Dalmatian," Jesper remarks. "We bred it like this." I ask if Hanne had sewn the stole herself. "Oh, no! This is really hard to do. If we want a coat made out of our mink, we have a tailor in China who will do it."

When we rejoin Hanne and Anders, I decide to bring up the elephant in the room; I ask them what they think about the animal rights controversy surrounding fur and if it touches their lives. At first they don't understand. "We love our mink," Hanne offers. "We take good care of them."

Jesper seems almost hurt by the question. "What I don't understand is hunting," he finally says.

"Even for food?"

"Well, I suppose, but so many people even here kill for fun, not food. It seems a waste of natural resources."

"And trapping?" I ask. "There is a big controversy over trapping where I live. People are trying to get the government to ban it on public lands because their pets get caught in the traps."

The whole family shudders. Hanne seems stricken. "I think trapping is just horribly cruel," she says.

⌐ ✑

The next morning, it is raining again. The brothers, who live together in a newly constructed house down the road, show up for breakfast at eight: hard breads, cheeses, jams, poached-in-the-shell eggs, and Danishes, the latter a special treat purchased for me. Soon Jesper and I are heading to the mink farm, located a short drive away. He unlocks the door to the long, low prefab building, and a heavy, pungent, overwhelmingly musky smell overpowers me—a very, it seems, female smell. Jesper says that, although all mink have a strong odor, this one is particular, produced only when the mink are pregnant. "Ja, a sweet smell," he says, "not a bad smell," though I am not so sure. In just a few minutes, it has deeply permeated my hair and clothing.

In front of us, row upon row of two-tiered wire cages are set on tables about five feet above the ground; most of them appear to be empty. I spot a flash of white, and then it is gone. What is most astonishing is the sound, or lack thereof. Though Jesper told me that there are 2,200 creatures in this building, all I hear is the steady rain hitting the roof. To listen is to wonder if they are even here. Jesper approaches a cage, opens it, lifts a pile of straw. A white animal scurries out of his reach into the more open part of the enclosure, where I can see it. Standard dimension for cages in Denmark is approximately thirty-six by twelve by seventeen inches, with a nesting box mounted outside. (Cages less than eight inches wide are prohibited in Denmark and Norway.) The ones here seem to be larger.

"This is where she will have her puppies," Jesper says, pointing to the nesting box. "When she gives birth, she will pull out all her winter fur to line her nest." The mink comes to the bars and looks at me curiously. Her eyes are pink, her face sweet, her fur pure white. I touch her with my finger through the bars; she is soft as Hanne's coats, perhaps softer, and without temperature. I note the dark circles around her eyes. "Glasses," Jesper calls them; it is a sign that she will give birth soon. The females, he tells me, are half the size of the males. When they are pregnant, the law stipulates only one animal per cage. Between June and November, when the puppies are separated, there can be up to four. He warns me not to stick my finger in the cage again and shows me the scars on his hands. "To be bit is not funny." But when he holds open the door to her cage, the mink backs up. "The cage is her home," Jesper explains. "She doesn't want to leave it."

One of the most common misconceptions about mink farming is that these are wild animals trapped behind bars and thus, distressed. Like sheep, chickens, cows, and dogs, farmed mink are a product of a hundred or more generations of breeding—for color, size, quality of fur, and, like many domesticated animals, docility. Mink who don't adapt to the cage, who seem anxious or distressed, are not bred again, Jesper says. In 2011, according to the *Copenhagen Post*, "unknown persons" broke into a mink farm on the island of Funen and released as many as three thousand minks into the countryside. Funen forest manager Søren Strandgaard predicted that actions like this can have a disastrous effect on the ecosystem, especially on native birds, but pointed out that the minks suffer too: "Most of the minks that have been let out will starve to death. They're used to being fed, and very few of them will be capable of finding their own food." In the end, all but about one hundred were either captured again or killed because they had become aggressive and dangerous. "If left alone without an adequate food source, half the mink would eat each other," Jesper says. "That's nature."

While we are talking, Anders enters the barn and goes straight to a small tractor. He cranks the engine, and the thousands of cages suddenly fill with mink standing on their hind legs, waiting for food. Jesper points out the mash in the tractor bed. Gray-brown, it looks worse than mud. "Oh, that doesn't look very appetizing," I say.

"It doesn't taste very good either. But *they* like it."

It used to be that one person could take care of three hundred mink; now, however, because of mechanization each farmer can manage twelve hundred. I watch Anders trundle up and down the rows, squirting a palm-size dollop of mink food atop each cage from a hose: exactly 175 grams. The mink are eating about 10 percent of their body weight each day now. What they eat, how often, how many to a cage, how many times they are checked on during breeding (every twenty minutes to make sure they aren't fighting) is regulated by the government. "That's why Danish mink is the best in the world," Jesper says. I watch Anders pull a mink out of a cage and hold it in front of him. He is wearing thick leather gloves. "What's he doing?" I ask.

"He's pulling a fish bone out of her teeth," Jesper remarks. When his father feeds, he says, he's also paying acute attention. He notices if food from the day before hasn't been eaten, who doesn't come out to feed. "He sees everybody," Jesper explains. "He can see in their eyes if they're sick." Females are bred, at the most, three times, because after three years they seem to have more and more "birth difficulties." Each year, about fifteen to twenty, around 4 percent, die from childbirth or complications of pregnancy.

Not being a farmer, it takes me a while to think like one. "So these are all females? Where are the males?"

"We kill them when they are done fucking," Jesper says matter-of-factly.

I try not to laugh at this response, precisely because Jesper isn't trying to be funny. "So where do you get the males for breeding?"

Jesper is patient. He doesn't even roll his eyes. "From the babies." He pauses for a second, thinking of what will be helpful. "Sometimes we trade with other farms. In that way, we can change out half the males."

I watch him tease one mink with a blade of straw. "Do you ever get attached to them?"

"Ja, especially when a mother dies and you have to take care of the little ones. Sometimes we have fifty of them. They can eat by them-selves, but they can't keep warm. So we have a heat lamp. Ja, the puppies are easy to get attached to. Each has its own personality, like everything does."

I spot a mink lying on her back like an otter, resting her head against the side of the cage as if it were a pillow. "Look!"

"Ja," he says, "it is so sweet. She's relaxing. Sometimes when they are breeding, the male will sit back like that against the cage with its tail between its legs and suck on the tip. He makes a noise. *Mmmmm,*" Jesper demonstrates.

"So they sometimes bite each other?" I am thinking about the ani-mal rights photos of minks with sores and bitten-off ears.

"We have to watch carefully to make sure the pups aren't biting each other. When they're changing their coats, from summer to winter, sometimes they get agitated. I don't know why, but they do."

The pregnant minks have all disappeared under their nests again. "It's true," Jesper muses, "the females also can't get along sometimes.

And when we're breeding them, we have to check on the male and female, who are together in the same cage, every twenty minutes. It's the law."

"Why?"

"So they don't kill each other! If they can't get along, we have to take him out and bring her someone else."

"You check them even in the night?"

"Nooooo. We are not allowed to let them be together in the night without supervision." I laugh at his wording, but he is absorbed in the complications of breeding. "It is not so predictable. That spotted mink stole I showed you? Before the disease, we had two of the spotted ones. They had a difficult time breeding because that breed of mink, they are born deaf. The male makes a sexy sound, but she can't hear it."

We have been talking about mink sex for ten minutes now. When I ask Jesper about those who aren't chosen to breed next year, he leads me to the killing machine, an enclosed metal barrel to which a diesel engine is attached. This is it, he says. They wheel it to the cages instead of transporting the mink to it, which would traumatize them. The mobile unit is airtight and prefilled with cooled carbon monoxide gas. Thrown into the barrel, the mink immediately lose consciousness and are dead in less than thirty seconds. Jesper says the mink die so fast they don't cry out, nor, if a "breeder" is mistakenly dropped in, can it be saved, even a second later. "These are the racks," he says, pointing to wheeled shelves. "After they're dead, the bodies have to cool down before we skin them."

"Do you gut them?"

"No, *noooo*," he says, aghast. "We make a small slit, and we turn them inside out. The whole body is given for biodiesel. They make bone flour out of the bones."

The room seems remarkably free of blood, but Jesper disavows me of this idea. "Here is blood," he says, pointing at a faded starburst spatter on the drywall. "Not too much. A hundred ten thousand mink have been processed through this room, so not too much blood, given that."

Jesper, like many farmers, has had to learn to repair his own equipment. He shows me the expensive and highly specialized machines the family has purchased: the tumbler, which dries the wet skins with heat and sawdust; the fat scrapers; the stretcher. "How many minks does it take to make a mink coat?" I ask. "A hundred?"

"Noooo," he says. "About twenty to thirty. They don't look so big on the animal, but when we stretch them, they get really big." Sometimes a skin gets caught in the scraper or the stretcher, and it's ruined. If there are scars, they can't send the fur to auction. "There are always losses," Jesper says, none of which is less predictable than the market. It costs 300 kroner (about $45) to produce a single mink skin for auction, he tells me. Last night, watching the day's live stream, Jesper reported that some bundles were going for under 200 kroner a skin. I had glanced at the family for its reactions, but everyone was looking down at his or her plate.

Mink farmers in Denmark schedule their year around the dates of the Kopenhagen Fur auctions: January, February, April, a split auction in June. Jesper recites from memory the dates when furs have to be shipped. He talks to me so eagerly and in such detail that at one point the following day—chilled, almost faint from the heavy musk of the barns—my attention starts to flag. Yet I too have worked in the trades, as a baker for ten years, a house painter, a factory worker. I know how satisfying it is to produce things with one's hands, something we don't do much anymore in the United States. Breeding, feeding, cleaning, watering, euthanizing, skinning, scraping, tumbling the skins in sawdust, stretching, drying, shipping—and keeping track of how many skins of what kind and who gets bred to whom: so many steps, so many days of work, such expertise. The minks here at the Kvist Jensen farm, Jesper tells me, produce about fifteen tons of manure a year; the farm sells some to other farmers, and the rest they use to add nitrogen and phosphorus to their own soil. They used to spade it in by hand, but there is too much now. A neighbor cuts the manure into the soil with his mechanical spreader, and then plants their hay, cuts it, and

202 ~ *Putting on the Dog*

takes some for his own cattle. The rest of the hay lines the minks' beds. Keeping the minks alive surely involves even more labor than the killing and processing.

My last morning with the Kvist Jensens, leafing through a stack of books on the fur industry that Hanne and Anders left on the table for me, I stare at photos of fur-draped women and men, hip-hop stars and movie stars, and I admit that I am conflicted. Before now the wearing of fur had seemed outdated to me, gaudy where it was once glamorous, the glitzy material of Hollywood and Russian oligarchs. No one I know wears fur. Its lack of necessity makes it seem indulgent, intellectually misguided, an idea exemplified in tawdry expressions of status and heterosexuality. No longer do men customarily buy their women a fur to prove their worth. Conspicuous consumption seems less relevant to most of our lives. But how much of my attitude has been conditioned by the advertising budgets of PETA, the Humane Society of the United States (HMSUS), and Anima (a Danish animal rights organization)— over $16 million in 2016 in the case of PETA alone—which try to persuade us that wearing fur is unethical?

What are my ethics? I think I know, yet as with all ethical considerations, the issues are complex. Whether or not I wear fur is simply the easier, the more obvious question, one that I should probably, if I am honest with myself, extend to my use of any animal product, given that most of them eventually involve the loss of an animal's life. What constitutes an ethical human-animal relationship is the more difficult question. Do I sincerely wish that there were no more mink farmers like the Kvist Jensens? Am I ready to demand the extinguishing of all such rural knowledge, of this husbandry, passed between generations, of this *culture* of seasons, weather, tools, the farmers' "gear and tackle and trim," and instead to offer my homage to the chemists who make each day anew our pleather and polyester and faux fur? Or is this a question about the use of just *some* animals, or the scale of that use, or the specific use itself, and if so, why?

The Market

Kopenhagen Fur is located in Glostrup, a suburb about forty-five minutes by bus from central Copenhagen. As I travel farther and farther from downtown, my fellow passengers become older and less affluent, and more women on the street wear the hijab, evidence of Denmark's role as a home for the growing Syrian diaspora. The canals, the bakeries and organic supermarkets disappear, replaced with low-income housing and kabob stands. At my designated stop, I hail a cab and am dropped off a couple of miles away in the half-empty parking lot of a large, unmarked, nondescript warehouse. Inside, however, the halls are palatial—all chrome, polished hardwood, and marble, the landings of the spiral staircases stages for male and female mannequins modeling the latest innovations in fur. One mannequin sports a gorgeous blazer made of twisted ropes of white mink, another a thigh-high silk party dress trimmed with foot-long plumes of forest-green-dyed fox.

Nina Brønden Jakobsen, press consultant and my designated "handler" at the auction house, arrives seconds after I identify myself to the receptionist. Young, stylish, fluent in English, Jakobsen is tall, blue-eyed, with long, silky blond hair, a beauty in the Danish way. She wears tight stretch jeans, a dark wool wrap-around sweater, and faux alligator-skin high-heeled boots.

Because 90 percent of Denmark's mink skins are sold to China, there is now a special dining room downstairs that serves Chinese food. "You know, cow stomach and the like," says Jakobsen. The company pays for Mandarin lessons for its employees, and in April 2016, at Shanghai Fashion Week, it collaborated with Danish designer Jim Lyngvild to build a real mountain on a stage in the middle of the city where mink-draped Danish models brandishing swords and wearing chain mail headgear posed on the runway as Vikings and Valkyries. To further pamper its clients, the auction house has set up a mini-mall downstairs where the Chinese can buy high-end European jewelry, clothes, perfumes, and electronics when they take a break from their bidding.

Kopenhagen Fur is both a brand and an auction house, handling farmed furs from everywhere in the European Union (EU), although the majority of what it sells is Danish mink from its collective. Founded eighty years ago, the company is owned by members of the Danish Fur Breeders Association, selling, according to its website, 18.6 million mink skins a year for more than fifteen hundred farmer-owners.

After espresso and cake in the "European" cafeteria, Jakobsen takes me to the building's basement, which is filled with racks from which hang thousands of bundles of mink pelts of every possible color: white, gray, silver, black, "ranch brown," white with black flecks, the fabled palomino. Here and there, potential buyers, wearing lab coats and surgical gloves, are inspecting them. She walks me past deeply red fox pelts from Finland and Norway, each almost as tall as I am. (Fox are not domesticated and therefore don't adapt to their cages. For that reason, fox farms are banned in Denmark and the Netherlands, and, effectively, in Sweden.)

Here, she invites me to finger chinchilla skins, fragile and light as dandelion puffs. The chinchilla is "a rodent from the Andes whose fur falls apart if it gets wet," Jakobsen says, "but tell that to Beyoncé, who can afford not to care!" Sable, black-brown and lustrous, is a species of marten trapped and sometimes farmed in Siberia. A kind of fur with a texture of heavily embossed swirls gets my attention. "Swakara," Jakobsen notes. Swakara is a brand name created for the pelt of the southwest African Karakul, a breed of sheep. According to the company's website, Swakara generates not only money but also goodwill. Swakara production provides approximately twenty thousand jobs in a dry region of Africa without any other viable agriculture. Kopenhagen Fur worked with Namibian sheep breeders and their government to devise a "Code of Practice ensuring the welfare of the Karakul sheep" that would be approved by the EU and thus fit in with standards of animal welfare. The sheep are also good for the land there, she says, helping to increase vegetation in extremely dry regions by stomping grass seeds further into the ground.

What I did not expect to encounter at this auction are the racks of green-, blue-, orange-, and fluorescent-pink-dyed sealskins that Jakobsen is now showing me. In fact, I am shocked. I was in high school in 1977 when the famous blond actress Brigitte Bardot posed for photographs lying on the ice in the Canadian Arctic, her arms cuddling a fluffy white baby harp seal. Paired with videos of hunters bludgeoning the infants to death—the conventional method of harvesting—the photographs were part of a campaign sponsored by Greenpeace to stop commercial seal fishing and became one of the pivotal moments in the emerging animal rights movement. Horrified by the images, thousands of people around the globe objected to what they saw as a slaughter of the innocents. The campaign resulted in a 1983 European ban on "white coat" skins, which are those from seals less than two weeks old, and, eventually, a 2009 ban on all seal products. Russia, Belarus, and Kazakhstan banned sealskins in 2009; Taiwan joined them in 2013. So is Kopenhagen Fur trading in illicit goods? Jakobsen anticipates my question, answering that "the Inuit Exception" to the European ban allows them to procure sealskins from Greenland natives, something, she notes, that they are proud of facilitating. How we got to the place where I, as an American, can stand in an auction house in Copenhagen, able to purchase a bundle of sealskins, after almost forty years of "seal wars" between activists, hunters, governments, and indigenous peoples, is a story that illustrates the complications involved in any discussion of fur.

➤

Fur seals have been hunted by indigenous people in the Arctic for at least four thousand years with little impact on their populations; commercial sealing, however, which began in the 1700s and exploded with the invention of the steamship in the nineteenth century, was devastating. "Alaska fur seals, which numbered about two million in 1870, had been hunted nearly to extinction" by the early twentieth century, says Alan Herscovici, author of *Second Nature: The Animal-*

Rights Controversy and executive vice president of the Fur Council of Canada. An international treaty signed in 1911 by the United States, England, Canada, and Japan helped to rebuild seal populations, yet greed, paired with new technologies such as "radar, scout planes and government icebreakers," lured people with little experience in the Arctic or with hunting, causing a new kind of violence to the animals and enormous waste. Still, harp seals were no longer endangered—a crucial point, says Herscovici.

Enter Greenpeace. Hitherto, the environmental organization's mission had been conservation of threatened species. The campaign against seal hunting—the films, the photo ops with celebrities— appealed to people's moral sense. It shifted the emphasis from protecting animals to the question of whether we have the right to inflict suffering on animals for profit. Patrick Moore, director of Greenpeace at the time, explained the shift: "It's not the same as the conservation of whales or the preservation of an endangered species of tiger, or something.... What the seal hunt represented was the paramount focus for public attention on the need to change our basic attitude and relationship to nature and to the species that make it up." This thinking precipitated the distinction between *animal welfare*—providing for an animal's physical needs—and *animal rights*. Proponents of animal rights believe that animals have a right to exist in and of themselves.

When the seal wars began, pitting hunters against animal rights activists and environmental groups, very few people were thinking about the impact on indigenous people in Canada and Greenland, who share the same harp seal populations. For the Inuit in both countries, seals were an important food source as well as material for the crucial clothing they needed to protect themselves from the Arctic cold; in modern times, they also sold furs to supplement their subsistence lifestyle. With the seal bans in place, most Inuit communities were financially destroyed. Ironically, Inuits in Greenland, whose seal-hunting practices did not involve the killing of "white coat" seals, still suffered the consequences. Consumers did not understand the difference between "white coat" and adult sealskins, so they avoided sealskin altogether. Prices fell drastically; the sealskin market collapsed.

For the Inuit, the bans were a classic case of colonialist thinking: Europeans imposing their rules without any comprehension of indigenous life or any efforts made to include them in the decision-making. For environmentalists, the bans alienated some of their strongest potential allies, indigenous people who are most affected by the very pollution, oil drilling, damming, mining, and development that environmental organizations are committed to fighting. As Herscovici says, "Inuit and other hunting people study and respect animals because their lives literally depend on them. It is when we are no longer dependent on our environment, or think we're not, that contact is lost and, with it, respect for other life."

It took almost thirty years, but eventually attitudes changed. The Inuit Exception, amending the 2009 EU ban on all seal products, enabled auction houses like Kopenhagen Fur to deal directly with the Greenland Inuit at a fair price, albeit a price subsidized by the Greenland government. Greenpeace in turn apologized for promoting the universal bans: "Our campaign against commercial sealing did hurt many, both economically and culturally," writes Joanna Kerr, executive director of Greenpeace Canada, in a June 15, 2014, blog post. "Though the campaign was directed against the commercial hunting of seals—and not the small-scale, subsistence hunting carried out by Northern Indigenous and coastal peoples—we did not always communicate this clearly enough. The consequences of that, though unintended, were far-reaching." Inuit hunters in Nunavut and the Northwest Territories of Canada were recently included in the Exception. In the United States, however, trade in sealskins remains prohibited by the Marine Mammal Protection Act.

Jakobsen leads me to a man working at a table stacked high with pearl and white mink pelts. Frederik is a sorter, "the most important job in the company," I am told. Each skin is assigned a lot number according to its quality: Velvet, and Velvet 2, 3, and 4, and Classic; Velvet 4 is the best, and Classic is of a lower quality. "We are the only auction house in the whole world with this kind of system," says Jakobsen proudly. For every lot number there might be hundreds of skins in the basement; one lot could include minks from hundreds of different farms. "It's like saying, 'This skin is representative of this whole wagon. Trust us; they all look like this.' If the buyer gets home and says, 'Oh my god, they don't look like the one you showed me,' they'll never come here again," she explains. Sorting is therefore a highly specialized skill. Frederik has been working here for thirty years. He can grade a fur in a glance, searching it for scars, bare patches, tears. If there are any, he places the fur to the side. Not for the last time do I hear that it costs around 300 kroner to make one mink skin. "We don't get many bad ones," Jakobsen says. "If you've made a mink skin that doesn't even make Classic, you've lost money. Maybe you can sell it off to make a key chain or something."

"Ask him how many he can grade in an hour."

She translates: "He says that in the past few years, minks are getting bigger, so it takes longer to grade them. Better food, better care, he thinks." The sorter holds up two mink skins to show us the difference between male and female. As Jesper had said, the male is almost twice as big.

Jakobsen continues: "The Chinese buy fifty to sixty thousand skins at an auction. We get sometimes twenty-six million skins through in one year. In China, they raise maybe double that. Chinese still come here to buy ours because it is better, because the sorters do their jobs so well. Few Chinese furs come into the EU. They go to Russia and their own people."

When we come at last to the auction, it feels anticlimactic. No Italian furriers in fisticuffs with Beijing factory owners, no diamond-wearing celebrities or Russian counts. Not even any furs—on the podium or on the backs of buyers. The amphitheater-like room is windowless; its rows of designer seats and tables are U-shaped, so all have perfect sight lines to the five auctioneers on the podium. On the wall, clocks proclaim the time in London, Paris, Beijing, and New York, an old-fashioned gesture considering that everyone here has a laptop and at least one phone. The room can fit eight hundred people, and on the busiest days, it does. The seats are occupied mostly by Chinese men in white shirts and black slacks, although here and there a Frenchman or German bends over his or her coffee, looking exhausted. No one, in fact, looks excited: mostly tired, even bored. An electronic monitor flashes the lot number and name: White Male, Silver Female. The buyers know what quality by their catalogs, or perhaps they have gone below, as we did, and inspected the skins themselves. The auction moves fast and efficiently, conducted in English. Buyers raise their hands and shout, as at all auctions, and someone is declared the winner. A lot equals sixty pelts. A lot, Jakobsen says, is the minimum one can buy at the auction. In less than a minute, five lots of white males are sold for 250 kroner (about $37) a skin.

When prices were high, Jakobsen tells me—over $100—mink farmers were arriving at the auction in private helicopters. Every month there was a new record. At just one auction, they sold over $600,000 worth of skins. "Kopenhagen Fur was responsible for keeping the Danish economy alive!" (Jakobsen often speaks in laugh-filled exclamations.) "Right now it's the worst that it's been for the fur industry in decades," she states. "The prices were up, up, up, up, up; everyone was a millionaire, and then all of a sudden it went *boom* like this, and the prices were cut in half, and then one year ago we had an outbreak of plasmacytosis, and everyone had to put down all of their animals, disinfect everything, and then buy new animals. It's taken some farmers generations to make that exact kind of mink, really short hair and so on, a special male and a special female, and trying to breed them, and to make that particular kind of color. And then if you have to kill all of them, they've lost so much money!"

Overproduction is another factor behind the drop in mink prices. When they were high, people in other countries without strict regulations, such as Poland, gave up their cows and crops for mink, flooding the market. China's economy was suffering and its winters were becoming warmer, which also took a toll on the market. Some people point to the changing identities of women, who no longer need fur as proof of a man's love. And as much as everyone at Kopenhagen Fur wants to avoid the topic, antifur legislation is still hurting the industry. In 2011, Oslo banned fur on its runways during Fashion Week, the first city to do so. In 2014, a high-end nightclub in London named Mahiki banned the wearing of fur by its patrons. On the other hand, things are quite different from the years between 1985 and 1990, when antifur sentiment was responsible for a 75 percent drop in fur sales in Britain. "Fur Is Back in Fashion and Debate," writes Alex Williams in his headline for the July 3, 2015, issue of the *New York Times*. In 2015, the design house Fendi presented a "fur only extravaganza." Seventy-three percent of the world's 436 fashion shows that year featured fur. Young people, especially, are interested. "It's a tug of war," explains Dan Matthews, vice president for media at PETA. "The fur trade focuses on young designers like PETA focuses on young consumers."

"So no protests this year?" I ask Jakobsen.

"No, not this year. We do, however, get a lot of protests. I have to explain to a lot of my friends, a lot of people I don't know, and even some of my family, why I do what I do."

"What do you say?"

"But I don't know what to say! I try to tell people to go see a mink farm." She pauses. "If they are still against fur after they have seen a mink farm, then I respect that. But if they are simply against it, without knowing, I find that difficult."

"Look at that," I whisper, pointing to two older women walking out the door in full-length mink coats. "Finally! Someone wearing fur."

Jakobsen laughs. "Those two, they work in the kitchen. They are our cooks!"

The next afternoon, I am sitting in the auction house cafeteria with Jakobsen and Lone (pronounced Luna) Lyhneand, and they are trading mink-lore. "There is an old joke," Jakobsen says. "'How does a woman get mink?' Answer: 'The same way the mink does.' In other words, she has to sleep with him for it."

"Mink is popular, but fox is also, especially in Russia," Lyhneand interjects. "Fox looks good in photographs and movies because the hair is quite long. When you see it on catwalks it can look almost 3-D."

"In the '50s, Marilyn Monroe wore only white mink. Audrey Hepburn wore black," Jakobsen says.

"A man gets fox for his mistress, they say, and mink for his wife," Lyhneand adds.

In her early fifties, Lyhneand is from western Jutland and still retains the slow and melodic speech rhythms that Jesper exhibited, though she has lived in the city for decades. Rendered in English, which she speaks less fluently than Jakobsen but no less serviceably, the cadence makes her sound ingenuous, which perhaps she is. Lyhneand grew up on a mink farm. "When I was a child," she says, "I had a mink on my shoulder always. I took him to school with me, just everywhere. He was black. One day, he was missing. But a neighbor had a chicken farm…" She rolls her eyes.

Jakobsen had wanted me to meet Lyhneand as an example of one of few women working in the fur industry. Lyhneand's title is technical policy manager, which means she does a bit of everything: teaching the sorters and farmers how to grade skins, flying to China to help farmers to improve their animal welfare practices and to learn how to bid at the auction. She talks to them via Skype while they attend the auction by live stream. During our interview, Lyhneand is interrupted at least every five minutes by someone from management dropping by our table with an urgent question, or a buyer on her cell phone, pleading for advice. "I think I need a new title," she says and rolls her eyes again.

I ask Lyhneand if she wears mink. "An average mink coat costs 20,000 kroner [about $3,000]. If it's long, it's more expensive. It depends on what designer made it, of course," she says. "I have a boxer. If I had mink, I might come home, and it would be destroyed. He is the kind of dog that would open a bottle of champagne while I was gone and wreck the house."

"Ask a farmer how many mink coats his wife has. Are you kidding me?" adds Jakobsen. "Farmers usually can't afford to wear mink."

"Has the mink farm changed much since you were a child?" I ask Lyhneand.

"More educated people coming in, perhaps," she answers. "All the rules about how to breed and how to feed. You have to make sure you feed them good so they think, 'There is a lot of food in this area; I will have a lot of pups.' It used to be one farmer did it one way, another a different way. Everything today is more structured."

She glances at Jakobsen. Something has made her uneasy, perhaps simply that I am an outsider and I am taking notes. I notice her conversation becoming more scripted. "Farmers here are interested in animal welfare; they want the animals to have a good life."

To put her at ease, I tell her I spent three days with the Kvist Jensens in Jutland and that theirs seemed like a model farm. "What is it like in China?" I ask. "Does China support the same welfare regulations as in Denmark?"

"Many farms in China have found out that they can't produce good mink skins by just growing them; they are asking questions, how to breed them, how to treat them." Wrong question, I realize. Lyhneand is even more suspicious, and now, in addition, clearly irritated. "You know, we don't have any secrets here at Kopenhagen Fur. We try to share our knowledge with everyone. You have mink farms in the States as well. Their auction is in Toronto. I have a small mink farm myself. I imported one hundred minks from the United States."

Jakobsen tries to smooth things over. "What Lone is saying is that, in America, you're really good at making the black short-haired skins;

but now we are making the best short-hairs in the world!" When Lone doesn't respond, Jakobsen decides to confront the issue head-on. "The two biggest fallacies about the fur industry is that wild mink are put in cages and that we skin them alive."

"All the people who are against us," Lyhneand says with sudden passion, "they have opened cages on the mink farms sometimes!"

In 2009, a documentary called *Inside Out of a Fur Farm* aired on Danish television, instigating tremendous public outcry against Kopenhagen Fur. "If you wanted to do a documentary about 9/11, you wouldn't get al-Qaeda to do it, right?" Jakobsen complains. "But they hired Anima to get the footage." At the time, she was a graduate student in communications. She was horrified by the animal abuse depicted, as most people were. But when the company didn't apologize, when they actually sued Anima for not telling the truth in the video and they won, she was intrigued. She decided to write her master's thesis on how the company communicated during the crisis. Her research involved visiting a mink farm, which was revelatory for her: "People were actual people, and they weren't these awful criminals that they were pictured as."

Lyhneand looks more than a little disturbed after Jakobsen's confession. "After the film, it changed how we operated. We started to open up."

Jakobsen is still visibly aroused. "There is a video on the internet of a fox being skinned alive. I think it's from China, but I think it's fake. It's horrible. Why would you do that? You can get your fingers bitten off! But these journalists, they ask us, 'So after you skin the mink, how long before the hair grows back out?' There is so much ignorance!"

"What do you think Anima's motivation is?" I too have heard that many "animal snuff films" made by PETA and others are shot in places other than where they say they are or, even worse, that some of the abuses are staged. Who is to know?

"I think it is to make sure that we don't use animals in any way," Jakobsen says. "Pets or anything."

Lyhneand has been thinking quietly. "I think it is easy to target the fur industry because many people cannot afford to wear fur."

All three of us are quiet now. I am wondering, is that it? Is it really because we can afford leather shoes and down coats and wool sweaters that we are not against them? "What do you think about trapping?" I think to ask Lyhneand.

"I don't know anything about trapping because we have never done that in Denmark. I don't like trapping, to be honest; I love animals. I hate when they don't treat animals right. It's terrible to hear these stories."

The Clothes

On the quay, in the water-lit neighborhood of Nyhavn, surrounded by docked wooden boats and pastel-painted townhouses built in the seventeenth century, a young woman, thin as a model, with stylish holes in her jeans, wears a T-shirt and over it, a full-length black mink coat. She stares at us, almost, I would say, defiantly. It is the first mink coat I have seen on the streets—though I was told I would see many more if it were January rather than April. Still, the wind is fierce and cold today, and the woman looks enviably warm. In Russia, Korea, and China, fur is still common and even increasingly popular. But not here. Last night, I had dinner with Danish friends, older, radical, socialist lesbian-feminists, and I asked them if they would wear mink if they could afford it. "No!" was their collective outcry. When I asked them why, they didn't say they thought raising mink was bad; instead they told me that they would never get away with it. They would be challenged on the street. "People would spit on you," they said.

Full disclosure: Kopenhagen Fur paid for my train ticket to the mink farm. Jakobsen arranged the visit, and she has been my tour guide for three days in a row. I imagine the company extends the same courtesy to many of the journalists who come to inquire about the industry. After all, Jakobsen and Jespersen work in public relations, which means that they are not only mediating the company's exchanges with the public but also working to change the public's attitude toward fur at a time when PETA, Anima, HMSUS, and countless other organizations are posting new ads against it daily. As in most political struggles, accumulating allies is more profitable, and more ingenious, than continuing to confront one's enemies head-on.

The Kopenhagen International Center for Creativity (KICK), where I am meeting Jakobsen today, plays a central role in this strategy. Established by Kopenhagen Fur at the height of the mink comeback in 2013, the center sponsors young and emerging designers from around the world, giving them access to "luxury materials" they could never afford to experiment with, as well as support and training from expert furriers. (Saga Furs, in Finland, also has its own design center, doing much the same work.) "This is the largest fur showroom in the world!" Jakobsen exclaims when I catch up with her in the lobby. "But first we are going to have an interview with Birgitte. She is the team leader for Fur Fabulous, one of the arms of the center responsible for promoting the designs."

We enter an elegant conference room lined with display racks on which hang swatches of material, most of it mink dyed every conceivable color and transformed with such exotic techniques—shearing, braiding, roping, shaving—that much of it is simply no longer recognizable as fur. A gleaming hardwood table is set with white espresso cups. When Birgitte and her assistant arrive, it is evident that they are disappointed. I am clearly not one of the fashionistas they are used to entertaining. Nevertheless, Birgitte, who is wearing a tight black dress and stilettos, runs through her speech.

"This is the final destination where we work with the skins. Last stop before the red carpet. Downstairs you will see how they work the fur. Our furriers are constantly pushing the boundaries. We have more than two thousand techniques at the moment. Kopenhagen Nexus, which is the department of KICK I am heading, is more commercially focused in the sense that we are not so much about the red carpet and the catwalks; we are more about getting the fur beyond the high street and into the main street."

"*Really?*" I say, staring at her impossibly long fingernails, painted a dark maroon.

"We don't believe that fur should be something only the very rich can wear," she says. "We believe that it is a beautiful, accessible material for more people and more varied incomes. Of course, it is a luxurious material; it should remain that way. However, we believe we can be more strategic in how we use it, to stimulate the designers to use *small amounts of fur* as extra add-ons. As part of a pocket on a cashmere coat, for instance, or trim on the collar of a dress. We collaborate with a lot of the established fashion houses around Europe who have never used fur before or are lacking in ideas of how to use fur in more fun ways. We help them see fur as a justifiable material. At the moment, we have seventeen collaborations. Some in Denmark, of course; some in the Middle East, in Korea and China, one in Italy. Normally, in a two- to three-year collaboration, the designer learns everything there is to know about the fur processes."

Birgitte's department, it says on KICK's website, also makes the showroom's styles and samples "available to significant people and media platforms related to the worldwide fashion industry," meaning that people like Lady Gaga can request to borrow anything in the showroom (and she has). But I am more interested in Birgitte's use of the word *justifiable*.

"You have to convince people it's affordable and also that it is *justifiable?*" I know that I am being unfair, reacting cynically, as I haven't done at any other time on this trip. Perhaps it is the fashion world itself, its air of exclusivity—ironically, the same reason many people object to mink. "By *justifiable*, you must mean countering people's objection to fur at all?"

"I suppose it is fair to say that there is a certain amount of controversy surrounding fur. I think Kopenhagen Fur is very good at letting people know how the company is run." She glances at me warily. I wonder if

Birgitte has had to intern at a farm. She decides to continue: "Of course, many of these design companies are worried about sales points, about how their customers, sometimes in foreign countries, are going to perceive the use of fur. A lot of what we do here has to do with communication as well. Animal welfare, transparency: these are the messages and values that we're trying to get out to more people."

"Fake fur does a lot more damage to the environment," I say, trying to show her I am fair-minded. "All those petrochemicals that synthetics are made from."

"Yes," Birgitte says, brightening, "and the pollution they cause, the fact that they are not biodegradable, that they don't last, the energy it takes to manufacture them. But to be perfectly honest with you, we're dealing with *fashion people*, and if the price is right, they will love fur, regardless."

Jakobsen breaks into the conversation. "Fur *is* a luxury product. It is artisanal. The processes take time. The fashion industry asks us, How fast can you make a jacket? A couple weeks? No, we can't. And if the animals are being treated right, there is a cost to that too."

I decide to take Birgitte at her word, to believe she believes in what she is selling. "What are the premier qualities of fur for you?"

She relaxes. This is her territory. "First, it is three-dimensional. There is no other material that even comes close to that fact. Especially when you start mixing it with other material. And then the heritage is worth mentioning as well. The cultural heritage. Mankind has worn it throughout all ages. And there is no fur product that has not been through many, many hands, from the farm to the auction house to the manufacturer sitting in Greece or Turkey. Every fur item is unique. You can't duplicate it. And when you sew it together, you really need to be experienced and see the nuances in the skins. It's really a science and an art at the same time."

"Does the royal family borrow your furs?" I ask.

I am glad I have finally made Birgitte laugh. "No," she says, "they have plenty of their own."

⌐⌐

Armani decided to drop all use of fur beginning with its fall 2016 line. Hugo Boss (whom Jacob Kvist Jensen worked for), Tommy Hilfiger, Guess, Calvin Klein, Ralph Lauren, and Stella McCartney, among many other designers, have also pledged to stop using fur. Yet there are plenty of designers who still love it. Inside KICK's fur fashion showroom are examples of Birgitte's mink for Main Street: a gray wool coat trimmed with flamboyant swathes of teal-dyed mink; repeating stripes of aqua mink on the cuffs of a long-sleeved dress; the tongues of two white leather tennis shoes fashioned out of fuzzy puffs of mink; and, perhaps as a joke, fur lampshades! A baseball jacket, pieced together with mink dyed in team colors, hangs below mink berets and a pale silk blouse with a mint mink collar. The young designers have clearly been having fun. Why not, when mink is free, which it will never be for the rest of their lives. Mounted on a wall, in a Plexiglas case, is a life-size snowy owl made of spotted mink. I ask Birgitte if I can examine it more closely. She demonstrates that when you unscrew its head, you find a flask concealed inside.

Jakobsen has one last stop for me, the workshop itself, where the designers spend their days learning how to create clothing with both traditional mink and mink manipulated in ways no one has imagined before. It is a quiet day, Jakobsen apologizes as we enter a wide room bright with sunlight pouring in the windows, filled with long work-tables and mannequins wearing sealskin, mink, chinchilla. A lot of the furriers are off for holiday, she explains, and they are in between designers. Two women work at sewing machines especially designed with needles sharp enough to pierce the leather. One shows me the tiny stitches that bind the skins together at their edges, miraculously without any visible seam.

I am introduced to Thomas Andersen, head furrier at the design center, a friendly, middle-aged man who shows us a tunic made of overlapping flaps of bright orange sealskin, looking somewhat like the scales of a tropical fish; a short flecked chinchilla jacket that resembles the snowy owl upstairs; and a zippered men's coat sewn entirely of white, black, and gray mink with the Norse name Astrid splayed across the front. "Hip-hop," Andersen explains. Hip-hop and rap stars form a large part of his clientele.

"If I can ask a dumb question, what exactly is a furrier?" I ask.

"A furrier is one who is realizing the style: choosing which kind of skins to use, where to place them on the coat, and then stretching the skin, nailing the skin, sewing the skins together, adding the lining, everything. I know how to do everything. I'm from the old generation. I am what they call a cutter. Here, I do the cutting, and I have two seamstresses to do the sewing. Of course, you must calculate how many skins go into one piece of clothing. So much is about square centimeters." I think of what Birgitte said, about each piece of fur clothing having gone through hundreds of hands. Even today a fur coat can't be mass-produced. Every pelt is different and must be handled differently. Yet to be a furrier in Europe or America is rare today. Most fur from fashion designers is sent to places where there are still expert furriers, such as Greece, Turkey, and, increasingly, China. Montreal used to be called the "Fur Capital of the World," not only for the availability of skins but also because of the hundreds of furriers who immigrated from places like Greece and Armenia in the first half of the twentieth century. In the early twenty-first century, there are only about a dozen practicing furriers left in Montreal.

I ask Andersen to name his favorite fur.

"I'm a mink idiot," he chuckles. "We can do anything with it. It doesn't shed. Its leather is really strong. It lasts a long, long, long time. [Sixty years is the average lifespan of a mink coat.] You can stretch it and it doesn't break. If we make a coat, and it's ten centimeters short, we just pull. Chinchilla, on the other hand, is a very fragile material."

While we have been talking, Jakobsen has slipped on a cropped, silver mink jacket with a huge pink mink flower appliqué. She interrupts us to say, "Maybe this is finally the jacket I should start saving for!"

The Trap

Every autumn or so, I trap packrats in live cages when they migrate from their homes in the wild to the shelter of my garage. Some years I have caught up to nine, one at a time, then driven them to undisclosed locales where I, with trepidation, release them to their fates. I know, while I am doing this, that I am interfering with the lives they have established, separating young from their parents, depositing them where they disrupt the ecosystem I artificially place them in. And yet . . . Pack rats have chewed giant holes in my wooden doors, shat on every available service, left their telltale, *really* unpleasant odor everywhere, stolen screws and jar lids, and gnawed my battery cables to shreds. I probably should have killed them, but I don't have the nerve, though I toss the dead bodies of mice into the bushes with abandon after I find them in the traps I set inside my car.

Humans trap animals to eat, eradicate disease, protect habitat, control pests, manage wildlife, and, of course, to wear their fur. Fox—blue, silver, red, gray—raccoon, mink, chinchilla, sable, squirrel, nutria (much like a rat), muskrat (rat), ermine, beaver, wolf, coyote, and opossum are all trapped and killed for their pelts, mostly in Canada, Russia, and the United States, countries where the majority of the world's wild fur—not farmed fur—comes from. Coyote provides trim on the hoods of high-end parkas like those sold by Canada Goose, and muskrat lines cuffs on homemade coats for the Yupiit. Furbearers are transformed into hats, gloves, and coats for people who live in cold climates everywhere on earth.

Ask anyone in the North: there is nothing warmer than fur. It protects the face from frostbite, disrupts strong winds, and repels life-threatening moisture. Although only about 15 to 20 percent of fur used in the clothing industry comes from wild rather than farmed fur, most rural people in North America know someone who has trapped or is currently trapping animals. Given that the beaver trade kept the colonies in Canada and America afloat for their first hundred years, trapping is part of our national heritage. (The fact that most of the trapping was done by indigenous people who traded with the Europeans, and consequently, contracted smallpox and other diseases that wiped out entire villages, is also part of our heritage, as is the fact that opportunistic Europeans were drawn here because in the late 1500s their own beaver populations, through centuries of trapping, had gone extinct.)

Traps for furbearing animals come in three main types: leghold traps, which are self-explanatory; body-gripping traps, such as the Conibear, which is a larger version of my mouse trap, designed to break the spinal cord immediately; and snares, which are nooses laid on the ground with bait. A snare eventually strangles an animal that struggles against it. With leghold traps, and sometimes snares, the animal remains alive until the trapper arrives to "dispatch" it. Animal rights organizations object to trapping animals for the same reason they object to fur farming: it causes suffering and results in the killing of animals, in this case wild ones, for a vanity product they view as unnecessary. Trapping, however, is not often subject to the same attacks as fur farms, because it is an individual and itinerant activity.

Wildlife managers claim that no endangered species are ever trapped and that there are more furbearing animals in North America now than there were when Europeans first landed, although who knows how this could be proven. They say that mink, fox, beaver, and river otter have not only recovered from the greed of the fur trade's bang-up years—1600s to 1800s—but in some cases have increased their populations. They say that trapping helps to keep species from overpopulating and is therefore an important wildlife management tool. "All animal populations produce more offspring than are needed to replace their own numbers. The excess must be eliminated one way or another," writes Herscovici, claiming that too many animals in an area can result in species starvation and disease. Too many of one kind can also have an effect on the other species in the area. (Antifur organizations say, on the other hand, that killing coyotes doesn't help with predation because coyotes self-regulate their births, and that, eight years after the ban in Colorado, livestock predation had actually dropped 62 percent.)

Greg Linscombe, a research biologist with the Louisiana Department of Wildlife and Fisheries, says that without trapping, the overpopulation of nutria and muskrats would result in the destruction of his state's wetlands. "It's naive to believe that if you leave everything alone, nature will be all right," he said. "In the southeastern United States, beaver cause $100 million in damage annually to roads, farmlands, and timber. In Alaska, the arctic fox is trapped to protect an endangered species of Aleutian Canada goose. And raccoons present a serious rabies problem up and down the Atlantic coast."

The arguments accumulate. The International Fur Federation states that the trapping industry is well-regulated and that abuses are rare. The Agreement on International Humane Trapping Standards, which was signed by Canada, Russia, and the EU in 1997, ensures, they say, that most trapping is done in the most humane way possible. The fur industry in the United States also claims that trapping is a "well-regulated industry," but in fact there is no national set of regulations: each state is left to stipulate its own rules. According to a 2016 survey by the Association of Fish and Wildlife Agencies (AFWA), approximately 70 percent of states offer trapper education, but only twenty-one states say it is mandatory. Minimum age for a trapping license varies from zero to sixteen. Some states don't require a license at all if trapping on one's own property, especially for non-game species like coyotes, weasels, and skunks. Over 90 percent of states don't restrict how many traps can be set, and half have no limits on animals taken. Seventy-five percent don't regulate how an animal is killed. Although many states require that trappers check their traps frequently (requirements vary from every hour to once a week), for obvious reasons, compliance is impossible to gauge. There is the very real problem of enforcement of any regulations at all, given that trappers work in rural and wilderness areas, far from major roads and often in very poor weather. Footloose Montana, a nonprofit working to ban trapping on public lands, calls trapping the "least regulated activity" in the state.

Antitrapping organizations have two main objections. The first is that nontarget animals, like eagles, deer, bear, mountain lions, and, most distressingly for some, people's pets, get caught in the traps, often getting injured and even killed. In a recent editorial, Zack Strong of the Natural Resources Defense Council states that between 2010 and 2014 eighty-nine mountain lions, three grizzly, twelve black bears, four wolverines, three lynx, twenty-one bobcat, thirty-one river otters, nine deer, and fifty-eight dogs were caught in traps in Montana alone. In Idaho, a 2011–12 survey found that for every wolf that was trapped, 1.2 other animals were incidentally captured. Many of these animals died or were injured severely enough to be put down. The second objection is that traps and snares are barbaric in that animals undergo extreme pain and distress, sometimes for prolonged periods. Although most trappers check their traps frequently—it is in their interest to do so to protect the pelt—the fact is that no one has yet developed a "cruelty-free" trap, and not for lack of trying.

In 1925, the same year the National Anti-Steel Trap League was founded in the United States, the National Association of the Fur Industry offered a reward of $10,000 to anyone who could invent a "humane" trap. In 1949, the American Humane Association extended the offer to 1979. No one was able to claim either. In 1958, the Conibear trap was invented by a Canadian trapper and promoted as humane because it kills animals quickly. It does—*if* the animal enters the trap correctly, headfirst, and if the trap is the right size for that animal. The steel plates slam shut on the body, hopefully the neck, but in some cases the trap injures and does not kill, leaving animals to suffer. The Association for the Protection of Fur-Bearing Animals claims there is no such thing as a quick-kill trap that works for all species. The dangers of leghold traps are well known. Many countries have banned the use of leghold traps, but as the fur industry has noted, there haven't been furbearers of significance in those countries for a long time.

What about Herscovici's argument that trapping and hunting is a bulwark against industrial development and that taking away rural and indigenous peoples' right to earn a living in traditional ways is arrogant and imperialistic? "Just like the slave traders were forced to find new livelihoods, so will the furriers, fur farmers and trappers," says Dan Matthews, PETA's antifur campaign coordinator. Herscovici counters: "To tell people to buy synthetics is to tell thousands of trappers (many of them Native Indians) that they should live in cities and work in factories rather than stay in the woods. It is difficult to see how such a shift can help heal the nature/culture split, which the ecology movement began by criticizing."

But whose livelihoods, exactly, are we talking about? In the United States, there are approximately 250,000 registered trappers in an average year. When fur prices are high, as they were in 2013, those numbers can triple. In Canada, roughly 25,000 indigenous people out of about 60,000 register as trappers. This does not include those trappers whose states don't require them to obtain licenses for coyotes or other predatory animals. According to an article by Tom Reed, the National Trappers Association defines the average North American trapper as a man working alone, thirty-seven years old, with a high school diploma, who often needs to supplement his income, especially in the winter, when other jobs, such as construction, farming, ranching, or logging, are on hold. Although animals like bobcats can bring in more than a thousand dollars each, most trappers are like Toby Walrath, president of the Montana Trappers Association, who, in his account for Outdoorlife.com, states that he is like most "small-time trappers who enjoy the challenge of trapping and the opportunity to sell a few pelts to buy more traps and pay for a tank or two of gas to fuel our next check of the trapline." Coyote pelts—which sell for about fifteen dollars in a good year—dominate the Montana Trappers Association annual fur sale, Walrath says. In other states, where there are plentiful, more lucrative furbearers like fox, mink, and beaver, the story is different. Still, no one is getting rich here.

The industry says that, whether wild or farmed, fur is "natural and renewable, regulated to ensure animal welfare, made from animals that are abundant, not endangered, and thus sustainable, and it is long-wearing and biodegradable, unlike synthetics." Synthetics—polyester, nylon—which now make up 60 percent of the global market for textiles, are made from plastic, which is derived from oil. Eighty percent of synthetics are nonbiodegradable, although they do break down: the plastic fibers end up in the landfill or, via our washing machines, in our waterways, and eventually in our food. Microfiber pollution, found in all five major ocean gyres and along coasts worldwide, kills marine life and plants and might well be "the biggest environmental problem you've never heard of," according to *Guardian* reporter Mary Catherine O'Connor. Experiments found that a single synthetic garment could shed 1,900 microfibers a wash.

Animal rights organizations, on the other hand, say that the trapping of furbearing animals is cruel, indiscriminate, and unnecessary and that "trapping regulations are weak and extremely difficult to enforce, particularly because the number of enforcement officers assigned to this responsibility is disturbingly inadequate." In British Columbia, for example, one field officer may be assigned to approximately 4,247 square miles. Activists are hard on trapping and fur farms alike. Besides their claims that animals are abused, neglected, and sometimes killed cruelly, they say that mink farms are environmentally harmful, requiring more energy and producing more toxins than textile production. How do we balance these opposing views?

I am looking for a middle path, I guess. While it seems self-righteous and ignorant, let alone criminal, for urban and often wealthy people to attack farmers and furriers by releasing minks or setting businesses on fire, or by outlawing the means of income for some of the poorest and least powerful people on earth, it also seems that these actions have brought more scrutiny and regulations and oversight. Have they not called attention to countries or even individual farms or practices that need to change? Undercover videos of animal abuse at mink farms in Denmark have resulted in annual, statutory veterinarian visits and a set of strict animal welfare rules, created in cooperation between Kopenhagen Fur and the Danish Society for the Prevention of Cruelty to Animals. Since the 1990s, most countries have adopted national and international laws in an effort to improve the lives—and deaths—of animals we use. In 2010, President Barack Obama signed the Truth in Fur Labeling Act, which requires any fur coming into the United States to specify what species it is and the country of origin. In this way, people who want to know where and how their clothing comes to them—just as more and more of us try to know more about what food we're eating—can make conscientious choices.

Yet the logical conclusion to the animal rights platform, as opposed to an animal welfare platform, is that we don't have the right to use animals for anything at all. PETA, the largest animal rights organization, with over five million members worldwide, says as much: "Animals are not ours to eat, wear, experiment on, use for entertainment, or abuse in any other way." When I first began thinking about this book, I knew that fur would be the most challenging material to write about. Even if we eat meat, even if we farm and fish, even if we keep our dogs on leashes and covet leather bags and strings of pearls, even if we sleep in robes made from the spinning bodies of worms or slip our feet into socks knitted from the sheared wool of lambs, fur alone brings us face to face with the fact that we need to kill for it. Fur is the least transformed of all animal products, including even meat itself. It is also the most metaphorical. A woman who wears fox *is foxy*. She is a *vixen*. Which means she is animal, driven by hunger, thirst, sex, and fear of death and violence. Danger is, of course, part of fur's allure, as well as the reason it repulses us. Does anyone really believe that banning the trapping, hunting, or raising of animals is going to banish death and suffering? Perhaps instead of asking whether the use of animals in the making of our clothing is right or wrong, it would be more helpful to reframe the question.

"There is a real need for more intelligent discussion about the socio-ecological role of the fur trade in modern society," writes Herscovici in a personal email to me. Herscovici, whose grandfather came to Canada in 1913 as a "fur craftsperson" and whose father worked in the industry his whole life, has been thinking and writing about the ethics of wearing fur for more than thirty years. His was the first serious critique—and is still one of the very few—of the animal rights movement from an environmental and human rights perspective. "My message," he writes, "is that people working with animals should speak out about what they do, so the media and public can hear both (or, rather, the many) sides of these complex issues." Herscovici's respect for the Canadian Cree, in particular, with whom he has worked in his role as vice president of the Fur Council of Canada, illuminates one of these issues: "[They confront] the fundamental existential problem that human life is impossible without killing, and resolve it by affirming the limitations that must order and restrain such killing." He continues, "In religious terms, overharvest is considered a form of disrespect, which will cause the animals to leave an area."

My Assiniboine friend Mandy, who was born on the Fort Peck reservation in northeastern Montana, recently showed me a suitcase in which she keeps her powwow regalia. She pulled out two mink skins: two slim brown females, shiny, sleek, and, of course, soft. They are a gift from her grandmother, who wore them tied to her braids. Mandy also retrieved a pair of moccasins her grandmother had made out of deerskin, fully beaded with "greasy yellows" and an old-time green the shade of grass. She pointed to where the pattern was repaired by her mother with newer beads, the old colors no longer available. When I shared with Mandy the photos of the cages at the Danish mink farm I visited, she was horrified, not by the cages, nor by the fact that the minks were going to be killed, but by the sheer number of them. Let me make this clear: Mandy was horrified by what she saw as a lack of restraint, by the mass production of so many animals' lives.

Conclusion

Last spring, when a friend mentioned a course currently being offered at a tribal college in old-time brain tanning—using an emulsion of animal brains and water to soften and preserve a hide—I immediately said I wanted to sign up. She raised one eyebrow: "Melissa, first you have to shoot the deer." At the time, I had considered that funny, funny in a humbling yet illuminating way, evidence of the distance between her indigenous thought and mine, the shift in consciousness and language we accomplish when we separate the animal that is alive from the dead—beef tenderloin, not flesh located near the cow's backbone and kidneys; leather, not skin; chicken nuggets, not...not what? Did I think that I would show up in class and there would be a pile of dead deer for me to choose from? I appreciated the reminder, but some part of the lesson had still been lost on me.

Most of us rely on others to provide our clothing, just as I had expected the college to supply the deer. Few of us remember how to sew on a button, let alone how to procure the leather for our shoes or grow cotton for our T-shirts. Yet this morning, watching the white-tail doe with her twin fawns out my window as they browse my hollyhocks down to stubs, I realize that my friend had also doubted my ability to kill anything. It weighs less than I do, this thin, wide-eyed, really individual animal, this *deer person*. Could I? And if not, why not? Is it because I somehow feel that it would be wrong?

At the heart of this question—whether or not it is right to utilize animals for the materials they provide for us, including for food, clothing, and labor—is whether we believe our human lives are more valuable than theirs. Indeed, "most arguments about animal ethics or animal rights," as Clare Palmer writes in the *Oxford Handbook of Animal Ethics*, have to do with the "moral status" of animals or, more importantly, their "moral significance" as compared with human beings. Nineteenth-century writer Jeremy Bentham was one of the first Western philosophers to argue that animals do have moral standing. As a proponent of utilitarianism—the theory that an action is right or wrong depending on its effect on the majority—his reasoning was based on the fact that animals are *sentient*. They can smell, taste, see, hear, and feel pain as well as happiness; therefore their happiness must be considered when we make decisions affecting their lives. "The question is not, Can they *reason?* nor, Can they *talk?* but, Can they *suffer?*" he wrote. "*We owe it to these animals themselves*, not those humans who might be affected by what we do, to consider their pleasures and pains and, having done so, to ensure that we never make them suffer without good reason."

There have been disputes on this matter, as we expect among philosophers. Some utilitarians exclude animals that do not have the same cognitive abilities as humans—"worms, honeybees, lobsters." Others counter that if consideration is determined by cognition, developmentally disabled or brain-damaged people, and even babies, could be experimented on or killed or even eaten. (Today scientists have discovered that even the lowly worm has a nervous system similar to ours: according to Carl Savino, author of *Beyond Words: What Animals Think and Feel*, it has "connectivity patterns also found in the human brain.") In 1975, Peter Singer expanded on Bentham's ideas in his highly influential *Animal Liberation*. In this book he introduced the idea that all sentient beings have "inherent value." Animal lives are not, therefore, reducible to the uses we have for them; rather, they are valuable by virtue of their simply being alive. *Speciesism*, a term Singer popularized, is therefore, like racism or sexism, morally indefensible.

In 1983, Tom Regan, author of *The Case for Animal Rights*, took it a step further. Animals were never, he said, to be treated as mere resources for others, even if it is for the benefit of the common good. Recognized as one of the intellectual founders of animal rights theory, he believes that certain animals have rights because they are "subjects of a life": because they are like us in that "what happens to them matters to them," they have a "basic moral right to respectful treatment." Regan is an "abolitionist." He argues for vegetarianism and an end to all practices that utilize animals in any way, including clothing, sports, entertainment, and scientific experimentation.

What rights do animal rights philosophers grant animals? Tom L. Beauchamp, in "Rights Theory and Animal Rights," proposes the following list:

the right to not be caused pain or suffering

the right to not be traumatized by controllable human activities (such as slaughterhouses)

the right to be protected against harmful side effects of controllable human activities (such as the spraying of pesticides and herbicides, farming that produces dangerous waste, and pollution-causing construction projects)

the right to not be placed at risk of serious pain, injury, or death in "sport" activities (such as cockfighting, bullfighting, and dogfighting)

the right to not be placed at risk of serious pain, injury, or death in the testing of human products (including cosmetics, pharmaceuticals, and chemicals)

Beauchamp suggests we add, for any wild animal, the right to not have one's habitat destroyed; or, for any domesticated animal, the right to adequate food, water, shelter, exercise, and rest, as well as to maintain relationships with other animals of its kind.

"Animal rights" is a moral theory that now serves as the foundation for an international movement with the same name. Over ten million people have joined the animal rights movement in America alone. Regan claims it is "among the fastest-growing progressive causes in America, [a movement that] espouses uncompromisingly abolitionist goals." PETA, the Humane Society, Farm Animal Rights Movement, Animal Liberation Front, Animal Legal Defense Fund, Nonhumans First: thirty-eight national and international organizations are listed on a recent Wikipedia site alone. Animal rights activists have worked to end cruel practices, introduce regulations, and transform the buying habits of millions of consumers. Some countries, under pressure from activists, have banned farming of furbearers. Some have passed laws mandating adequate space for farm animals, recognizing the rights of cattle, pigs, and chickens to move freely. In Sweden, for instance, chickens have a right to free range.

I suppose I am like many people: an abolitionist, a reformist, and a believer in the status quo depending on the animal and the situation. Though I might think of myself as an abolitionist when it comes to live-plucked down or the trapping of bobcats with steel-jawed legholds—now an industry claiming the lives of over fifty thousand American animals a year, most of them destined for international high-end markets—I also value the "complex world of intention, creation, dependence, and vulnerability" that is reflected in the relationship between sheep and their shepherds, the sustainable pearl farmers in Mexico and their oysters, the sericulturalists and their silkworms in Japan. And there is this: the earth is all we have. We must eat it, drink it, and wear it. Cars, couches, movies, smartphones, vaccines, schools, sweaters, shoes, hats: we manufacture our products out of earth's essential ingredients. To believe that we do no harm by abstaining from animal products is to tell ourselves a lie.

In 2010, 85 percent of textiles produced worldwide were woven from only two sources: cotton and polyester. Both are responsible for widespread pollution of waterways, soils, and air. Both consume enormous amounts of resources. Let us start with the growing of cotton, which is the world's most profitable nonfood crop, accounting for huge swaths of agricultural land in most developing countries. In addition to the dangers that monoculture causes—reduced resistance to disease, destruction of previously diverse ecosystems, depletion of soil—the growing of cotton consumes 11 percent of pesticides used worldwide, many of which are dangerous, causing health problems for workers and those downstream. Cotton also requires lots of water. The World Wildlife Fund estimates that it takes 20,000 liters (5,283 gallons) of water to produce enough cotton to make a T-shirt and a pair of jeans. It is estimated that 97 percent of the water in Pakistan's Indus River goes into the growing of cotton. Chemicals and dyes used in the manufacture of cotton garments also take their toll on workers and the watersheds where factories are located.

Synthetics come in two forms, those made from "natural polymers" or molecules derived from wood fibers such as bamboo or beech, and synthetic polymers that are dependent on hydrocarbons. Textiles made from natural polymers include viscose, lyocell, and acetate. Although the source materials are carbon neutral, the rest of the process, wherein the natural fibers are bleached and dissolved in various acids and sulfates, results in harmful emissions. Synthetic polymers include polyester, nylon, acrylic, and polypropylene. Polyester has now surpassed cotton as a textile, doubling production in the last fifteen years. "The agents used in the manufacture of polyester," Kate Fletcher, author of *Sustainable Fashion and Textiles* and professor at the London College of Fashion, "are petrochemicals and arguably its chief impacts stem from the political, social and pollution effects of the petrochemical industry." Polyester also consumes large amounts of energy in its production and releases harmful emissions into the air, water, and soil. Nylon also depends on petrochemicals. Fletcher states that nitrous oxide released from just one nylon factory in England was responsible for 3 percent of the country's greenhouse gas emissions.

One of the largest impacts of synthetic clothing comes not from its manufacture but from its "end use." Americans annually discard approximately 9.3 million metric tonnes (20.5 million pounds) of clothing and other textiles into our waste management systems. The majority of synthetics are not biodegradable. They sit in our landfills, leaching chemicals and microfibers into our water and our soils, and eventually pollute our waterways and impact animal and marine life in streams, rivers, and ultimately the ocean. Another "end use" is laundering. Cotton and synthetics need to be laundered often. Machine washing and tumble drying cause their own environmental damage: the more we wash our clothes, the more water and energy we consume. Dryers consume five times more energy than washing machines. Laundering a polyester blouse uses six times the energy it took to make it. Dyes and chemicals used in the processing and growing of cotton and in the manufacturing of synthetics, let alone the microfibers released with each washing, join the water table when clothes are rinsed.

In comparison to animal products, which are biodegradable and more durable and need far less laundering, and, if grown sustainably, do not leach pesticides into the ecosystem, the supply chain for synthetics comes with environmental problems at every turn. In our quest to do no harm to animals, many of us have unintentionally ignored the harm caused by the alternatives and have neglected the benefits to the land, animals, and rural people that animal products provide. As Becky Weed of Thirteen Mile Lamb and Wool Company writes, "We have allowed an entire industry of petroleum-based synthetic fibers to induce cultural amnesia about wool's superior qualities." This issue, like all other issues that ask us to take responsibility for what we consume, is complex. The clothing industry has one of the longest and most complicated supply chains in manufacturing. Many ecologists—and those working in animal ethics—are beginning to acknowledge the naïveté of thinking that there is one easy solution or that one fabric—or one practice or one theory—would enable us to clothe ourselves more wisely on this earth.

In *The Omnivore's Dilemma* and *The Botany of Desire*, Michael Pollan visits slaughterhouses and feedlots, pesticide factories and laboratories, to investigate industrial agriculture and the damage it has done to both workers and animals. Urging us to be less disconnected from the food we eat, he offers clear, simple advice: "Eat food. Not too much. Mostly plants." The fashion industry is founded on what the poet Baudelaire called *fugitive beauty*, a beauty dependent on constant change that inevitably dictates the obsolescence of garments. Fashions go *out of fashion* quickly. Many are intended to be worn for only one season. "No industry has better perfected the cultural cycle of invention, acceptance and discard...and has so successfully delinked it from physical need or function," writes Fletcher. In 2007, due to the availability of cheap clothing in places like Target and Walmart, people bought a third more garments than they had just four years before. (More recent statistics state that Americans spent 14 percent more on clothing and footwear in 2016 than in 2011, a trend that seems to be replicated in the rest of the world.) Cheap clothing, regardless of what it is made from, demands that workers are paid poorly and that horrific accidents—like the Rana Plaza factory collapse in Bangladesh, which killed eleven hundred textile workers—continue to happen. Industrial manufacturing often means that animals are regarded as raw material and thus that their welfare and rights go unprotected. One would imagine that the last place to look for solutions to meeting these very real challenges would be the fashion industry itself.

Patterned after the Slow Food movement, which was initiated by Italian farmers in protest against McDonald's opening a franchise in the Piazza di Spagna in Rome, the Slow Fashion movement is an attempt by designers, manufacturers, and retailers to address similar concerns in the fashion industry. Fletcher, who coined the term in 2008, says slow fashion, as opposed to fast fashion, emphasizes buying from local and smaller sources, designing with sustainable materials, such as organic wool or cotton, and utilizing secondhand, recycled, and refurbished clothing. The movement encourages consumer awareness and responsibility, from knowing how and where and by whom one's garment is made, through caring for it environmentally, including making changes in laundering such as washing in cold water and air-drying, to deciding how a garment will be repaired or discarded in the end.

The Slow Fashion movement has created a pledge to help consumers think more deeply about the clothes they buy: "I pledge to slow down. To practice conscious consumption by learning more about where my clothing comes from, making decisions based on quality rather than quantity, supporting handmade, local, sustainable or secondhand fashion, caring for my clothes to make them last, and to live life better by living slower."

More and more people are signing on. Many brands, like Puma, have commissioned "Environmental Profit and Loss Accounts" that calculate environmental costs and make them public. Dana Thomas, in an article for the *New York Times*, states that many luxury brands are now capitalizing on the ethics involved in the making of a garment, targeting "cleaner fabrics (treatment is often chemical heavy), animal rights in leather and fur production, production transparency, safer manufacturing conditions and worker rights and a proactive look at the impact of climate change." Labels that proclaim organic cotton, traceable down, natural-dyed silk, and pesticide-free wool work as status symbols to advertise their wearers' politics—their love of the earth, of animals, their concern for the planet—rather than their wealth.

Throughout this book, I have returned again and again to indigenous ideas of reciprocity. Theodore Brasser, in *Native American Clothing*, writes, "Fundamental to the native worldview was the belief that spirits, or spiritual power, resided not only in human beings, but also in animals, plants, rocks, and other natural phenomena." Because their clothing, food, and shelter were derived from these sources, consecration "was what produced the desired results and the well-being of the people." Contemporary ecology reaffirms this view: that the natural world is responsive to human care for it and that we are dependent on its health for our own survival. Reciprocity begins with awareness. It is guided by respect and restraint. It always involves an expression of gratefulness. With reciprocity in mind, I would like to end this book with my own version of Pollan's advice: "Buy clothes. Not very many. Made mostly from animals and plants. Then cherish and care for them."

Notes

INTRODUCTION

Page 1: *Scientists speculate that we lost*   Melissa A. Toups et al., "Origin of Clothing Lice Indicates Early Clothing Use by Anatomically Modern Humans in Africa," *Molecular Biology and Evolution* 28, no. 1 (2011): 29–32.

Page 2: *Our first sunscreen*   John Noble Wilford, "In African Cave, Signs of an Ancient Paint Factory," *New York Times*, October 14, 2011.

Page 2: *"Such substances as wood, hide"*   Eric Delson et al., *Encyclopedia of Human Evolution and Prehistory*, 2nd ed. (New York: Garland, 2000), 527.

Page 2: *The earliest chipped stone tools*   Michael Balter, "World's Oldest Stone Tools Discovered in Kenya," *Science Magazine*, April 14, 2015.

Page 2: *Bone awls, perhaps the oldest*   Ian Gilligan, "The Prehistoric Development of Clothing: Archaeological Implications of a Thermal Model," *Journal of Archaeological Method and Theory* 17, no. 1 (2010): 50.

Page 3: *Eyed needles, however*   Ralf Kittler, Manfred Kayser, and Mark Stoneking, "Molecular Evolution of *Pediculus humanus* and the Origin of Clothing," *Current Biology* 13, no. 16 (2003): 1414–17.

Page 3: *According to Ralf Kittler*   Ibid.

Page 3: *Further studies by Melissa A. Toups*   Toups et al., "Origin of Clothing Lice."

Page 3: *Collectively, these findings affirm*   Gilligan, "The Prehistoric Development of Clothing," 16.

Page 3: *"Specialized cold-weather clothing"*   Mark Collard et al., "Faunal Evidence for a Difference in Clothing Use between Neanderthals and Early Modern Humans in Europe," *Journal of Anthropological Archaeology* 44B (2016): 235–46.

Page 4: *In fact, archaeologists analyzing faunal remains*   Ibid.

Page 4: *"Clothing may have allowed early modern humans"*   Kittler, Kayser, and Stoneking, "Molecular Evolution of *Pediculus humanus* and the Origin of Clothing."

Page 4: *A desire for adornment is also apparent*   Anna Gosline, "Ancient Beads Imply Culture Older Than We Thought," *New Scientist*, June 22, 2006.

Page 4: *An equally ancient workshop*   Wilford, "In African Cave, Signs of an Ancient Paint Factory."

Page 5: *"began to acquire psychosocial functions"*   Gilligan, "The Prehistoric Development of Clothing," 32.

Page 5: *cave bears, woolly-haired rhinoceroses*   Eric Delson et al., *Encyclopedia of Human Evolution and Prehistory*, 2nd ed. (New York: Garland, 2000), 514.

Page 5: *Humans shared the Americas*   Doug Peacock, *In the Shadow of the Sabertooth* (Oakland, CA: AK Press, 2013), 31.

Page 5: *Naia, the young girl*   Michael Greshko, "Ice Age Predators Found alongside Oldest Human in Americas," *National Geographic*, August 25, 2017.

Page 5: *"the animistic assumption"*   David Abram, *Becoming Animal: An Earthly Cosmology* (New York: Vintage, 2010), 77.

Page 6: *"The buffalo, elk, and birds in the air"*   John G. Neihardt, *Black Elk Speaks: Being the Life Story of a Holy Man of the Oglala Sioux* (Albany: State University of New York Press, 2008), 27.

Page 6: *He writes, "We fail to recognize"*   Abram, *Becoming Animal*, 41.

Page 6: *In medieval Europe, traders charged*   Barry Lopez, *Arctic Dreams: Imagination and Desire in a Northern Landscape* (New York: Scribner, 1986), 127, 140–43.

Page 7: *In "Fragments of the Heavens"*   Catherine Howard, "Fragments of the Heavens: Feathers as Ornaments among the Waiwai," in *The Gift of Birds: Featherwork of Native South American Peoples*, ed. Ruben E. Reina and Kenneth M. Kensinger (Philadelphia: University Museum of Archaeology and Anthropology, 1991), 54.

Page 8: *Putting on the dog is an American phrase*   "'Putting on the Dog' Originated at Yale in the 19th Century," Google News, August 9, 1998, news .google.com/newspapers?nid=1915&dat=19980809&id=NJZGAAAAIBAJ &sjid=dPgMAAAAIBAJ&pg=5490,1814679&hl=en.

1. LEATHER

Page 10: *An archaeological site in nearby northeastern Siberia*   Peacock, *In the Shadow of the Sabertooth*, 66.

Page 10: *The adjectives Yup'ik or Inupiaq*   Ann Fienup-Riordan et al., *Hunting Tradition in a Changing World: Yup'ik Lives in Alaska Today* (New Brunswick, NJ: Rutgers University Press, 2000), 166.

Page 10: *With approximately twenty-three thousand enrolled members*   Ann Fienup-Riordan, *Wise Words of the Yup'ik People: We Talk to You Because We Love You* (Lincoln: University of Nebraska Press, 2005), 244.

Page 10: *Along with the more northern Inupiat*   Fienup-Riordan et al., *Hunting Tradition*, 9.

Page 11: *As a hunter crept*   William W. Fitzhugh and Susan A. Kaplan, *Innua: Spirit World of the Bering Sea Eskimo* (Washington, DC: Smithsonian Institution Press, 1982), 142.

Page 12: *Sealskins were scraped and then soaked*   Ann Fienup-Riordan, *Yuungnaqpiallerput: The Way We Genuinely Live* (Seattle: University of Washington Press, 2007), 145.

Page 12: *Six to eight rabbits*   Vivian Beaver et al., *Skin Sewing for Clothing in Akula* (Alaska Historical Commission Studies in History No. 22, n.d.), n.p.

Page 12: *One of the most unusual—and essential—inventions of the Yupiit*   Fienup-Riordan, *Yuungnaqpiallerput*, 154.

Page 13: *"The seams are so airtight"*   Ibid., 134.

Page 17: *In addition, there are eight names*   Fienup-Riordan, *Yuungnaqpiallerput*, 25.

Page 20: *"A good knowledge of the local landscape"*   Lopez, *Arctic Dreams*, 287.

Page 22: *In Edna Wilder's book*   Edna Wilder, *Secrets of Eskimo Skin Sewing* (Anchorage: Alaska Northwest, 1976), 17, 93.

Page 22: *"We are no longer willing to be treated like artifacts"*   J. C. H. King, Birgit Pauksztat, and Robert Storrie, eds., *Arctic Clothing* (Montreal: McGill-Queens University Press, 2005), 25.

Page 23: *Men living north of the Kuskokwim*   Fitzhugh and Kaplan, *Innua*, 147.

Page 23: *"The ocean has eyes"*   Fienup-Riordan, *Wise Words*, 282.

Page 24: *which was a greater reciprocity*   Ann Fienup-Riordan, *Boundaries and Passageways: Rules and Ritual in Yup'ik Eskimo Oral Tradition* (Norman: University of Oklahoma Press, 1995), 3.

Page 24: *"People believed that thoughtful actions"*   Fienup-Riordan, *Hunting*, 12.

Page 24: *"No culture has yet solved the dilemma"*   Lopez, *Arctic Dreams*, 413.

Page 25: *"Our ancestors took great care"*   Fienup-Riordan, *Wise Words*, 43.

Page 25: *"the essential personhood of animals"*   Ibid., xxx.

Page 25: *"It was the gift"*   Lopez, *Arctic Dreams*, 191.

Page 25: *"Such [acts] of propitiation"*   Ibid., 113.

Pages 25–26: *its soul or* inua *enters an unborn animal*   Fitzhugh and Kaplan, *Innua*, 14.

Page 26: *Until the sixteenth century*   Josephine Barbe, *Leather: History, Techniques, Projects* (Atglen, PA: Schiffer, 2013), 8–9.

Page 29: *For most animals, skin is made up of*   Ibid., 24.

Page 30: *The roots and pores*   Ibid., 33.

Page 30: *The pig is the animal*   National Hide Association, *Hides and Skins* (Chicago: Jacobsen, 1970), 182.

Page 31: *"Leather flaws"*   Ibid., 36.

Page 31: *Like most skin*   Roy Thomson, "Skin, Leather and Tanning: Some Definitions," in *Leather Tanneries: The Archaeological Evidence*, ed. Roy Thomson and Quita Mould (London: Archetype, 2011), 3.

Page 32: *The Blackfeet might have been so named*   Barbe, *Leather*, 13.

Page 32: *Tutankhamun, buried in 1550 BC*   Ibid., 13.

Page 32: *The tanner's guild*   Ibid., 16.

Page 35: *Worldwide, however, 85 percent of skins*   Ibid., 29.

Page 36: *"Five years from now"*   National Hide Association, *Hides and Skins*, 70.

Page 36: *Currently, China and India*   Andrew Tarantola, "How Leather Is Slowly Killing the People and Places That Make It," *Gizmodo*, June 3, 2014.

Page 36: *about thirty-nine dollars a month*   Raveena Aulakh, "Bangladesh's Tanneries Make the Sweatshops Look Good," *Toronto Star*, October 12, 2013.

Page 37: *Because of journalists like Sean Gallagher*   Tarantola, "How Leather Is Slowly Killing the People and Places That Make It."

Page 37: *high instances of pancreatic cancer*   Ilya Veyalkin and Velentin Gerein, "Retrospective Cohort Study of Cancer Mortality at the Minsk Leather Tannery," *Industrial Health* 44, no. 1 (2006): 9–74.

Page 37: *A health assessment of 197 men*   Amit Pandey, Subodh Rastogi, and Sachin Tripathi, "Occupational Health Risks among the Workers Employed in Leather Tanneries at Kanpur," *Indian Journal of Occupational and Environmental Medicine* 12, no. 3 (2008): 132.

Page 37: *The average life expectancy*   Aulakh, "Bangladesh's Tanneries Make the Sweatshops Look Good."

Page 37: *tanning with leaves and herbs*   Paul J. Baskar, "Devastation by Leather Tanneries in Tamil Nadu," *Development in Practice* (Oxfam UK) 2, no. 2 (1992).

Page 37: *Processing 100 kilograms (220 pounds)*   Ibid.

Page 37: *In 2014 there were three hundred tanneries*   Pandey, Rastogi, and Tripathi, "Occupational Health Risks"; Sean Gallagher, "The Toxic Price of Leather," *Pulitzer Center on Crisis Reporting*, February 4, 2014.

Page 38: *In the city of Hazaribagh*   Tarantola, "How Leather Is Slowly Killing the People and Places That Make It."

Page 38: *Tannery runoff contains*   K. S. Shahzad, S. A. Akhtar, and S. M. Mahmud, "Prevalence of and Factors Associated with Asthma in Adult Male Leather Workers in Karachi, Pakistan," *European Journal of Epidemiology* 21 (2006): 292.

Page 38: *Hazaribagh is rated one of the five most toxic*   Tarantola, "How Leather Is Slowly Killing the People and Places That Make It."

Page 38: *Children are increasingly born*   Gallagher, "The Toxic Price of Leather."

Page 39: *in vats of bell pepper, red poppy*   Barbe, *Leather*, 21.

Page 39: *indigo, made from flowers native to Asia*   Ibid., 32.

Page 40: *Park Avenue Cordovan Oxfords*   Wailin Wong, "Chicago's Last Tannery," *Chicago Tribune*, December 26, 2014, www.chicagotribune.com/bluesky/hub/chi -distance-horween-tannery-bsi-hub-story.html.

Page 40: *And good horsehides are rare*   Ibid.

Page 41: *in 2012, according to the US Hide, Skin, and Leather Association*   "Trade Issues," US Hide and Skin and Leather Association, 2014, ushsla.org.

Page 41: *According to the World Statistical Compendium*   "15th Edition World Statistical Compendium 2013 for Raw Hides and Skins, Leather and Leather Footwear, 1993–2012," Food and Agriculture Organization of the United Nations, 2013, fao.org.

Page 41: *even unnatural, quality*   Barbe, *Leather*, 44.

Page 41: *"requires killing cows"*   Fran Hawthorne, *Ethical Chic: The Inside Story of the Companies We Think We Love* (Boston: Beacon Press, 2012), 22.

Page 42: *"This process eliminates"*   Ibid., 107.

Page 44: *"Both the fell cutter"*   Ibid., 18.

Page 45: *According to Human Rights Watch*   "Blood, Sweat, and Fear," Human Rights Watch, January 25, 2005, humanrightswatch.org.

Page 45: *Despite the Forest Code of 1965*   Lucy Siegle, "Luxury Leather and the Amazon," *Guardian*, March 3, 2013.

Page 46: *As Lucy Siegel writes*   Ibid.

Page 46: *For instance, shoe manufacturers*   Hawthorne, *Ethical Chic*, 27.

Pages 46–47: *raise the profile of ethics in global fashion*   "The GCC Brandmark," Eco -Age.com, 2013, https://eco-age.com/news/green-carpet-challenge-archive.

Page 47: *Leafing through a collection of fourteen academic essays*   Shari Benstock and Suzanne Ferriss, eds., *Footnotes: On Shoes* (New Brunswick, NJ: Rutgers University Press, 2001).

2. WOOL

Page 49: *"So powerful, in fact"*   Elizabeth Wayland Barber, *Women's Work: The First 20,000 Years* (New York: W. W. Norton, 1994), 45.

Page 50: *"The English word* robe"   Ibid., 290.

Page 50: *It takes the hair from three goats*   Joan Tapper and Gale Zucker, *Shear Spirit: Ten Fiber Farms, Twenty Patterns, and Miles of Yarn* (New York: Potter Craft, 2008), 135.

Page 51: *The word* cashmere   Ibid.

Page 51: *Eight times warmer than sheep's wool*   Marina Romanova, "Mongolia's Cashmere Industry," *Mongolia Briefing*, February 24, 2012.

Page 51: *Before continental Europe discovered it*   Michelle Maskielle, "Consuming

Kashmir: Shawls and Empires, 1500–2000," *Journal of World History* 13, no. 1 (2002): 27–33.

Page 51: *Their weaving was introduced to the French court* Maskielle, "Consuming Kashmir," 29, 35; "What You Didn't Know about Pashmina," *Indian Explorer*, November 14, 2012, indianroots.com.

Page 51: *Napoleon is said* Maskielle, "Consuming Kashmir," 39.

Page 51: *These goats, which can produce* Barbara Parry, *Adventures in Yarn Farming: Four Seasons on a New England Fiber Farm* (Boston: Roost Books, 2013), 202.

Page 51: *Then they were bred back to white* Tapper and Zucker, *Shear Spirit*, 75.

Page 52: *Most alpaca fiber, when not made into blankets* Ibid., 82.

Page 52: *Unprocessed wool from the vicuña* Carlos Valdez and Juan Karita, "Vicuña Roundup in Bolivia's High Plains," *Huffington Post Online*, October 14, 2002 (no longer available).

Page 52: *Every two or three years* Carlos Valdez and Juan Karita, "Sustaining Vicuña Populations through Community Involvement," *Horizons International Solution Site*, 2011.

Page 52: *According to the Oomingmak Musk Ox Producers' Co-op* *Qiviut Alaskan Handknits* (pamphlet), Oomingmak Musk Ox Producers' Co-op, Anchorage, Alaska.

Page 53: *Wool grows in clusters* D. J. Cottle, *International Sheep and Wool Handbook* (Nottingham: Nottingham University Press, 2010), 1.

Page 54: *Wild sheep and goats originated* Ibid.

Page 54: *over 1.2 billion domesticated sheep* Ibid., 37.

Page 54: *Paging through a field guide to sheep breeds* Deborah Robson and Carol Ekarius, *The Field Guide to Fleece: 100 Sheep Breeds and How to Use Their Fibers* (North Adams, MA: Storey, 2013).

Page 55: *over five hundred different breeds* Cottle, *International Sheep and Wool Handbook*, 5.

Page 56: *Sheep had to change a lot* Barber, *Women's Work*, 97.

Page 56: *In an essay titled "Ten Thousand Years of Crisis"* Paul Shepard, *The Only World We've Got* (San Francisco: Sierra Club Books, 1996), 202.

Page 57: *Biologists claim that dogs* Hal Herzog, *Some We Love, Some We Hate, Some We Eat* (New York: Harper, 2010), 105.

Page 57: *Most mammals, including humans* Stephen Budiansky, *The Covenant of the Wild: Why Animals Chose Domestication* (New York: William Morrow, 1992), 77–80.

Page 58: *According to* Biology Online Dictionary S.v. "thrive," biology-online.org/dictionary/Thrive, accessed October 29, 2018.

Page 58: *Selection of sheep for qualities* Cottle, *International Sheep and Wool Handbook*, 1.

Page 58: *Wild sheep, as I mentioned earlier, were predominantly hairy* Barber, *Women's Work*, 219.

Page 59: *These new "woolly sheep"* Ibid., 104, 210.

Page 59: *By 2300 BCE* Ibid., 211.

Page 59: *Crete began to use slaves* Ibid., 180.

Page 59: *Wool trading began in earnest* Cottle, *International Sheep and Wool Handbook*, 1.

Page 60: *1571: an English man could be fined* Barber, *Women's Work*, 574.

Page 60: *a tribe of Arabic Moors introduced a breed* Cottle, *International Sheep and Wool Handbook*, 9.

Page 60: *In 1492, Columbus brought a flock* "History of Sheep," International Wool Textile Organization, iwto.org/history-sheep, accessed October 29, 2018.

Page 60: *In 2006, there was one sheep for every six people on earth* Cottle, *International Sheep and Wool Handbook*, 37.

Page 61: *Their wool is known for being so fine* Parry, *Adventures in Yarn Farming*, 12.

Page 61: *Most large ranches in the West employ shearers* Rick Hampton, "Today's Shepherds Are Alone on the Range at Christmas," *USA Today*, December 23, 2010.

Page 64: *Wool refers to the entire fleece* Robson and Ekarius, *The Field Guide to Fleece*, 10.

Page 64: *Most usable wool falls* "Wool measurement," *Wikipedia*, https://en.wikipedia.org/wiki/Wool_measurement, accessed November 1, 2018.

Page 64: *In comparison, a human hair* "Understanding Micron Ratings," *Baldwin Filters*, March 2014, www.baldwinfilter.com/literature/english/TechTips/201403TechTipsMicronRatings.pdf.

Page 66: *The word* card *comes from the Latin* Barber, *Women's Work*, 36.

Page 67: *Not so long ago, all clothing* Ibid., 31.

Page 67: *The invention of the flying shuttle* "The Spinning Jenny: A Wool Revolution," Faribault Woolen Mill Company, faribaultmill.com, accessed October 29, 2018.

Page 70: *The American sheep industry loses* Budiansky, *The Covenant of the Wild*, 103.

Page 70: *issued 24,479 wolf-hunting licenses* "2013 Montana Wolf Hunting Season Report," Montana Fish, Wildlife and Parks, fwp.mt.gov, accessed October 29, 2018.

Page 70: *In Australia, a 3,307-mile fence* Thomas O'Neill and Medford Taylor, "Traveling the Australian Dog Fence," *National Geographic* 191, no. 4 (1997): 18.

Page 71: *In the Himalayas* Snow Leopard Conservancy, "Threats to Snow Leopard Survival," snowleopardconservancy.org, accessed October 29, 2018.

Page 71: *According to the United States Department of Agriculture* "Sheep and Lamb Predator and Nonpredator Death Loss in the United States, 2015," www.aphis.usda.gov/animal.../sheep/.../sheepdeath/SheepDeathLoss2015.pdf, accessed November 1, 2018.

Page 71: *"Our guard llamas have developed"* Tim King, "Predator Friendly Farming," *Maine Organic Farmers and Gardeners Organization*, Spring 2005, mofgo.org.

Page 71: *"In general," Weed writes* "Why Should We Care about the American Sheep

Industry?," Thirteen Mile Lamb and Wool Company, lambandwool.com, accessed October 29, 2018.

Page 72: *Predator Friendly took formal shape*   Matt Barnes, "Livestock Management for Coexistence with Large Carnivores, Healthy Land and Productive Ranches," Keystone Conservation, peopleandcarnivores.org/PC_2015_WhitePaper.pdf, accessed October 29, 2018.

Page 72: *"Rangelands have evolved"*   Ibid., 5.

Page 72: *"ranching in nature's image"*   Ibid., 3.

Page 73: *"Women dominate nearly every aspect"*   Herzog, *Some We Love*, 136.

Page 74: *"He never wanted his critters"*   "Testimonials," February 3, 2015, Bud Williams Stockmanship, stockmanship.com.

Page 77: *"The nineteenth century"*   John Berger, "Why Look at Animals?," in *Selected Essays* (New York: Vintage, 2003), 259.

Page 79: *New Zealand and Australia*   Cottle, *International Sheep and Wool Handbook*, 37.

Page 79: *In addition, China is the main raw wool importer*   Ibid., 38.

Page 79: *In the last fifty years, the domestic goat population*   Romanova, "Mongolia's Cashmere Industry."

Page 79: *China is now the largest producer of cashmere*   Ibid.

Page 80: *In a study published in* Conservation Biology   Joel Berger, Bayarbaatar Buuveibaatar, and Charudutt Mishra, "Globalization of the Cashmere Market and the Decline of Large Animals in Central Asia," *Conservation Biology* 27, no. 4 (2013): 683.

Page 80: *These wild animals*   Ibid., 680.

Page 80: *In Inner Mongolia alone*   Ibid., 683.

Page 80: *Even in Eastern Mongolia*   Ibid., 686.

Page 81: *"O come and live with me"*   Virgil, *The Ecologues*, trans. David Ferry (New York: Farrar, Straus and Giroux, 1999), 13.

Page 81: *In its tendency to idealize the rural*   Leo Marx, *The Machine in the Garden: Technology and the Pastoral Ideal in America* (London: Oxford University Press, 1964), 6.

Page 82: *His is the dream of an* improved *wilderness*   Ibid., 87.

Page 82: *"the systematic creation of animal deformities"*   Shepard, *The Only World We've Got*, 199.

Page 83: *"As soon as people began to kill wolves"*   Ibid., xviii.

Page 83: *"Draw me a sheep"*   Antoine de Saint-Exupéry, *The Little Prince* (New York: Harcourt, Brace & World, 1943).

3. SILK

Page 85: *for over twelve hundred years*   "The History of Nishijin," Nishijin Textile Industrial Association, 1997, nishijin.or.jp/eng/history/history.htm.

Page 86: *Greed for silk spurred*   Silk Center Kokusai Boeki Kanko Kaikan No. 1 Yamashita-cho, Naka-ku, Yokohama, Japan, silkcenter-kbkk.jp/museum/en/, accessed October 29, 2018.

Page 86: *The Empress Leizu*   "Leizu: Legendary Founder of China's Silk Industry," amazingbibletimeline.com/blog/leizu/#sthash, accessed October 29, 2018.

Page 87: *According to Dieter Kuhn's essay*   Dieter Kuhn, "Tracing a Chinese Legend: In Search of the Identity of the 'First Sericulturalist,'" *T'oung Pao*, 2nd ser., 70, nos. 4/5 (1984): 218.

Page 87: *fujigimono, a kind of work clothing*   Haru Matsukata Reischauer, *Samurai and Silk: A Japanese and American Heritage* (Cambridge, MA: Belknap Press of Harvard University Press, 1986), 70.

Page 87: *Older legends*   Kuhn, "Tracing a Chinese Legend," 217.

Page 87: *Yet the cult of Leizu*   Ibid., 241.

Page 87: *Silk cultivation flourished*   "History of Silk," Silk Road Foundation, silk-road.com/artl/silkhistory.shtml, accessed October 29, 2018.

Pages 87–88: *In the second century, according to legend*   Ibid.; "Japan," Facts and Details, factsanddetails.com/japan/cat20, accessed October 29, 2018.

Page 89: *"according to rituals and secrets"*   Alessandro Baricco, *Silk* (London: Harvill, 1997), 214.

Page 89: *"animal spirit" of a horse*   Kuhn, "Tracing a Chinese Legend," 233.

Page 90: *as Haru Matsukata Reischauer notes*   Reischauer, *Samurai and Silk*, 158–59.

Page 91: *After Japan closed its ports*   Ibid., 157.

Page 93: *Reischauer speaks of this in her account*   Ibid., 157.

Page 94: *They will weigh ten thousand times*   Sylvia A. Johnson, *Silkworms* (Minneapolis: A Lerner Natural Science Book, 1982), 22.

Page 94: *pheromones, the chemical substances*   Ibid., 10.

Page 95: *Of the 100,000-plus insects that spin cocoons*   Silk Center Kokusai Boeki Kanko Kaikan No. 1 Yamashita-cho.

Page 95: *a sticky substance called* sericin   Johnson, *Silkworms*, 26.

Page 95: *cocoons were very small*   Silk Center Kokusai Boeki Kanko Kaikan No. 1 Yamashita-chor.

Page 96: *Large landowners bought cocoons*   Reischauer, *Samurai and Silk*, 164.

Page 96: *According to Ron Cherry*   Ron Cherry, "History of Sericulture," Insects.org, insects.org/ced1/seric.html, accessed October 29, 2018.

Page 96: *"considered unpolluted"*   "History of Silk."

Page 96: *Ahimsa silk*   "Ahimsa (Peace) Silk," wormspit.com/peacesilk.htm, accessed October 29, 2018.

Page 97: *From one ounce of eggs*   "History of Silk."

Page 97: *a Buddhist priest's vestments*   Terry Satusuki Milhaupt, *Kimono: A Modern History* (London: Reaktion Books, 2014), 150.

Page 98: *In preindustrial days, before the availability of electric heat*   Reischauer, *Samurai and Silk*, 157.

Page 98: *"Dyeing the hemp cloth indigo blue"*   Amuse Boro Museum, Asakusa, Tokyo, amusemuseum.com/english/boro/index.html, accessed October 29, 2018.

Page 99: *Even as late as the beginning of the nineteenth century*   Milhaupt, *Kimono*, 87.

Page 100: *it was referred to as a* kosode   Ibid., 21.

Page 100: *For instance, geisha obi*   Brochure, Kyoto Museum of Traditional Crafts, 2015.

Page 101: *the traditional Japanese system referred to in literature*   "The Traditional Colors of Japan: Making Modern History," Tofugu, LLC, 2015, tofugu.com/2013/09/12/the-traditional-colors-of-japan-making-modern-history.

Page 101: *In feudal Japan*   Milhaupt, *Kimono*, 31.

Page 102: *"One word can create an environment"*   Hoshinaga Fumio, quoted in "A Conversation between Richard Gilbert and Timothy Green," *Rattle* 21, no. 2 (2015): 76.

Page 102: Kusakizome *is the word*   Brochure, Kusakizome Studio, Tomioka, Japan.

Page 103: *"I recall with nostalgia"*   Akira Yamazaki, *Nippon Hand Weaves in "Kusakizome Dyes"* (Kakio, Japan: Getuimekai, 1959).

Page 103: *"In a nation that esteems"*   Martin Fackler, "Old Ways Prove Hard to Shed, Even as Crisis Hits Kimono Trade," *New York Times*, February 9, 2015.

Page 104: *Today synthetic indigo*   "What Are Clothing Fabric Dyes Made Of?," wardrobeadvice.com/what-are-clothing-fabric-dyes-made-of, accessed October 29, 2018.

Page 106: *In his influential book*   Sōetsu Yanagi, *The Unknown Craftsman: A Japanese Insight into Beauty* (New York: Kodansha USA, 2013), 107.

Page 107: *"It is this beauty with inner implications"*   Ibid., 124.

Page 108: *"It is unlikely that the clothes we wear today"*   Ibid., 205.

Page 108: *"so widespread that a number of awakened people"*   Ibid., 144.

Page 112: *"It's a choice that cannot be taken lightly"*   Gail Tsukiyama, *Women of the Silk* (New York: St. Martin's, 1991), 77.

Page 112: *As in Tsukiyama's novel, at Tomioka*   Tomioka Silk Mill, Information Desk, Tomioka City, Japan, tomioka-silk.jp, accessed October 29, 2018.

Page 112: *From 1894 to 1912*   Milhaupt, *Kimono*, 107.

Page 113: *"to suit the average size"*   Tomioka Silk Mill.

Page 113: *Over a million trays of eggs*   Ibid.

Page 113: *In fact, demand for healthy silkworms*   Milhaupt, *Kimono*, 67.

Page 114: *Venice and Florence, in particular*   "Textile Production in Europe 1600–1800," Heilbrunn Timeline of Art History, metmuseum.org/toah/hd/txt_s/hd_txt_s.htm, accessed October 29, 2018.

Page 114: *In France, Louis XI ordered*   Jim McNeill, "History of the Silk Industry in the Touraine Region," *Social History in the Touraine* (blog), May 21, 2011, jim mcneill.wordpress.com/2011/05/21/history-of-the-silk-industry-in-the-touraine -region-france.

Page 114: *"Silk brocades and watered tabinets"*   W. G. Sebald, *The Rings of Saturn* (New York: New Directions, 1999), 283.

Page 114: *In 1623, James I*   Charles E. Hatch Jr., "Mulberry Trees and Silkworms: Sericulture in Early Virginia." *Virginia Magazine of History and Biography* 65, 1 (1957): 17–18.

Page 115: *Then, in 1844, blight wiped out*   Ibid.

Page 115: *In 1849, the* pébrine *pandemic*   Junko Thérèse Takeda, "Global Insects: Silkworms, Sericulture, and Statecraft in Napoleonic France and Tokugawa Japan," *French History* 28, no. 2 (2014): 207–25.

Page 115: *The nonnative European climates*   Tamil Nadu Agricultural University, agritech.tnau.ac.in/sericulture/disese%20mgt_silkworm.html, accessed October 29, 2018.

Page 115: *The* Bombyx mori *was introduced in 1771*   G. K. Rajesh, "Indian Sericulture: Past Glory and Future Challenges," *Silkwormmori* (blog), May 28, 2001, silkworm mori.blogspot.com/2011/05/indian-sericulture-industry-over-view.html.

Page 115: *Contemporaneous with these disasters, the Taiping Rebellion*   Milhaupt, *Kimono*, 66.

Page 115: *It was exactly then, in 1853*   Reischauer, *Samurai and Silk*, 168.

Page 115: *While the pébrine pandemic was doing its damage*   Takeda, "Global Insects," 213.

Page 116: *Japanese production doubled*   Reischauer, *Samurai and Silk*, 254.

Page 116: *In 1929, the United States imported*   Ibid., 256.

Page 116: *"apex of kimono production in Japan"*   Milhaupt, *Kimono*, 87.

Page 116: *In a 1925 survey of the Ginza*   Ibid., 230.

Page 116: *Back in Japan, because of the time-consuming work*   Ibid., 234.

Page 116: *In Nishijin, power looms were broken apart*   Tamara K. Hareven, *The Silk Weavers of Kyoto: Family and Work in a Changing Traditional Industry* (Berkeley: University of California Press, 2002), 29.

Page 117: *"By 1920, Nagano prefecture"*   Milhaupt, *Kimono*, 78.

Page 117: *it is said that Lady Diana's*   "The Silkworm Story: A Thread through History," *Growing with Science* (blog), November 21, 2008, blog.growingwith science.com/2008/11/the-silkworm-story-a-thread-through-history.

Page 117: *The houses are called* nagi-no-ne-doko   Harleven, *The Silk Weavers of Kyoto*, 12.

Page 117: *"Today," says Matsuo Hiroko*   Quoted ibid., 32.

Page 117: *According to Hareven, 40 percent*   Ibid., 39.

Page 118: takenoko seikatsu, *"bamboo shoot existence"*   Milhaupt, *Kimono*, 190.

Page 119: *In China, the decline in demand for raw silk*   Shelagh Vainker, *Chinese Silk: A Cultural History* (New Brunswick, NJ: Rutgers University Press, 2002), 204.

Page 119: *According to the Japanese Information Network*   Japan Information Network, "The Cocoon Strikes Back: Innovative Products Could Revive a Dying Industry," Trends in Japan, November 17, 2000, web-japan.org/trends00/hon bun/tj001117.html.

Page 120: *"preserving clothing as family heirlooms"*   Milhaupt, *Kimono*, 154.

Page 120: *According to* Trade Forum Magazine   International Trade Center, "Silk in World Markets," *International Trade Forum Magazine* 1 (1999), tradeforum.org/ Silk-in-World-Markets/#sthash.LpsZOAl1.dpuf.

Page 120: *"strolled the Ginza"*   Milhaupt, *Kimono*, 246.

Page 121: *India, the second largest producer*   International Trade Center, "Silk in World Markets."

Page 121: *After 4,700 years*   Cherry, "History of Sericulture."

Page 121: *There are about ten million silkworm growers in China*   "Silk in China," Facts and Details, factsanddetails.com/china/cat9/sub63/item342.html, accessed October 29, 2018.

Page 121: *Seven hundred thousand households in India*   "Silk," Natural Fibers, naturalfibres2009.org/en/fibres/silk.html, accessed October 29, 2018.

Page 121: *silk sells for roughly twenty times*   Rajesh, "Indian Sericulture."

Page 121: *Sericulture is also environmentally friendly*   Silk Center Kokusai Boeki Kanko Kaikan No. 1 Yamashita-chor.

Page 121: *Cotton accounts for 3 percent*   Tatiana Schlossberg, "Fig Leaves Are Out. What to Wear to Be Kind to the Planet," *New York Times*, May 24, 2017.

4. FEATHERS

Page 122: *"The fact [is], in more temperate regions"*   François Boucher, *20,000 Years of Fashion: The History of Costume and Personal Adornment* (New York: Abrams, 1987), 22.

Page 122: *If one distinguishes, as Boucher does*   Ibid., 9.

Page 123: *"Unlike paints or dyes"*   Thor Hanson, *Feathers: The Evolution of a Natural Miracle* (New York: Basic Books, 2011), 209.

Page 123: *Bird feathers gain their colors in two ways*   Ibid., 199.

Page 123: *The cardinal has to eat the redness*   David S. Scott and Casey McFarland, *Bird Feathers: A Guide to North American Species* (Mechanicsburg, PA: Stackpole Books, 2010), 39.

Page 123: *"When light hits a pigment-bearing feather"*   Hanson, *Feathers*, 199.

Page 123: *The number of bird species in the world*   Scott and McFarland, *Bird Feathers*, 4.

Page 123: *the number of birds close to 400 billion*   Hanson, *Feathers*, 4.

Page 123: *Feathers are considered part of the "integumentary" system*   Scott and McFarland, *Bird Feathers*, 13.

Page 123: *Feathers . . . are made of the protein keratin*   Hanson, *Feathers*, 67.

Pages 123–24: *Like hair, they grow out of the bird's skin*   Ibid., 71.

Page 124: *Once feathers reach their optimum size*   Ibid., 70.

Page 124: *Together, rachis, barbs, and barbicels form*   Scott and McFarland, *Bird Feathers*, 15.

Page 124: *Each bird has different kinds of feathers*   Ibid., 15–17.

Page 125: *In Hanson's book, those who believe feathers evolved for flight*   Hanson, *Feathers*, 117ff.

Page 127: *Often, farmers had to hire native girls*   Philip M. Parker, "The Feather Merchants," *Time* 57, no. 19 (1951): 94.

Page 127: *An ostrich egg incubator*   Sarah Abrevaya Stein, *Plumes: Ostrich Feathers, Jews, and a Lost World of Global Commerce* (New Haven, CT: Yale University Press, 2008), 3.

Page 127: *"Ostrich feathers were valuable commodities"*   Ibid., 117.

Page 127: *"colonial booty"*   Ibid., 22.

Page 128: *"empress hat"*   Parker, "The Feather Merchants."

Page 128: *At the market's height*   Ibid.

Page 128: *When the* Titanic *sank in 1912*   Stein, *Plumes*, 22.

Page 128: *Prior to the farms*   Ibid., 59.

Page 128: *It took six months to a year*   Ibid., 92.

Page 128: *As demand for ostrich feathers increased*   Ibid., 92.

Page 128: *In a story worthy of a crime novel*   Ibid., 5.

Page 128: *"In the Cape, over 90 percent of feather merchants"*   Ibid., 6.

Page 129: *The Dutch owned the farms*   Ibid., 43.

Page 129: *London, New York, and Paris, the centers of feather-related manufacturing*   Ibid., 13.

Page 129: *Twenty-two thousand people worked*   Hanson, *Feathers*, 176.

Page 129: *By 1915, Stein writes*   Stein, *Plumes*, 19.

Page 129: *"My amazement stemmed"*   Hanson, *Feathers*, 171.

Page 129: *The male indigo bunting*   Cornell University Lab of Ornithology, "The Basics: Feather Molt," April 20, 2008, allaboutbirds.org/the-basics-feather-molt.

Page 130: *"Birds wouldn't have developed beautiful"*   Scott and McFarland, *Bird Feathers*, 60.

Page 130: *traits like the lemon hue of the yellow warbler*   Geoffrey E. Hill, *National Geographic Bird Coloration* (Washington, DC: National Geographic, 2010), 172.

Page 130: *"When an ornithologist is asked why birds"*   Ibid., 189.

Page 130: *In one study of house finches*   Ibid., 174.

Page 130: *"extra-pair copulations"*   Ibid., 175.

Page 130: *Although most people have killed birds*   Scott Weidensaul, *Of a Feather: A Brief History of American Birding* (Orlando: Harcourt, 2007), 154.

Page 130: *"Market shooting for the table"*   Ibid., 136.

Page 130: *Weidensaul states that in the late 1890s, in the Everglades*   Ibid., 150.

Page 130: *In nine months, the London market*   William Souder, "How Two Women Ended the Deadly Feather Trade," *Smithsonian*, March 2013.

Pages 130–31: *If one included all species*   Weidensaul, *Of a Feather*, 151.

Page 131: *George Bird Grinnell*   Ibid., 150.

Page 131: *to instead buy "Audubonnets"*   Jenna Weissman Joselit, *A Perfect Fit: Clothes, Character, and the Promise of America* (New York: Holt, 2002), 158.

Page 131: *The movement Hemenway reinvigorated*   Weidensaul, *Of a Feather*, 160.

Page 131: *the Migratory Bird Act (1913)*   Stein, *Plumes*, 23.

Pages 131–32: *By the 1920s, merchants were going bankrupt*   Stein, *Plumes*, 23.

Page 132: *By the time World War I began*   Parker, "The Feather Merchants."

Page 132: *Some blamed Henry Ford*   Ibid.

Page 132: *But what really seems to have happened*   Hanson, *Feathers*, 190.

Page 132: *In Christopher Howell's poem*   Christopher Howell, "King of the Butterflies," in *Dreamless and Possible: Poems New and Selected* (Seattle: University of Washington Press, 2010), 205.

Page 133: *Five thousand years ago, the dried skins*   Hanson, *Feathers*, 167; Frances Berdan, "Circulation of Feathers in Mesoamerica," *Nuevomundo*, January 21, 2006.

Page 133: *Wearing them invoked awe*   Boucher, *20,000 Years of Fashion*, 10.

Page 133: *Bird catchers in the Hawaiian Islands*   Heather Pringle, "The Feather Cloak of Captain Cook," *Hakai Magazine*, February 1, 2016, hakaimagazine.com/article-short/feather-cloak-captain-cook.

Page 133: *After plucking the feathers they wanted*   "'Ahu'ula of King Kamehameha I," hawaiialive.org/realms.php?sub=Wao+Lani&treasure=355&offset=0, accessed October 31, 2018.

Page 133: *It is said that Kamehameha I*   George H. Fenwick, "Opening Statement," *Royal Hawaiian Featherwork: Na Hulu Ali'i*, ed. Leah Caldeira et al. (Honolulu: University of Hawai'i Press, 2016), 11.

Page 133: *although more common birds were sometimes killed*   Pringle, "The Feather Cloak of Captain Cook."

Page 133: *Feather regalia was considered sacred*   Caldeira et al., *Royal Hawaiian Featherwork*, 46.

Page 133: *So much time and expertise were demanded*   Pringle, "The Feather Cloak of Captain Cook."

Page 134: *It has recently returned to Hawaii*   Jay Jones, "Royal Cape Made from 20,0000 Bird Feathers Returns to Hawaii after 237 Years," *LA Times*, March 25, 2016.

Page 134: *The feather cloak of King Kamehameha I*   "'Ahu'ula of King Kamehameha I."

Page 134: *yellow feathers plucked from an estimated 80,000 birds*   Hanson, *Feathers,* 204.

Page 134: *Most of the feathers for the royal capes*   "'Ahu'ula of King Kamehameha I."

Page 134: *Today, according to George H. Fenwick*   Fenwick, "Opening Statement," 13.

Page 134: *Despite the unbelievable numbers of feathers*   Ibid.

Page 135: *"The bright blue feathers come"*   Claudia Brittenham, "Did the Maya and Aztecs Take Feathers for Headdresses from Birds Other Than Quetzals?," July 5, 2015, mexicolore.co.uk/aztecs/home/did-the-maya-and-aztecs-take -feathers-for-headdresses-from-birds-other-than-quetzals-1.

Page 135: *Aztecs, Maya, and Incas kept aviaries*   Hanson, *Feathers,* 206; Barry Lopez, *Crossing Open Ground* (New York: Vintage, 1989), 194.

Page 135: *But the quetzal can't survive in captivity*   Brittenham, "Did the Maya and Aztecs Take Feathers."

Page 135: *According to the organization Birdlife International*   BirdLife International, 2008, birdlife.org/datazone/sowb/casestudy, accessed October 31, 2018.

Page 136: *feather tributes were solicited by rulers*   Berdan, "Circulation of Feathers in Mesoamerica."

Page 136: *Aztec feather workers, called* amanteca   Brittenham, "Did the Maya and Aztecs Take Feathers."

Page 136: *"hierarchal movements of goods"*   Berdan, "Circulation of Feathers in Mesoamerica."

Page 136: *"A market exchange has an equilibrium"*   Lewis Hyde, *The Gift: Creativity and the Artist in the Modern World* (New York: Vintage, 2007), 11.

Page 136: *To be considered a gift, Hyde says*   Ibid., 4.

Page 137: *"a series of interconnected relationships"*   Ibid., xx.

Page 137: *"When we see that we are actors in natural cycles"*   Ibid., 23.

Page 137: *For hundreds of years, the Aztec*   Hanson, *Feathers,* 206.

Page 137: *Archaeological evidence of scarlet macaw feathers*   Berdan, "Circulation of Feathers in Mesoamerica."

Page 137: *Partners in Flight . . . estimates the quetzal population*   BirdLife International.

Page 137: *although the quetzal is the national bird*   "What Is the National Bird of Guatemala?," *World Atlas,* 2018, www.worldatlas.com/articles/what-is-the -national-bird-of-guatemala.html, accessed November 8, 2018.

Page 137: *In Mexico, Guatemala, Honduras*   Birdlife International.

Page 138: *According to the Environmental Literacy Council*   "Mesoamerica," Environmental Literacy Council, enviroliteracy.org/ecosystems/hotspots -of-biodiversity/mesoamerica, accessed October 31, 2018.

Page 138: *"These great towns and temples"*   "Travel Narratives," Center for History and New Media, George Mason University, chnm.gmu.edu/worldhistorysources/ unpacking/travelanalysis.html, accessed October 31, 2018.

Page 138: *"The image of Cortés burning the aviaries"* Lopez, *Crossing Open Ground,* 197.

Page 139: *As unheralded and mysterious as the down and feather industry is* Lily Hay Newman, "What's Good for the Goose," *Slate,* October 29, 2014, https://slate .com/business/2014/10/patagonia-the-north-face-and-cruelty-free-down-indus try-standards-for-ethical-down.html.

Page 139: *In 2000, in the latest count I can find* J. Kozák, I. Gara, and T. Kawada, "Production and Welfare Aspects of Down and Feather Harvesting," *World's Poultry Science Journal* 66 (2010): 768.

Page 141: *Domesticated ducks were probably originally bred from an Asian bird* Thor Hanson, personal interview, February 12, 2016.

Page 141: *The indigenous Muscovy duck* "7 More Domestic Animals and Their Wild Ancestors," *Encyclopedia Britannica,* britannica.com/list/7-more-domestic-animals -and-their-wild-ancestors, accessed October 31, 2018.

Page 141: *Geese are believed to be one of the very first birds* Kozák, Gara, and Kawada, "Production and Welfare Aspects of Down and Feather Harvesting," 770.

Page 141: *The greylag goose* (Anser anser) Roger Buckland and Gerard Guy, eds., "Feather and Down Production," in *Goose Production,* FAO Animal Production and Health Paper No. 154 (Rome: Food and Agriculture Organization of the United Nations, 2002), www.fao.org/docrep/005/Y4359E/y4359e0c.htm#bm12, accessed October 31, 2018.

Page 141: *China produces 80 to 85 percent* "Bright Future for China's Feather and Down Industry," *Poultry News,* December 14, 2009, thepoultrysite.com.

Page 143: *In Scandinavia, raiding the nests* Jon Sveinsson, "Real Eiderdown," eiderdown.com/files/eider_article.pdf, accessed October 31, 2018.

Page 143: *"An experienced collector"* Ibid.

Page 144: *In some places today, such as Iceland* Audubon Society, "Common Eider," Audubon Guide to North American Birds, audubon.org/field-guide/bird/common -eider, accessed October 31, 2018.

Page 144: *One standard-size pillow* Down Heaven, "Eiderdown Pillow," downheaven .com/eiderdown-pillows-detail.aspx, accessed October 31, 2018.

Page 145: *When killed for meat, only about 55 percent* Kozák, Gara, and Kawada, "Production and Welfare Aspects of Down and Feather Harvesting," 768.

Page 145: *I had read in Hanson's book* Hanson, *Feathers,* 98.

Page 146: *In most slaughterhouses, geese are killed* Buckland and Guy, "Feather and Down Production."

Page 146: *"Live-plucking is only"* Adriana Stuijt, "Ikea Drops Live-Plucked Chinese Down Bedding from Shops," *Digital Journal,* February 17, 2009, www.digital journal.com/article/267439.

Page 147: *Responsible Down Standard* "H&M, Eddie Bauer, The North Face, Marmot and Other Leading International Brands Commit to More Responsible

Down," *Business Wire*, October 21, 2014, www.businesswire.com/news/
home/20141021005275/en/HM-Eddie-Bauer-North-Face-Marmot-Leading.

Page 147: *In May 2016, People for the Ethical Treatment of Animals*   Charlie Lunan,
"New Down Standard Faces Fight with PETA," *SportsOneSource Media*, June 3,
2016, responsibledown.org.

Page 148: *Four Paws recently released a statement*   Ibid.

Page 148: *Made from the fatty liver of ducks*   J. Kenji López-Alt, "The Ethics of Foie
Gras: New Fire for an Old Debate," Serious Eats, seriouseats.com/2015/01/foie
-gras-new-fire-for-an-old-debate.html, accessed October 31, 2018.

Page 148: *Because of their higher fill power*   Kozák, Gara, and Kawada, "Production
and Welfare Aspects of Down and Feather Harvesting," 769.

Page 148: *During the Middle Ages, live-plucking*   Ibid.

Page 148: *In the wild, birds molt*   Buckland and Guy, "Feather and Down Production."

Page 148: *Today live-plucking is illegal*   Kozák, Gara, and Kawada, "Production and
Welfare Aspects of Down and Feather Harvesting," 767.

Page 148: *Since 1999, force-feeding*   Buckland and Guy, "Feather and Down
Production."

Page 148: *As of 2012, China has no laws prohibiting cruelty*   Christopher Peak, "A
Heavy Problem for the Feather Industry," *Good: A Magazine for the Global Citizen*,
November 3, 2014.

Page 151: *Apsáalooke does not mean "crow"*   Frank B. Linderman, *Plenty-Coups: Chief
of the Crows* (Lincoln: University of Nebraska Press, 2002), 28.

Page 151: *"We followed the buffalo herds"*   Ibid.

Page 152: *A person had to earn the right*   Ibid., 31.

Page 152: *According to Plenty Coups, the style*   Ibid., 102.

Page 152: *One man wears a bustle*   Murton McCluskey, *Your Guide to Understanding
and Enjoying Powwows*, rev. ed. (Helena: Montana Office of Public Instruction,
2009), https://opi.mt.gov/Portals/182/Page%20Files/Indian%20Education/
Indian%20Education%20101/PowWows.pdf, accessed October 31, 2018.

Page 153: *A good dancer is one who keeps*   Ibid.

Page 153: *Many of the dances are patterned*   Ibid.

Page 153: *In 1882, the US Indian Office*   Gabriella Treglia, "Using Citizenship to
Retain Identity: The Native American Dance Bans of the Later Assimilation Era,
1900–1933," *Journal of American Studies* 47 (2012): 777.

Page 153: *In 1921 and 1923, a decree was issued*   Ibid., 781.

Page 153: *The federal ban on Sun Dance participation*   "Outlawing American Indian
Religions," Native American Net Roots, February 28, 2010, nativeamericannet
roots.net/diary/380, accessed October 31, 2018.

Page 154: *As of 2007, the bald eagle*   "Migratory Bird Program: Permits," US Fish and
Wildlife Service, last modified March 9, 2017, fws.gov/migratorybirds/mbper-
mits/regulations/BGEPA.PDF.

Page 154: *US Secretary of the Interior C. B. Morton announced*   Ruth Flower, "Department of Justice Policy on Eagle Feathers," Friends Committee on National Legislation, October 25, 2012, fcnl.org/issues/nativeam/doj_eagles.

Page 154: *Still, it wasn't until October 2012*   "Justice Department Announces Policy on Tribal Member Use of Eagle Feathers," US Department of Justice, October 12, 2012, www.justice.gov/opa/pr/justice-department-announces-policy-tribal -member-use-eagle-feathers, accessed November 9, 2018.

Page 154: *"While the right to possess eagle parts"*   Ibid.

Page 155: *In 2016, a Crow man pleaded guilty*   Claire Johnson, "Pleading Guilty, Crow Agency Man Says Killing of Bald Eagle Was for 'Cultural Use,'" *Billings Gazette*, April 7, 2016.

Page 155: *In 2012, a Blackfoot woman*   Duncan McCue, "Rachel CrowSpreadingWings Fights Charges of Trafficking Eagle Feathers," *CBC News*, February 18, 2014.

Page 156: *The song is a Sun Dance song*   Albert White Hat Sr., "Wiowang Wacipi Olowan: Sun Dance Songs," *Cannupa Olowan*, n.d., 22.

Page 156: *"least in strength but strongest of mind"*   Linderman, *Plenty-Coups*, 37.

Page 156: *"It was so small," he recounted*   Ibid., 80.

Page 157: *"Eagle feathers pushed our culture forward"*   Tristan Picotte, "Opinion: Lakota Values Soar with the Eagles," *Environmental Health News*, October 1, 2014.

Page 157: *"Any fool can see that feathers are beautiful"*   Kenneth M. Kensinger, "Why Feathers?," in *The Gift of Birds: Featherwork of Native South American Peoples*, ed. Ruben E. Reina and Kenneth M. Kensinger (Philadelphia: University Museum of Archaeology and Anthropology, 1991), 42.

5. PEARLS

Page 159: *in Persia pearls were called* murwari   Steve King, "Naked Lustre," *Vanity Fair*, July 2009.

Page 159: *In China, people believed they fell from clouds*   Beatriz Chadour-Sampson with Hubert Bari, *Pearls* (London: Victoria and Albert Museum, 2013), 153.

Page 159: *Pliny the Elder... thought they were formed*   Kiyohito Nagai, "A History of the Cultured Pearl Industry," *Zoological Science* 30 (2013): 783–93, BioOne.org.

Page 159: *"tears of the moon"*   Mario Monteforte and Micheline Cariño, "Episodes of Environmental History in the Gulf of California: Fisheries, Commerce, and Aquaculture of Nacre and Pearls," in *Latin American Landscapes, Land between Waters: Environmental Histories of Modern Mexico*, ed. Christopher R. Boyer (Tucson: University of Arizona Press, 2012), 250.

Page 159: *the oldest pearl necklace was made in Persia*   King, "Naked Lustre."

Page 159: *some shell beads are 100,000 years old*   Chadour-Sampson, *Pearls*, 9.

Page 159: *Out of ten thousand wild oysters*   Ibid.

Page 159: *The first pearl beds were discovered*   American Museum of Natural History,

"Diving for Pearls," www.amnh.org/exhibitions/pearls/obtaining-pearls/diving-for-pearls, accessed October 31, 2018.

Page 160: *Gulf pearls are large and white*   Chadour-Sampson, *Pearls*, 15.

Page 160: *During the wars of the Roman Empire*   Fred Ward, "The History of Pearls," *Nova*, December 29, 1998, pbs.org/wgbh/nova/ancient/history-pearls.html.

Page 160: *Two pearls approximated the worth of 1,875,000 ounces*   Ibid.

Page 160: *special songs...called the* nahham   Chadour-Sampson, *Pearls*, 19.

Page 160: *"The diver's only equipment"*   Ibid., 20.

Page 160: *Using two ropes*   Gabi Logan, "Pearl Diving in Qatar," *USA Today*, April 17, 2017.

Page 160: *Chinese were harvesting freshwater pearls*   James L. Sweaney and John R. Latendresse, "Freshwater Pearls of North America," *Gems and Gemology* (Fall 1984): 126.

Page 161: *The Bajau, or Badjao, people*   Johnny Langenheim, "Last of the Sea Nomads," *Guardian*, September 17, 2010.

Page 161: *Japanese* ama *or "women of the sea"*   Sean O'Hagan, "Is the Tide about to Turn for Japan's 'Women of the Sea?,'" *Guardian*, December 28, 2011.

Page 161: *they are called* kaito   Tresi Nonno, "On the Etymology of Word Ama," *Cultural Anthropology and Ethnosemiotics* 1, no. 3 (2015): 19–25.

Page 161: *Descendants of seafaring nomads*   Anne McDonald and Kaori Brand, "Japan's 'Ama' Free Divers Keep Their Traditions," *Our World*, May 7, 2010, https://ourworld.unu.edu/en/japans-ama-free-divers-keep-their-traditions.

Page 161: *In 1956, there were 17,611 ama*   Michael Gakuran, "Ama—The Pearl Diving Mermaids of Japan," Gakuranman, November 5, 2013, http://gakuran.com/ama-the-pearl-diving-mermaids-of-japan/.

Page 161: *Most of the traditional* ama *are now past middle age*   O'Hagan, "Is the Tide about to Turn for Japan's 'Women of the Sea?'"

Page 162: *With sea temperatures having risen 1.68 degrees*   McDonald and Brand, "Japan's 'Ama' Free Divers Keep Their Traditions."

Page 162: *The labia-like organs of the oyster*   Millie Creighton, "Consuming Rural Japan: The Marketing of Tradition and Nostalgia in the Japanese Travel Industry," *Ethnology* 36, no. 3 (1997): 239–54.

Page 162: collars *of pearls resting directly on her throat*   American Gem Society, "About Pearls," americangemsociety.org/en/pearls, accessed October 31, 2018.

Page 163: *The famous Pearl Carpet of Baroda*   Chadour-Sampson, *Pearls*, 150.

Page 163: *In 1498, on Columbus's third voyage*   Monteforte and Cariño, "Episodes of Environmental History in the Gulf of California," 345.

Page 163: *There he encountered Guaiqueri Indians*   "Margarita Island," *Encyclopedia Britannica*, www.britannica.com/place/Margarita-Island, accessed November 9, 2018.

Page 163: *By 1525, Margarita Island became a Spanish colony*   Ibid.

Page 164: *"a landscape strewn with putrefying oysters"*   Molly A. Warsh, "Enslaved Pearl Divers in the Sixteenth Century Caribbean," *Slavery and Abolition* 31, no. 3 (2010): 356.

Page 164: *Slaves were locked in their huts*   Ibid., 347.

Page 164: *The air in divers' lungs*   Kevin Dawson, "Enslaved Swimmers and Divers in the Atlantic World," *Journal of American History* 92, no. 4 (2006): 1346.

Page 164: *They were also attacked by sharks*   Warsh, "Enslaved Pearl Divers," 349.

Page 164: *From 1513 to 1540, approximately 120 million pearls*   Ibid., 347.

Page 164: *The Indian and African slaves*   Dawson, "Enslaved Swimmers and Divers," 1350.

Page 165: *One of the world's most famous pearls*   Gem Select, "The Story of 'La Peregrina, the Wandering Pearl,'" last updated August 16, 2017, gemselect.com/other-info/la-peregrina-pearl.php.

Page 165: *Hernán Cortés landed near Veracruz*   Charles C. Mann, *1491: New Revelations of the Americas before Columbus*, 2nd ed. (New York: Vintage, 2011), 141.

Page 165: *or Triple Alliance*   Ibid., 127.

Page 165: *Tenochtitlan was bigger than Paris*   Ibid., 143.

Page 165: *"Absent smallpox"*   Ibid., 146.

Page 165: *There . . . they encountered Indians*   Monteforte and Cariño, "Episodes of Environmental History in the Gulf of California," 249.

Page 166: *When word arrived that new pearl beds*   Ibid., 356.

Page 166: *"Light filtered down through the water"*   John Steinbeck, *The Pearl* (New York: Bantam, 1974), 21.

Page 166: *The Indians of Baja*   Monteforte and Cariño, "Episodes of Environmental History in the Gulf of California," 251.

Page 166: *"eliminate overexploitation"*   Ibid., 253.

Page 166: *"so intensively that the wild stocks"*   Ibid.

Page 167: *There were far too many to be eaten*   Ibid.

Page 167: *"A description of competing boats"*   Warsh, "Enslaved Pearl Divers," 355.

Page 167: *Modernized diving equipment*   Monteforte and Cariño, "Episodes of Environmental History in the Gulf of California," 246.

Page 167: *By the early 1900s, in the Sea of Cortés*   American Museum.

Page 170: *Although they can more easily be dislodged*   American Museum of Natural History, "Diving for Pearls."

Page 170: Pinctada fucata martensii, *typically found*   "Akoya Cultured Pearls," Sustainable Pearls, 2012, sustainablepearls.org, accessed November 9, 2018.

Page 171: *These two oysters share the same waters*   "History," Perlas del Mar de Cortéz, www.perlas.com.mx/en/historia.php, accessed November 9, 2018.

Page 171: *In 1903, Gastón J. Vives*   Monteforte and Cariño, "Episodes of Environmental History in the Gulf of California," 246.

Page 172: *Within nine years the company had become*   Ibid., 259.

Page 172: *In 1914, the Mexican Revolution*   Ibid., 246.

Page 172: *In fifteen years the oysters were depleted*   Ibid., 247.

Page 172: *Black-lipped and rainbow-lipped oysters*   Ibid., 249–50.

Page 173: *Natural, uncultured pearls form*   American Museum of Natural History, "Diving for Pearls."

Page 174: *The technique was first developed*   Nagai, "A History of the Cultured Pearl Industry," 783.

Page 174: *To wit, the Chinese induced Buddha-shaped blisters*   Ibid.

Page 174: *The result was nacre-covered*   Ibid., 787.

Page 174: *Japanese businessman Kokichi Mikimoto*   Ibid., 784.

Page 174: *Mikimoto's secret method*   King, "Naked Lustre."

Page 174: *Mikimoto pearls began to appear*   Monteforte and Cariño, "Episodes of Environmental History in the Gulf of California," 250.

Page 174: *"Jewelers were aghast"*   Nagai, "A History of the Cultured Pearl Industry," 784.

Page 174: *In 1952 he patented*   Monteforte and Cariño, "Episodes of Environmental History in the Gulf of California," 247.

Page 174: *A former dentist, Otokichi Kuwabara*   Nagai, "A History of the Cultured Pearl Industry," 790.

Page 176: *McLaurin-Moreno describes traditional pearl-seeding*   "Pearl Seeding Operation and Pearl Harvest," Cortez Pearl, https://cortezpearl.mx/pages/virtual-pearl-farm-tour-seeding-operation-pearl-harvest, accessed November 9, 2018.

Page 178: *Sustainability is defined by the World Commission*   "Sustainable Development," General Assembly of the United Nations, www.un.org/en/ga/president/65/issues/sustdev.shtml, accessed November 9, 2018.

Page 178: *"The Triple Bottom Line"*   "The Triple Bottom Line," *Economist*, November 17, 2009.

Page 179: *"protection of the biosphere"*   "Five Sustainability Principles for Marine Cultured Pearls" (version 2), July 2014, Sustainable Pearls, www.sustainablepearls.org/sustainability-principles/sustainability-principles/.

Page 179: *Cartier and Saleem Ali report that one oyster*   Laurent Cartier and Saleem Ali, "Pearl Farming as a Sustainable Development Path," *Solutions* 3, no. 4 (2012): 30–34.

Page 180: *"Cultured pearl farming is one of the few"*   Saleem H. Ali and Laurent E. Cartier, "China's Pearl Industry: An Indicator of Ecological Stress," *Our World*, January 23, 2013.

Page 180: *"There is a clear link between poverty eradication"*   Ibid.

Page 180: *"The most effective forms of conservation"*   Cartier and Ali, "Pearl Farming as a Sustainable Development Path."

Page 181: *"Pearl farming is an extremely tough job"*   Andy Müller, "A Brief Analysis of the Global Seawater Cultured Pearl Industry: Past, Present, and Future," Hong Kong Jewelry and Gem Fair (Asia World Expo), September 12, 2013, chinata trading.com, accessed February 20, 2016.

Page 182: *Unlike oysters, mussels can be seeded*   Ali and Cartier, "China's Pearl Industry."

Page 182: *In the 1980s China became the world's biggest producer*   Ali and Cartier, "China's Pearl Industry."

Page 182: *by 2010 it was harvesting an astonishing 1,500 tonnes of them*   King, "Naked Lustre."

Page 183: *Off the coast of Guangdong*   Ibid.

Pages 183–84: *Manure and fertilizer are often added*   Ibid.

Page 185: *Chadour-Sampson notes that Pliny the Elder*   Chadour-Sampson, *Pearls*, 39.

Page 185: *Some queens had up to thirty-three necklaces*   Ibid., 98.

Page 185: *Crafted out of 139 European glass faux pearls*   Lynda Resnick, "The One True Copy of Jackie Kennedy's Pearls," One for the Table, oneforthetable.com/Stories/the-one-true-copy-of-jackie-kennedys-real-fake-pearls.html, accessed October 31, 2018.

Page 186: *"I only like fake jewelry"*   Susan Jane Jewels, "Costume Jewelry Pearls: History and How Coco Chanel Made Them Fashionable," susanjanejewels.com/costume-jewelry-pearls-history-coco-chanel, accessed October 31, 2018.

6. FUR

Page 187: *In 1996, an activist*   Alex Williams, "Fur Is Back in Fashion and Debate," *New York Times*, July 3, 2015.

Page 187: *"Fur is Toxic"*   Rosy Cherrington, "London Fashion Week: Nearly Naked Models Stage Anti-fur Protest with PETA," *Huffington Post*, February 19, 2016.

Page 187: *In a 2009 article in the* Guardian   Elizabeth Day, "Would You Rather Go Naked? Not Any Longer," *Guardian*, November 22, 2009.

Page 188: *"That's a beautiful fur. You'd look so much better without it."*   Ibid.

Page 188: *The Animal Liberation Front claimed responsibility*   Jill Gerston, "Face-Off over Fur: Animal-Rights Groups, Claiming That Furs Are a 'Sadist Symbol,' Not a Status Symbol, Have Launched a Campaign to Shame Wearers into Taking Them Off. But the $1.8 Billion Fur Industry Is Fighting Back," *Philadelphia Inquirer*, June 11, 1989, philly.com, accessed April 3, 2016.

Page 188: *But indigenous people in Canada*   Alan Herscovici, *Second Nature: The Animal-Rights Controversy* (Toronto: Stoddart, 1985), 132.

Page 189: *According to a Canadian government report*   Department of Environment and Conservation, Newfoundland Labrador, "Fur Farming," env.gov.nl.ca/env/env_assessment/projects/Y2003/1101/1101_registration_background.pdf, accessed October 31, 2018.

Page 189: *Most of the world's mink and fox*   Pierre-Henry Deshayes, "Controversial Nordic Farms Flourish on Fur Comeback," *Philly.com*, February 18, 2014.

Page 189: *By contrast, during the same year in the United States*   Fur Commission USA, "Mink Farming," furcommission.com/mink-farming-2, accessed October 31, 2018.

Page 191: *mink had already been farmed in the United States for 130 years*   Ibid.

Page 197: *Standard dimension for cages in Denmark*   "Code of Practice for the Care and Handling of Mink: Review of Scientific Research on Priority Issues," Mink Code of Practice Scientists' Committee, May 2012, National Farm Animal Care Council.

Pages 197–98: *"unknown persons" broke into a mink farm*   "Thousands of Mink Escape from Fur Farm," *Copenhagen Post*, August 2, 2011.

Page 198: *"Most of the minks that have been let out"*   Quoted ibid.

Page 200: *The mobile unit is airtight and prefilled*   "Fur Farming."

Page 204: *Kopenhagen Fur is both a brand and an auction house*   Kopenhagen Fur, kopenhagenfur.com, accessed October 31, 2018.

Page 204: *fox farms are banned in Denmark*   "Fur Bans," Fur Free Alliance, www.furfreealliance.com/fur-bans/, accessed November 9, 2018.

Page 205: *The campaign resulted in a 1983 European ban*   International Fund for Animals, "Ending Trade in Seal Products," ifaw.org/united-states/our-work/seals/ending-trade-seal-products, accessed October 31, 2018.

Page 206: *"Alaska fur seals, which numbered"*   Herscovici, *Second Nature*, 46.

Page 206: *"radar, scout planes and government icebreakers"*   Ibid., 73.

Page 206: *"It's not the same as the conservation of whales"*   Ibid., 91.

Page 206: *animal welfare—providing for an animal's physical needs*   "Animal Welfare: What Is It?," American Veterinary Medical Association, 2018, www.avma.org/KB/Resources/Reference/AnimalWelfare/Pages/what-is-animal-welfare.aspx, accessed October 31, 2018.

Page 206: *For the Inuit in both countries*   Herscovici, *Second Nature*, 70.

Page 207: *"Inuit and other hunting people study"*   Ibid., 103–4.

Page 207: *It took almost thirty years*   "Trade in Seal Products," European Commission, March 8, 2017.

Page 207: *"Our campaign against commercial sealing"*   Joanna Kerr, "Greenpeace Apologizes to Inuit for Impacts of Seal Campaign," June 25, 2014, greenpeace.org.

Page 207: *Inuit hunters in Nunavut and the Northwest Territories of Canada*   "Trade in Seal Products."

Page 207: *In the United States, however, trade in sealskins*   "Marine Mammal Protection Act," US Fish and Wildlife Service, www.fws.gov/international/laws-treaties-agreements/us-conservation-laws/marine-mammal-protection-act.html, accessed November 9, 2018.

Page 210: *Overproduction is another factor behind the drop*   Deshayes, "Controversial Nordic Farms Flourish."

Page 210: *Some people point to the changing identities*   Carol Dyhouse, "Skin Deep: The Fall of Fur," *History Today* 61, no. 11 (2011).

Page 210: *In 2011, Oslo banned*   Tracy McVeigh, "Animal Rights Campaigners Protest as Fur Comes Back into Fashion," *Guardian*, March 1, 2014.

Page 210: *different from the years between 1985 and 1990*   Dyhouse, "Skin Deep."

Page 210: *In 2015, the design house Fendi*   Williams, "Fur Is Back in Fashion and Debate."

Page 210: *"It's a tug of war"*   Ibid.

Page 218: *Armani decided to drop all use of fur*   Fur Free Alliance, "Luxury Brand Armani Goes Fur Free," March 22, 2016, furfreealliance.com.

Page 218: *Hugo Boss . . . , Tommy Hilfiger, Guess*   "Fur Free Retailer," Fur Free Retailer, 2018, https://furfreeretailer.com, accessed November 9, 2018.

Page 219: *Montreal used to be called*   Morgan Lowrie, "Montreal Furriers Still Practicing Trade amid Changing Times," *Canadian Press*, March 4, 2016.

Page 219: *Sixty years is the average lifespan*   Ibid.

Page 220: *Fox—blue, silver, red, gray*   "Trapping Regulations," International Fur Trade Association, wearefur.com, accessed October 31, 2018.

Page 220: *Although only about 15 to 20 percent of fur*   Ibid.

Page 221: *opportunistic Europeans were drawn here*   Eric Jay Dolin, *Fur, Fortune, and Empire: The Epic History of the Fur Trade in America* (New York: W. W. Norton, 2010), 22.

Page 221: *A snare eventually strangles an animal*   "Trapping."

Page 221: *Wildlife managers claim*   "AFWA Final Trapping Report," Associated Fish and Wildlife Agencies, 2005, fishwildlife.org, accessed April 30, 2016.

Page 221: *"All animal populations produce"*   Herscovici, *Second Nature*, 124.

Page 222: *Antifur organizations say . . . that killing coyotes*   Footloose Montana, footloosemontana.org, accessed October 31, 2018.

Page 222: *Greg Linscombe, a research biologist*   Quoted in Gerston, "Face-Off over Fur."

Page 222: *The International Fur Federation*   International Fur Federation, wearefur .com, accessed October 31, 2018.

Page 222: *The fur industry in the United States*   "2016 Summary of Furbearer Trapping Regulations in the United States," Associated Fish and Wildlife Agencies, www.fishwildlife.org/download_file/view/738/1213, accessed November 10, 2018.

Page 222: *According to a 2016 survey*   Ibid.

Page 223: *Footloose Montana, a nonprofit*   "MT Trapping Regulations," Footloose Montana, www.footloosemontana.org/trapping-season-2011-12/mt-trapping -regulations/, accessed November 10, 2018.

Page 223: *In a recent editorial, Zack Strong*   Zack Strong, "Time for Daily Trap Checks to Be the Rule in Montana" (editorial), *Independent Record*, June 7, 2016.

Page 223: *In Idaho, a 2011–12 survey*   Peter Backus, "Montana, Idaho Trappers Catching More Than Just Wolves," Ravalli Republic, March 3, 2013, https://raval lirepublic.com/news/local/article_c32b206e-8384-11e2-9dbf-0014a4bcf887a.html, accessed November 10, 2018.

Page 223: *In 1925, the same year the National Anti-Steel Trap League*   Tom Reed, "Is Trapping Doomed?," *High Country News*, April 12, 1999.

Page 223: *In 1958, the Conibear trap was invented*   Ibid.

Page 223: *The Association for the Protection of Fur-Bearing Animals*   Association for the Protection of Fur-Bearing Animals, "Trapping and Wildlife," thefurbearers .com/trapping-and-wildlife, accessed October 31, 2018.

Page 224: *"Just like the slave traders"*   Gerston, "Face-Off over Fur."

Page 224: *"To tell people to buy synthetics"*   Herscovici, *Second Nature*, 140–41.

Page 224: *In the United States, there are approximately 250,000 registered trappers*   Reed, "Is Trapping Doomed?"

Page 224: *In Canada, roughly 25,000*   Fur Institute of Canada, "Canada's Fur Trade: Fact & Figures," fur.ca/fur-trade/canadas-fur-trade-fact-figures, accessed October 31, 2018.

Page 224: *According to an article by Tom Reed*   Reed, "Is Trapping Doomed."

Page 224: *Although animals like bobcats can bring in more than a thousand dollars*   Toby Walrath, "The Fur Trade: The Journey from Trap to Market," *Outdoor Life*, February 2016.

Page 224: *Coyote pelts—which sell for about fifteen dollars in a good year*   Walrath, "The Fur Trade."

Page 225: *The industry says that, whether wild or farmed*   Fur Council of Canada, "Fur Is Green," furisgreen.com, accessed October 31, 2018.

Page 225: *Eighty percent of synthetics are nonbiodegradable*   Ibid.

Page 225: *Microfiber pollution, found in all five major ocean gyres*   Mary Catherine O'Connor, "Inside the Lonely Fight against the Biggest Environmental Problem You've Ever Heard Of," *Guardian*, October 27, 2014.

Page 225: *"trapping regulations are weak"*   Association for the Protection of Fur-Bearing Animals, "What Is Wrong with Trapping," thefurbearers.com, accessed October 31, 2018.

Page 226: *annual, statutory veterinary visits and a set of strict animal welfare rules*   Kopenhagen Fur, "Animal Welfare in Danish Mink Farming," kopen hagenfur.com/responsibility/animal-welfare, accessed October 31, 2018.

Page 226: *In 2010, President Barack Obama signed*   Williams, "Fur Is Back in Fashion and Debate."

Page 226: *"Animals are not ours"*   People for the Ethical Treatment of Animals, "Issues," www.peta.org/issues, accessed October 31, 2018.

Page 227: *"[They confront] the fundamental existential problem"*   Herscovici, *Second Nature*, 60.

Page 227: *"In religious terms, overharvest is considered"*   Ibid., 63.

CONCLUSION

Page 229: *"most arguments about animal ethics or animal rights"*   Clare Palmer, "The Moral Relevance of the Distinction between Domesticated and Wild Animals," in *The Oxford Handbook of Animal Ethics*, ed. Tom L. Beauchamp and R. G. Frey (Oxford: Oxford University Press, 2011), 704.

Page 229: *"The question is not"*   Jeremy Bentham quoted in Tom Regan, *Defending Animal Rights* (Urbana: University of Illinois Press, 2001), 14.

Page 229: *"worms, honeybees, lobsters"*   R. G. Frey, "Utilitarianism and Animals," in Beauchamp and Frey, *The Oxford Handbook of Animal Ethics*, 175.

Page 229: *"connectivity patterns also found in the human brain"*   Carl Savina, *Beyond Words: What Animals Think and Feel* (New York: Henry Holt, 2015), 32.

Page 229: Speciesism, *a term Singer popularized*   Regan, *Defending Animal Rights*, 15.

Page 230: *Animals were never, he said, to be treated*   Ibid., 43.

Page 230: *Regan is an "abolitionist"*   Ibid., 45.

Page 230: *Tom L. Beauchamp, in "Rights Theory and Animal Rights"*   Tom L. Beauchamp, "Rights Theory and Animal Rights," in Beauchamp and Frey, *The Oxford Handbook of Animal Ethics*, 215.

Page 230: *Beauchamp suggests, we add, for any wild animal*   Ibid.

Page 231: *"among the fastest-growing progressive causes in America"*   Regan, *Defending Animal Rights*, 40.

Page 231: *Some have passed laws mandating adequate space*   Beauchamp, "Rights Theory and Animal Rights," 217.

Page 231: *In Sweden, for instance*   Ibid.

Page 231: *over fifty thousand American animals a year*   Rachel Bale, "Trapping Bobcats for Fur in the U.S. Is Going Strong—and It's Grisly," *National Geographic*, January 15, 2016.

Page 231: *In 2010, 85 percent of textiles*   Kate Fletcher, *Sustainable Fashion and Textiles: Design Journeys* (London: Routledge, 2014), 8.

Page 232: *The World Wildlife Fund estimates*   World Wildlife Fund, "Cotton: Overview," worldwildlife.org/industries/cotton, accessed October 31, 2018.

Page 232: *Synthetics come in two forms*   Fletcher, *Sustainable Fashion and Textiles*, 12.

Page 232: *Although the source materials are carbon neutral*   Ibid., 19.

Page 232: *Polyester has now surpassed cotton*   Ibid., 14.

Page 232: *"The agents used in the manufacture of polyester"*   Ibid., 16.

Page 232: *Fletcher states that nitrous oxide*   Ibid., 18.

Page 233: *Americans annually discard approximately 9.3 million*   Ibid., 116.

Page 233: *Machine washing and tumble drying*   Mattias Wallander, "T-shirt Blues: The Environmental Impact of a T-Shirt," *Huffington Post*, September 2, 2102.

Page 233: *Dryers consume five times more energy*   Ibid.

Page 233: *Laundering a polyester blouse*   Fletcher, *Sustainable Fashion and Textiles*, 92.

Page 233: *"We have allowed an entire industry"*   Becky Weed, "What Kind of Place Is Thirteen Mile Farm and Who Runs It?," Thirteen Mile Farm, 2013, lambandwool.com.

Page 233: *The clothing industry has one of the longest*   Fletcher, *Sustainable Fashion and Textiles*, 51.

Page 234: *"Eat food. Not too much."*   Quoted in "How to Eat: Diet Secrets from Michael Pollan (and Your Great-Grandma)," *Houston Chronicle*, January 23, 2010, michaelpollan.com/reviews/how-to-eat, accessed October 31, 2018.

Page 234: *"No industry has better perfected"*   Fletcher, *Sustainable*, 140.

Page 234: *In 2007, due to the availability of cheap clothing*   Kate Fletcher, "Slow Fashion," *Ecologist*, March–April 2015.

Page 235: *The Slow Fashion movement has created a pledge*   "Slowfashioned," Creative Commons, 2016, slowfashioned.com, accessed August 28, 2016.

Page 235: *Many brands, like Puma*   Fletcher, *Sustainable Fashion and Textiles*, 24.

Page 235: *Dana Thomas, in an article for the* New York Times   Dana Thomas, "Luxury Brands Focusing on a Sustainable Future," *New York Times*, December 2, 2015.

Page 235: *Theodore Brasser, in* Native American Clothing   Theodore Brasser, *Native American Clothing: An Illustrated History* (Buffalo: Firefly Books, 2009), 88.

Acknowledgments

My gratitude and respect goes to Barbara Ras, who first proposed the marvelous concept behind *Putting on the Dog*. Thank you, Barbara, for your astute editor's eye and your confidence in me.

Thank you to the Kendeda Fund for its generous support during the writing of this book.

Acknowledgment also goes to Mara Naselli, whose reading of the manuscript helped me step back from the project and see it in a broader light; to Sheila Black, who provided critical inspiration and guidance at the very beginning of this journey; to Christi Stanforth, whose brilliant copyediting was a lesson and a gift; and to the hardworking staff at Trinity University Press for making it all happen.

I would know nothing if it weren't for those who so generously shared their expertise and love of animals and materials with me:

All those in the Yup'ik village of Kusigluk and the town of Bethel who shared with me their homes, their salmon, their *akutag*, their beautiful clothing, and their histories: Charlie Issac, Anna Barbara Charles, Wassillie Berlin, Vivian Beaver, Bertha Hoover, Bertha Brink, Sam Twitchell, Olga Kinegak, Lucy Crow, and Cauline Ferguson.

Gary Thomas of High Plains Sheepskin, Colin Wheeler of the Nugget

Company, and Brent Richman, owner of Milligan Canyon Meats, who taught me about contemporary methods of tanning.

Anne Perkins and Marie Suthers, faculty in the Anthrozoology Department at Carroll College, Helena, Montana, for helping me to understand the scope of the human-animal bond.

The hardworking research librarians at Carroll, who met my questions and odd requests with seriousness and humor—Heather Navratil, Christian Frazza, Karla Hokit, and Terence Kratz.

The shepherds and sheep people of Montana: Karen Davidson, Stephanie Sater, Kammy Johnson, Cathy Campbell, Cindy Kittredge, Becky Weed, John F. Baucus, Jeanne Decoster, and Roberto Enrique Ninahuanca Tocas.

Thor Hanson for his extremely helpful book *Feathers: The Evolution of a Natural Wonder*, and for his invaluable correspondence.

Mike Jetty and M. L. Smoker at the Indian Education for All offices of Montana's Office of Public Instruction for keeping me honest and for sharing their knowledge and humor.

Daniel Uretsky and Matthew Betcher of Allied Feather & Down of Los Angeles for discussing with me all things feathered.

Douglas McLaurin-Moreno at Perlas del Mar de Cortéz for his openness, humor, and invaluable perspective, and for giving so much of his time.

Søren Jessing Jespersen and Nina Brønden Jakobsen of Kopenhagen Fur for taking a chance on me. Both of you are informed, fair-minded, and delightful.

The Kvist Jensens of Hvide Sande—Hanne, Anders, Jesper, and Jakob—for their trust, their hard-earned knowledge of mink, and their wine and fish dinners, and for opening their lovely home on the North Sea to me.

Members of the Silk Tour and its codirectors, Glennis Dolce and Takada Hirata, and Fumiko Satoh, Shaku Yuho, the Tatehiko Yamazaki family, Yaeko Asami, Eriko Okamato, Wataru and Nobue (Azuma)

Hiraishi, and Yae Inoue—artists all. I could not imagine a more generous and richer introduction to Japan.

Thank you. Quyana. Arigatou gozaimasu. Gracias. Tak. Ahó.

I am forever grateful to Rusty Morrison, Bryher Herak, and Robert Baker, my first readers, who provided magical ladders when I was buried deep in information and whose vision and intelligence are extraordinary.

Thank you to all my friends for their patience when I neglected them or when they heard more than I'm sure they wanted to about sheep and oysters.

And to my adventurous, brave, and transcendent traveling companions, Lorna Milne, Nancy Daniels, Jo Smith, and Bryher, my gratitude and love.

Index

abalone, 162. *See also* mollusks
abattoir. *See* slaughterhouses
"abolitionists," 230, 231
Abram, David, 5
Africa, 128–29
    ostriches in, 127–29, 131–32
    prehistoric, 2–5, 54, 57
    sheep in, 54, 60, 204
    silkworms in, 115
African Karakul, 204
African slaves, 164–66, 185. *See also* slavery
Agreement on International Humane
    Trapping Standards, 222
Ahimsa silk, 96
aigrettes, 130
Akoya pearls, 170, 174, 182
Akula, Alaska, 16–18
Alaska, 9, 10, 13–15, 19, 222
Alaska fur seals, 205
Alaska Natives, 10, 15, 52, 53. *See also*
    "Eskimos"; Inupiaq; Yupiit/Yup'ik people
    ethnic terminology, 10
Ali, Saleem, 179, 180
Allied Feather & Down, 139–42, 146–47, 150
alpaca, 52
alum, 32, 105
aluminum, 32, 43
ama (Japanese divers), 161–62
Amami Oshima, 103, 106
Amazonian rainforest, 45–47
American Humane Association, 223
American Indian Religious Freedoms Act,
    154
Anchorage, Alaska, 13–14

Andersen, Hans Christian, 189, 191
Andersen, Thomas, 218–19
anesthetization of animals before slaughter,
    45, 146
angora (material), 51
Angora goat, 51
Angora rabbits, 51–52
Anima (Danish animal rights organization),
    202, 213, 215
animal cruelty, 45, 146, 148, 149, 213. *See also*
    animal welfare; live-plucking
    in trapping, 196, 223, 225. *See also* trapping
animal ethics, 41, 46–47, 96, 202, 227–30,
    233, 234. *See also* animal rights; animal
    welfare; animals and humans
Animal Liberation (Singer), 229
animal rights, 196, 227, 229–31. *See also*
    animal ethics
    vs. animal welfare, 206, 226
    industrial manufacturing and, 234
animal rights arguments, 229–30
animal rights organizations, 147–48, 188,
    202, 213, 215, 221, 225, 226, 231
    fraud, 146, 147, 213
    videos, 147, 189, 205, 213, 225–26
animal rights photos, 146, 199, 205
animal welfare, 45, 149–50, 204, 217,
    225, 226. *See also* animal ethics; traps,
    "humane"
    vs. animal rights, 206, 226
    Canada and, 188, 206, 222, 223, 225, 227
    farmers' interest in, 212
    industrial manufacturing and, 234
    meaning of, 206

mink farms and, 197–200, 213, 227. *See also under* animal welfare activists
animal welfare activists, 187
  fur farms and, 213, 221, 224, 225
  gender, 73, 187
  mink farms targeted by, 188–90, 197–98, 210, 213
  trapping and, 187, 225
  violence and vandalism, 188–90, 197–98, 213, 214
animal welfare practices in China, 146, 211–13
animal welfare protests, 187, 210
animal welfare regulations, 147, 189, 204, 205, 210, 223, 231. *See also* Responsible Down Standard
  in China, 148, 212
  in Denmark, 193, 197, 204, 212, 226
animals and humans, relationship between, 55. *See also* mutualism
  humans as animals, 55
  killing animals, 23–25, 41, 96, 146, 188, 196, 221, 226, 227. *See also* birds: killing; mink: killing; predators: killing; slaughterhouses; trapping
  respect toward animals, 6
anthrozoology, 55
antibiotics, raising sheep without, 68, 78
antitrapping organizations, 223
Apsáalooke/Crow Nation, 150–52, 155, 157
Arafune Cold Storage, 113
artisans, 136. *See also* craftspeople
  in Japan, 92, 98, 99, 101, 106, 107, 117
ash, burning, 109–10
auction houses, 190, 203–4, 207–9, 211, 217. *See also* Kopenhagen Fur
auctions, 165, 185
  China, the Chinese, and, 208, 209, 211
  Kopenhagen Fur, 188, 190, 194, 201, 203–5, 207–9, 212
  mink skins sold at, 195, 201, 208, 209
  minks sold at, 195, 208, 212
  Nina Brønden Jakobsen and, 203, 205, 208–9, 211, 212
  pelts sold at, 195
  seal products sold at, 205, 207
  wool sold at, 75
Australia, 70, 79, 170, 171, 179, 180
Aztec Empire, Spanish conquest of, 138, 165, 166
Aztecs, 135–38

Bacochibampo Bay, 169, 173, 180, 181
Badjao, 161
Baja California Pearl and Shell Breeding Company (CCCP), 171–72

Bajau, 161
bald eagle, 154, 155
Bangladeshi tanneries, 37, 38, 57
Barbary ostriches, 128
barbicels (feathers), 124
barbs (feathers), 124
Barnes, Matt, 72
Baucus, John F., 73, 76
Baucus, Max, 73, 76
beads
  bone, 4, 6
  shell, 159, 174–76
  tusk, 14
beamhouse, 42. *See also* slaughterhouses
bearded seals, 17–18, 23
bears, 5, 70, 75, 221, 223
Beauchamp, Tom L., 230
beauty, 23, 107, 234
Beaver, Vivian, 20, 21
beaver populations, 29, 221
beaver trade, 220–21
beavers, 16, 28–29
  coats, 28
  destruction caused by, 222
  fur trade and, 221
  trapping, 29, 220
Bentham, Jeremy, 229
Berdan, Frances, 135–36
Berger, John, 77
Beringia, 10
Berlin, Wassillie, 19–21
Betcher, Matthew, 142–43, 145–50
Bethel, Alaska, 13, 14
biomimicry, 129
bird feathers. *See* feathers
birds, 123. *See also specific species*
  breeding, 129–30, 135
  colors, 123, 130
  domesticated, 141, 148
  killing, 130, 131, 133, 139, 142, 145, 146, 154, 155
black-lipped oyster (*Pinctada mazatlanica*), 170, 171
bladders, seal, 23, 25
bleaching pearls, 179, 185
blister pearls/mabe pearls, 176, 177
bobcats, 31–32, 223, 224, 231
Bombyx mori (domestic silkmoth), 86, 88, 89, 96–97, 115. *See also* moths
bone beads, 4, 6
Boucher, François, 122
bovine hides, 40, 46. *See also* cowhide
"Boy Who Lived with the Seals, The" (Yup'ik story), 23–26
boycotts, 38, 116
Brand, Kaori, 162

Brasser, Theodore, 235
Brink, Bertha, 22
British Empire, 59–60, 114
Brittenham, Claudia, 135
Buddhism, 96–97, 107
Budiansky, Stephen, 70
butterflies, 132

cages, 220
    mink, 193, 197–200, 213, 227
    oyster, 169, 172, 173
    regulations on, 197
    size, 149, 173, 197
calamus (feathers), 124
calfskin, 30
California, Gulf of. *See* Sea of Cortés
Campbell, Cathy, 69–70, 73, 78
Canada, 189, 206, 207, 219
    animal welfare activism and, 188, 206, 222,
        223, 225, 227
    indigenous people in, 22, 153, 188, 206,
        207, 224
    trapping, trappers, and, 188, 189, 220,
        222–25
Canadian Cree, 227
carding wool, 66–68
Caribbean, 163–65, 167
caribou, 11, 12, 22, 29
Cariño, Micheline, 165–66
Cartier, Laurent E., 179, 180
cashmere, 50–52
    economics, 71, 79
    etymology of the term, 51
    growing of, 71, 79
    Mongolia and, 50, 71, 79
    overview and nature of, 50–51
    produced in China, 71, 79–80
cashmere market, 79–80
cashmere sweaters, 50–51, 79
caterpillars, 93, 116, 120. *See also* silkworms
cattle, 41–48, 78. *See also* cowhide
Chadour-Sampson, Beatriz, 160, 185
Charles, Anna Barbara, 18
chickadee, 156
child labor, 36, 37
China, 86–89, 94, 100. *See also under* Japan
    animal welfare practices, 146–49, 211–13
    animal welfare regulations, 148, 212
    cashmere produced in, 71, 79–80
    clothing manufacture moved to, 89
    colors and, 101. *See also* dyeing
    decline in demand for raw silk, 119
    desire to spread silk production, 87–88
    down production, 141
    down supply chain in, 126
    duck meat consumption, 126, 141

ducks in, 126, 141, 145, 149
economy, 38, 79, 86, 195, 208, 210
feather production, 141
folklore and legends about, 86
fur and, 203, 208, 214, 216, 219
geese in, 126, 141–42, 146, 148–49
goats in, 71, 80
Japan and, 87–89, 91, 116
leather industry, 36, 38, 79
mink farms, 212
mink products sold to, 195, 203
pearls in, 159, 160, 168, 174, 178, 180–83,
    185
regulations, 79
sericulture, 114, 115
sheep in, 79, 80
silk exports, 87–89, 91, 120, 121
silk weavers and, 117
silk work, 112
silkworm growers, 121
sweaters manufactured in, 79
tanneries, 34, 36
wild landscape transformed into
    profit-making machine, 79–80
women in, 112, 119, 121
wool and, 71, 79
chinchilla, 204, 218–20
Chinese, 203, 209
    auctions and, 208, 209, 211
Chinese Americans, 14
Chinese goose, 141. *See also* geese: in China
chrome-tanned leather, 35–38
chromium sulfates, 32, 36, 37
chromium waste and contamination, 37, 38.
    See also chromium sulfates
climate change, 177–78, 235
cloth (and cloth making), 98–108
    Chinese, 113
    dyeing, 98, 102, 103, 106, 111, 120
clothe, defined, 1
clothes washing. *See* laundering
clothing, 236. *See also specific topics*
    vs. costume, 122
    functions, 4–5
    in historical context, 1
clothing designers. *See* fashion designers
clothing manufacture, history of, 2–4
coats (animal), 199. *See also* undercoats
    clothing made from, 51
    goat, 50, 51
    sheep, 55, 59, 61–63, 78
coats (clothing), 9, 11, 12, 55, 149, 219, 220.
    See also jackets
    animal welfare activists and, 188
cocoons, 89, 114–17
    archaeological excavation of, 97

in China, 86–87
Hiraishis and, 93–98
in Japan, 89, 93–99, 111–13, 116, 119, 120
spinning, 93–95
Columbus, Christopher, 60, 163
combing, 66–68
commensalism, 57
conditioning, 39. *See also* finishing
Conibear/body-gripping traps, 221, 223
conservation, 72, 179–80, 206
of pearl farms, 179–80
of species, 52, 137, 167, 206
conservation areas for birds, 193
conservation organizations, 72, 137
contour feathers, 124
Cook, James, 133–34
corium, 29–30
corrected grain (finishing), 39
Cortés, Hernán, 60, 138, 165, 166
Cortés pearl, 178, 182–83
costume *vs.* clothing, 122
cotton
contrasted with down, 146
contrasted with silk, 121
contrasted with wool, 53, 68
dyes and, 232, 233
environmental impact, 121, 146, 231–33
organic, 234, 235. *See also* pesticides
water resources used in growing, 121, 146, 231–32
cotton clothes, washing, 233
cotton textiles, 231–32
courtship display (birds), 129–30
cowhide, 30–32, 34, 40–42, 46–48. *See also* cattle
coyote pelts, 220, 224
coyotes
killing, 71–72, 221
population, 71–72, 221–22
predation, 69–72, 221–22
shepherds and, 71, 73
trappers, trapping, and, 220, 222, 224
crafts, 104, 107. *See also* mingei
craftspeople, 87, 103, 107. *See also* artisans
Crete, 59
Crow, Lucy, 15
Crow Fair, 150, 152, 154, 158
Crow Nation (Apsáalooke), 150–52, 155, 157
CrowSpreadingWings, Rachel, 155
"cultural uses" of eagles, 155. *See also under* Native Americans
cultured pearl farms, 168, 177, 180
cultured pearls, 170, 173–78, 181, 182
freshwater, 178, 182, 185
culturing pearls, 180–82. *See also* pearl farming

definition and nature of, 174
inventor of the procedure of, 162

Danish, 190, 193–96, 203, 214
mink and, 198, 204, 214, 227
Danish Society for the Prevention of Cruelty to Animals, 226
Darwin, Charles, 130
Day, Elizabeth, 187
death, animal. *See also under* animals and humans
Yup'ik and, 23, 25–26
deCoster, Jeanne, 60–61, 63–65
deforestation, 45–47, 137
Denmark, 189, 193, 213. *See also* Kopenhagen Fur
animal welfare regulations, 193, 197, 204, 212, 226
economy, 191, 209
farms, 188, 227
mink farms, 192–93, 201, 225–26
mink in, 191, 195
mink production, 189, 195
mink skins, 203, 204, 208
dermis, 29–30
desertification, 79, 80
designers. *See* fashion designers
developmental psychology of animals, 57–58
Dewar, Victoria, 22
Díaz del Castillo, Bernal, 138
dingoes, 70, 71
diving, underwater. *See* pearl divers
Dōgen, 97
dogs
livestock guardian, 69–70
as predators of sheep, 70
Dolce, Glennis, 91, 92, 96, 97, 102, 106, 119
domesticated animals, 56, 127, 141, 148, 197. *See also* dogs
cattle, 41–42, 46. *See also* cattle
ostriches, 127
reintroduced into the wild, 55
sheep, 46, 53, 54, 58, 60. *See also* sheep
silkworms, 93. *See also* silkworms
traits/qualities that humans prefer in, 58
domestication of animals, 49–60, 81, 82, 86
animals participating in their own domestication, 57–58
Anne Perkins and, 55–58
defined, 56
as a form of mutualism, 57, 58, 70
Neolithic revolution and, 56–57
neotony and, 57–58
women and, 53, 60
and wool, 56

dorozome. See mud-dyeing
down. *See also* traceable down
  Allied Feather & Down, 139–42, 146–47,
    150
  in China, 126, 141
  from ducks, 141–43, 146
  environmental impact, 146
  goose, 125, 141–46, 149
  Hungary and, 141–43, 145
  Responsible Down Standard (RDS), 147,
    149, 150
down feathers, 124. *See also* feathers
down insulation, 124, 125, 141, 143–45
down jackets, 126, 139, 142, 145
duck feathers, 11, 126, 141, 143
duck meat and ducks raised for human
  consumption, 141, 142, 145, 148, 149
ducks
  in China, 126, 141, 145, 149
  cruelty to, 146, 148, 149
  down from, 141–43, 146
  species and breeds, 141, 143
dyed cowhide, 30
dyeing, 100–101, 104, 106, 110. *See also*
  finishing; indigo dyeing
  cloth, 98, 103, 106, 111, 120. *See also*
    kusakizome
  in Japan, 109, 110, 116
  leather, 29–32, 34–37, 39–41
  mud-dyeing, 103, 106
  sheep, 34
  silk, 88, 91, 95, 97, 98, 100–106, 109–11,
    116, 121
  wool, 51, 53, 59, 64–67, 79
  work of, 111, 116
  Yamazakis and, 102–6
dyeing rooms, 67, 104, 105
dyes, 183
  colors, 29–32, 34, 40, 51, 59, 95, 110–11,
    123, 183, 203, 205, 215, 218. *See also*
    indigo dyeing
  cotton and, 232, 233
  environmental impact, 79, 183
  names of, 102–3
  natural, 39, 41, 64, 67, 85, 101–6, 109, 235
  synthetic chemical, 36, 64, 79, 103
  used in synthetic clothing, 233

eagles, 154–58
earrings
  ivory, 14, 19, 122
  pearl, 160
ecologists, 56, 82, 178, 233
ecology, 137, 178, 233–36. *See also specific*
  topics
  sheep, 69–81

ecosystems, sustainability of, 178. *See also*
  sustainability
Edo period, 95, 99
eggs, 127, 148
  silkworm, 87, 88, 93–97, 113, 115
egrets, 130, 131
Egypt and Egyptians, 32, 51, 160
eider (*Somateria mollissima*), 143, 144
eiderdown, 143–45
Elemental Affects, 61
environmental impact, 121, 146, 235. *See also*
  conservation; deforestation; filtering;
  overfishing; sustainability; water
  pollution; wool products
  of cotton, 121, 146, 231–33
  of dyes and dyeing, 79, 183
  of mink farms, 225
  of synthetics, 145–46, 217, 225, 231–33
  of tanneries, 37, 38. *See also* chromium
    waste and contamination
environmental regulations, 79
"Eskimos," 10, 17, 18, 20, 22, 25. *See also*
  Alaska Natives; Inuit
ethics. *See also* animal ethics
  in fashion industry, 46–47
Eugénie de Montijo (Empress Eugenie),
  127–28
evolutionary history of humans, 1–2

fabric. *See* textile materials
Fackler, Martin, 103
fake fur, 217
fake pearls, 174, 181–82, 185–86
fashion, 122, 195, 202, 217. *See also specific*
  topics
  slow *vs.* fast, 234–35
fashion designers, 46–47, 212, 215, 216, 218,
  219, 234
fashion industry, 46–47, 216–19, 234
fashion shows, 85, 121, 210
Fashion Week, 187, 203, 210
feather market, American, 130–31
featherpillows, 138–39. *See also* pillows
feathers. *See also* plumes
  antiplumage bills designed to stop trade
    in, 131
  biomimicry and human attraction to,
    129
  colors, 123, 143
  compared with hair, 123–24
  dyeing, 123, 126, 128
  eagle, 154–58
  evolutionary functions, 124–25. *See also*
    Feathers
  killing birds for. *See* birds: killing
  Native Americans and, 154–57

nature of, 123–26
ostrich, 127–29, 131
and shelter, 138–50, 157
shape and anatomy, 124
spirituality and, 150–58
status and, 132–38, 157
as symbol, 122–27, 157
terminology, 124, 129
types of, 124
washing, 126
ways they gain their colors, 123
women and, 127–29, 131, 132
Feathers: The Evolution of a Natural Miracle
(Hanson), 123–26, 145
Fenwick, George H., 134
Ferguson, Cauline, 14–15
fermentation, 98, 103, 110
fertilizer, 68, 183–84, 201
Fienup-Riordan, Ann, 13, 23–25
filature factories, 91, 112, 121
fill power, 144, 145, 148, 149
filoplumes (feathers), 124
filtering
    environmental toxins and, 38, 146
    oysters, 137, 179–80
finishing, leather, 34, 35, 39–40. *See also*
    dyeing
    steps in the process of, 39
    terminology, 39
fishing, 180, 205. *See also* overfishing
    regulations on and prohibitions against,
        172, 180, 193. *See also* seal bans
flaying, 42. *See also* skinning: live
fleece, 27, 52, 62–66, 146
flight feathers, 124
foie gras, 148
Footloose Montana, 222–23
force-feeding, 148
Forest Code of 1965, 45–46
Four Paws, 147–48
fox farms, 204
foxes, 204
Fuji-san, 108–9
full grain (finishing), 39
Fumio, Hoshinaga, 102
fur, 225. *See also specific topics*
    banned, 210
    China and, 203, 208, 214, 216, 219
    designers that have pledged to stop using,
        218
    fake, 217
    as luxury material, 188, 215, 216, 237
    PETA and, 202, 210, 215
    produced at family-owned farms, 189
    in Russia, 189, 211, 214, 220
    worn so that the animals can be seen, 8

fur clothing, 214–19. *See also* coats; jackets;
    specific topics
    ways of producing, 189
    women and, 8, 12, 187, 202, 210, 211
fur controversy, 187–88
fur farms, 189–202. *See also* mink farms
    animal rights activists and, 213, 221, 224,
        225
    banned, 189, 204
    fox, 204
fur market, 203–14
fur seals, 205
furbearing animals, 189, 220, 221. *See also*
    specific animals; specific topics
    trapping, 221, 223–25. *See also* trapping
furriers, 215, 218–19, 224, 225

Ganges River, 37–38
gavage, 148
geese, 220
    in China, 126, 141–42, 146, 148–49
    down from, 125, 141–46, 149
    in Europe, 141–42, 146
    feathers from, 11, 126, 142, 145, 149
    history, 141
    human consumption of, 126, 141, 142, 145,
        148
    in Hungary, 141–43, 145, 146
    live-plucking, 146, 148
    slaughtering, 146
    species and breeds, 11, 141, 222
geese farms, 141–42, 148–50
geisha, 88, 118
gender roles and gender differences, 73. *See*
    also women
"gifted" *vs.* "given," 157
Gilligan, Ian, 4–5
global warming, 177–78, 235
goat hair, 50–51
goat populations, 79, 80
goats, 79–82
    cashmere and, 50–51. *See also* cashmere
    evolutionary history, 54
    humans and, 58, 81, 82
    in Mongolia, 71, 79, 80
    origins and history, 54, 57
    predators, 70, 71
    wool and, 50–51, 53, 66, 79
goatskin, 30, 32, 39
goose farms. *See* geese farms
grading fleece, 61, 63
gray wolf (*Canis lupus familiaris*), 57, 70. *See*
    also wolves
Green Carpet Challenge, 46–47
greenhouses, 67, 93
Greenland Inuit, 205–7

Greenpeace, 205–7
Grinnell, George Bird, 131
grizzly bears, 75, 223
Guatemala, 137
Guaymas, Mexico, 169–81
Gucci, 47, 195
Gunma prefecture (Japan), 89–91
"gut raincoat" (imarnitet), 12–13

hair
    animal, 50–52. See also kemp; wool; specific
        animals
    human, braided with pearls and nacre
        shells, 165–66; dyeing, 109; feathers
        worn in, 151, 157
hair dyes, human, 183
"hairdressing ceremony," 112
Hanson, Thor, 123–26, 129, 132, 145, 148
Hareven, Tamara K., 117
harp seals, 205, 206
hats, 16, 29, 127, 131, 132
Hawaii, 133–37
Hawthorne, Fran, 41
Hazaribagh, Bangladesh, 38, 46
headdresses, 135–38, 153
health hazards, 36–38, 45
Heart Butte, 157
heavy metals, 79, 140, 179, 183
Hemenway, Harriet Lawrence, 131
Herscovici, Alan, 205–7, 221, 224, 227
Hide and Skin Handbook (National Hide
    Association), 36, 41
hide cellars, 42
hide(s), 15, 16, 26, 30–31, 36, 44, 54. See also
    tanneries; tanning
    beaver, 28
    bovine, 40, 46. See also cowhide
    costs and pricing, 35
    country, 42
    drums stretched with, 151
    etymology of the term, 26
    handling, 37
    horse, 40
    occupational safety and, 37
    overview, 26–31
    portion discarded as waste, 38
    preservation, 2, 228
    sheep, 54
    softening, 228
    sold to global market, 45
    stretched. See stretching
    subcutis and, 30
    terminology, 26–27
    uses of the term, 26
    wearing, 3
Hilger Ranch, 60, 64, 65, 69, 73
Hill, Geoffrey E., 130

Himalayas, cashmere grown in, 50, 71
Hiraishi, Nobue (Azuma), 92–94, 96–98
Hiraishi, Wataru, 92–98
Hirata, Takuo (Hirata-san), 91–92, 98, 100,
    105, 106, 109, 111, 118, 120, 121
Hiroko, Matsuo, 117
Hoover, Bertha, 21–22
horsehides, 40
Horween, Skip, III, 40
Horween Leather Company, 40
hot-stuffed (finishing), 39
Howard, Catherine, 7
Howell, Christopher, 132
Humane Methods of Livestock Slaughter
    Act, 45
"humane"/quick-kill traps, 222, 223
humane slaughtering methods, 44–45, 146
Hungary, geese and down in, 141–43, 145,
    146, 148
hunter-gatherer societies, 10–11, 56
hunting, Eskimo view of, 25
Hvide Sande, Denmark, 190–93
Hyde, Lewis, 136–37

Icelandic sheep, 78
imarnitet ("gut raincoat"), 12–13
India, 87–89, 163. See also Himalayas
    cashmere market, 71, 80
    economics/finances, 36, 38, 59, 89, 121
    industrial waste and pollution, 38
    sericulture, 96, 114, 115, 121
    tanneries/leather industry, 36–38
indigenous people. See Inuit; Native
    Americans
indigenous worldviews, beliefs intrinsic to,
    23–26
indigenousness, 6
indigo
    Japanese. See Persicaria tinctoria
    synthetic, 104, 111
indigo dyeing, 39, 67, 98, 102–4
    Fumiko Satoh and, 110–11
indigo farmers, 110
Indigo Master. See Satoh, Fumiko
Indigofera tinctoria. See indigo
Industrial Revolution, 51, 54, 67
Inoue, Yae, 102
insulation, down, 124, 125, 141, 143–45
intestines, animal, 12
Inuit, 205–7. See also Alaska Natives;
    "Eskimos"
Inuit Exception to the EU ban on seal
    products, 205, 207
Inupiaq, 10–12, 22, 25–26
Isabella of Spain, 163
Issac, Charlie, 17
itajime shibori (indigo dyeing), 111

"Italian leather" (high-quality leather), 46
Italy, 234
  leather and, 34–36, 46
  silk and, 113–15
  as wool producer, 59
ivory, 6
  walrus, 6, 10, 14, 19, 23
ivory jewelry, 10, 14, 19, 122
ivory labrets, walrus, 6, 23

jackets. *See also* coats (clothing)
  down, 126, 139, 142, 145. *See also* down
  fur, 195, 217. *See also* mink jackets
Jakobsen, Nina Brønden, 203–5, 208–15,
  217–19
  on animal cruelty, 213
  auctions and, 203, 205, 208–9, 211, 212
  Lone Lyhneand and, 211–13
  mink and, 204, 208–15, 218, 219
James I, 114
Japan, 87, 91–93, 149. *See also* kimonos;
  Kyoto
  artisans, 92, 98, 99, 101, 106, 107, 117
  vs. China as preeminent exporter of silk,
    89, 91
  climate, 93
  cocoons in, 89, 93–99, 111–13, 116, 119, 120
  colors and, 101. *See also* dyeing
  down products, 146
  dyeing in, 109, 110, 116
  Edo period, 95, 99
  folktales and mythology, 90, 94
  indigo farmers, 110
  oysters and, 160–62, 167, 174, 180
  pearls and, 160–61, 168, 174. *See also* Akoya
    pearls
  ports, 91, 115
  sakoku (isolationist foreign policy), 19, 115
  seals and, 206
  sericulture, 93, 115–17, 119, 231
  silk availability, 113
  silk consumption, 120
  silk fabrics exported from China to, 87. *See*
    also China: silk exports
  silk-growing, 99
  silk industry, 89. *See also* Tomioka Silk Mill
  silk production, 87–88, 116, 120
  silkworms, 99, 113, 115–16, 231
  social order in Edo society, 101
  storage of silkworm eggs, 113
  trade with China, 91
  World War II and, 116
Japan Silk Center, 106
Japanese clothing, 97, 98
  preserving clothing as family heirlooms,
    129
Japanese fashion, 100

Japanese Folk Crafts Museum (Nihon
  Migei-kan), 108
Japanese indigo (*Persicaria tinctoria*), 110.
  See also indigo dyeing
Japanese underwater diving, 160–62
Japanese women, 99, 109, 112, 113, 117, 120,
  161, 162. *See also* women
  in industrial labor force, 112, 119
  reeling silk, 98, 99, 112–14, 119–21
Japan's "Ama" Free Divers Keep Their
  Traditions (video), 162
Japonaise au bain, La (painting), 120
Jefferson, Thomas, 82
Jespersen, Søren Jessing, 190, 214–15
Jetty, Mike, 155–57
jewelers, 174
jewelry, 159, 181, 186. *See also* earrings
  fake, 186. *See also* fake pearls
  ivory, 10, 14, 19, 122
  pearl, 169, 174, 176, 186. *See also* pearls
Jews in feather industry, 128–29
Johnson, Kammy, 53–54
jugs (mesh lambing pens), 73, 76

Kamehameha I, 133, 134
kangaroos, 71
Kanpur, India
  tanneries in, 37–38
Kashmir, 51
Kasigluk, Alaska, 16, 20–21
kayaks, 11–13
kemp, 56, 58, 59
Kennedy Onassis, Jacqueline, 185, 186
Kensinger, Kenneth, 157
keratin, 53, 123, 146
Kerr, Joanna, 207
kimono fashion shows, 85, 121
kimono shops, secondhand, 117–18
kimonos, 85–87, 100, 105, 116, 119–20
  antique, 119
  autographing, 118
  bartering, 118
  buses giving free rides to those wearing,
    121
  colors, 8, 86, 88, 101–2, 119
  cost, 102, 103, 116
  dyed, 8
  evolutionary history, 100
  Japanese women adopting Western dress
    in lieu of, 117
  in Kyoto, 88, 121
  materials used to make, 98, 120
  production, 98
  resurgence, 120–21
  silk immortalized via, 89
  in Tokyo, 116, 120
  worn for special family occasions, 120–21

King, Steve, 163, 182
Kirchner, Thomas (Shaku Yuho), 97
Kittridge, Cindy, 78, 80
knifeman (cattle slaughter), 44
kon-zome, 110
Kopenhagen Fur, 190, 195, 201, 203, 209, 213, 215, 216
  animal welfare and, 204, 213, 226
  auctions, 188, 190, 194, 201, 203–5, 207–9, 212
  finances, 209
  fur farms, 190, 212, 214
  Greenland Inuit and, 207
  Kwasny and, 190, 203–5, 212, 214
  and the media, 190, 213
  mink and, 204, 210, 212, 214, 215
  Nina Brønden Jakobsen and, 203–5, 209, 212–14
  overview, 204
  seal products and, 205, 207
  secrecy, disclosure, and, 190, 212, 213, 216
  sheep and, 204
  Søren Jessing Jespersen and, 190, 214–15
Kopenhagen International Center for Creativity (KICK), 215, 216, 218
Kopenhagen Nexus, 215–16
Korea, 88, 117, 214, 216
kosode, 100. See also kimonos
Kuhn, Dieter, 87
kusakizome, 102, 103, 109
Kusakizome Studios, 104
Kvist Jensen, Anders, 190, 191, 194, 196, 198, 202
Kvist Jensen, Hanne, 190, 193–94, 196, 197, 202
Kvist Jensen, Jakob, 194, 195
Kvist Jensen, Jesper, 190–94, 202
Kyoto, Japan, 85, 88, 91, 93, 97, 117, 121. See also Nishijin

La Japonaise au bain (painting), 120
La Manga, 168
La Paz, 166, 167
La Peregrina pearl, 165
lambing pens, mesh, 73. See also jugs
lambs, 33–34. See also Thirteen Mile Lamb and Wool Company
  defined, 33
  at Hilger Ranch, 69, 70, 73
  number harvested, 33
  organic, 68
  predators and, 70, 71
  at Sieban Ranch, 73–77
  sold for food, 33, 63
lambskin, 33, 34

lanolin, 52, 63, 66, 79
larvae, 173. See also spat collection
laundering, 225, 233, 235
lead (sea ice), 20
leather. See also hide(s); tanneries
  cowhide, 30–32, 34, 40–42, 46. See also cowhide
  dyeing, 29–32, 34–37, 39–41
  ethical, 46–47
  etymology of the term, 26
  Italy and, 34–36, 46
  as luxury good, 37, 40, 41, 47
  meanings and uses of the term, 26
  overview, 31–41
  shoe, 30, 40, 41, 46–48
"leather flaws," 30–31
leather industry. See also finishing
  in China, 36, 38, 79
  finances, 36, 38
  in India, 36–38
leghold traps, 221, 223, 231
Leizu, Empress, 87
leks, 129
leopards, snow, 70–72
Linscombe, Greg, 222
Little Prince, The (Saint-Exupéry), 83–84
live-plucking, 45, 131, 133, 143, 146–49
llamas, 52, 71
Lopez, Barry, 20, 24, 25, 138
luxury materials/luxury goods, 8, 41, 47, 215–17. See also under fur; leather
Lyhneand, Lone, 211–14

mabe pearls, 176, 177
mabushi, 94–95
mammoth hide, 26
mammoth tusk, 14
mammoths, 5, 6, 10, 13
Mann, Charles C., 165
mantle (mollusc), 175–77
Manuel de Ocio, 166
manure, 183–84, 201
Margarita Island, 163–64
Marine Mammal Protection Act of 1972, 9, 207
maroquinerie, 39
Marx, Leo, 81, 82
mating behavior. See courtship display; mink: breeding/reproduction
Matthews, Dan, 210, 224
mawata, 100, 111
McDonald, Anne, 162
McFarland, Casey, 129–30
McLaurin-Moreno, Douglas, 168–72, 184
  background, 169

on China, 181
  on dyes, 183
  on global warming, 177–78
  jewelry and, 185, 186
  on Mexico, 168–69
  overview and description of, 168
  oysters and, 170, 171, 173, 175–78, 182,
    184–85
  pearls and, 170, 171, 176–79, 181–86
  professional work, 181
  shells and, 175–78, 182–84
  spat collection and, 173
merino wool (and clothing), 60, 61, 68
merinos, 54, 60, 70
metals, heavy, 79, 140, 179, 183
Mexican Revolution, 172
Mexico, 167. *See also* Guaymas
  Douglas McLaurin-Moreno on, 168–69
  feathers and birds in, 135–37
  Hernán Cortés's expedition to, 165, 166
  pearl diving banned in, 172
  pearl farmers in, 231
  pearl harvesting, 166
micro farms, 149
microfiber pollution, 146, 225, 233
Mikimoto, Kokichi, 162, 174
Mikimoto Island, 162
Mikimoto Pearl Museum, 162
Milhaupt, Terry Satsuki, 116–18, 120
Milligan Canyon Meats, 42–45
Milne, Lorna, 6, 9, 11, 13, 14, 18, 19, 21
mingei (hand-crafted art of ordinary people),
  106–7
mink, 188, 189
  breeding/reproduction, 192–93, 195–200,
    212
  China and, 195, 203, 212
  dyed, 215, 218
  history, 191
  Jakobsen and, 204, 208–15, 218, 219. *See
    also* Jakobsen, Nina Brønden
  killing, 192, 196, 198–200
  sold at auctions, 195, 208, 212
  spotted, 200
  stretching, 219
  trapping, 12
  women and, 210, 211, 214
mink cages, 193, 197–200, 213, 227
mink coats, 196, 201, 214, 219
mink farms, 190–94, 202, 209–15, 225, 227.
  See also auctions
  animal welfare and, 197–200, 213, 227
  finances, 189, 194, 209
  Jakobsen and, 209, 213–15. *See also*
    Jakobsen, Nina Brønden

Lone Lyhneand and, 211–13
  number of, 189
  targeted by activists, 188–90, 197–98, 210,
    213
mink jackets, 195, 219
mink prices, 194
  drop in, 194–95, 209–10
mink skins, 227
  Danish, 203, 204, 208
  economics, 201, 208
  sold at auctions, 195, 201, 208, 209
mink stole, 195–96, 200
mohair, 51
mollusks, 170, 173
Mongolia, 50, 71, 79–80
  cashmere and, 50, 71, 79
Montana, 27, 68, 151
  Kwasny in, 7, 13, 27, 42, 53–55, 65, 67, 78,
    109, 125
  trapping in, 222–24
Montana Fish, Wildlife and Parks, 70
Montana Trappers Association, 224
Montebello, California, 139–40
Monteforte, Mario, 165–66
Montezuma, 135, 136
Montreal, 219
Moore, Patrick, 206
morality. *See* animal ethics
moths, 93–97. *See also Bombyx mori*
Mount Fuji, 108–9
mountain lions, 69, 70, 75, 223
mouton, 16, 29, 40. *See also* wool
mud-dyeing, 103, 106
mudrooms, 15, 193
mukluks, 10, 15, 16
mulberry leaves, 89, 93, 96, 98, 115
mulberry stems, 87
mulberry trees, 86, 91, 92, 96, 113, 114, 121
Müller, Andy, 181
musk ox, 13–14, 52–53
muskrats, 12, 15, 220, 222
mussels, 170, 173, 174, 176, 182, 184
mutualism (biology), and domestication of
  animals, 57, 58, 70

nacre, 165–66, 171–74, 176
Nagano prefecture, 117
Naia (skeleton), 5
Namibia, 204
Napoleon, 51
National Association of the Fur Industry,
  223
Native American celebrations and dances,
  prohibitions against, 151–54
Native American Clothing (Brasser), 235

Native Americans, 166. See also Alaska
  Natives; Canada: indigenous people in
  clothing, 165–66
  at Crow Fair, 150
  eagles and, 154–57
  enslaved, 164
  feathers and, 154–57
  oysters harvested by, 166–67
  pearls and, 163, 164, 166
  spirituality, 150–58, 235
  stewardship of the sea, 166–67
Nebraska Beef, 45
necklaces, 122
  pearl, 159, 182, 185, 186
Neolithic revolution, 56–57
neotony
  defined, 57–58
  domestication of animals and, 57–58
Newkirk, Ingrid, 187–88
Nihon Migei-kan (Japanese Folk Crafts
  Museum), 108
Nishijin (district in Japan), 85, 116, 117
nishijin-ori, 85
Nishijin Silk Center, 85
Nobue Azuma, 92–98
North Face, 139
North Pacific Fur Seal Convention of 1911,
  206
Nugget Company, 31–34, 39, 40
Nunachuk, 19–21
nylon, 232. See also synthetics

Obama, Barack, 226
occupational safety and health, 36–38
  standards, 37, 45
ocean acidification, 178
Ocio, Manuel de, 166
Okamato, Eriko, 106
Okonogi, Sensei, 99
Oomingmak Musk Ox Producers' Co-op,
  52, 53
organ sewing. See skin sewing
Orinasu-Kan textile museum, 85–86
ostrich feathers, 127–29, 131
ostriches, 127–29, 131–32
overfishing, 174, 180, 193
oysters. See pearl oysters

packrats, 43, 220
painting, 4, 6, 39, 40, 86, 104, 123, 183. See
  also finishing
palapa, 169, 173, 181
Palmer, Claire, 229
Palmer Musk Ox Farm, 53
parka feathers, 11
parkas, 5, 6, 13, 15, 21–22, 149

children's, 11, 12, 15
  colors, 9, 11, 15
  dyed, 6
  Lucy Crow and, 15
  materials, 9, 11–13, 15, 21–23, 149, 220
  production process, 12
  styles, 6, 9
"partnering with the animal," 55
pastoral life, 81–83. See also shepherds
Paul John, 25
Pearl, The (Steinbeck), 166
pearl beds, first discovery of, 159
pearl divers, 160–62, 164–67, 172
  enslaved, 164–66
  ordeals experienced by, 160, 185
  pearl diving, banned in Mexico, 172
pearl earrings, 160
pearl farming, 168, 174. See also culturing
  pearls
  cultured, 180. See also cultured pearl farms
pearl farms, 167–73. See also cultured pearl
  farms
  environmental impact, 183
  sustainable. See sustainable pearls
Pearl Myth, 159–67
pearl necklaces, 159, 182, 185, 186
pearl oyster cages, 169, 172, 173
pearl oyster shells, broken/cracked-open,
  163, 166
pearl oysters, 172–73. See also specific topics
  breeding, 171, 173
  Douglas McLaurin-Moreno and, 170, 171,
    173, 175–78, 182, 184–85
  Japan and, 160–62, 167, 174, 180
  killed, 176, 179
  native, 173, 180
  overview and nature of, 170
  types of, 170–71
pearl rope, 163
pearl-seeding. See seeding: pearls
pearls. See also cultured pearls
  Akoya, 170, 174, 182
  in China, 159, 160, 168, 174, 178, 180–83,
    185
  colors, 170
  cost, 181
  Douglas McLaurin-Moreno and, 170, 171,
    176–79, 181–86
  dyed, 179, 183
  fake, 174, 181–82, 185–86
  freshwater, 160–61, 178, 181–83, 185
  Japan and, 160–61, 168, 174. See also Akoya
    pearls
  mabe/blister, 176, 177
  myths about the origin of. See Pearl Myth
  natural, 163, 167, 172–74, 177, 179

shells and, 159, 163, 170–71, 174, 176, 182, 183
sustainable, 178–86
terminology, 159
pébrine, 115
Peking duck, 141
people, profit, and planet (3Ps), 178–79
People for the Ethical Treatment of Animals (PETA), 226
budget, 202
films and other videos, 147, 213
Four Paws and, 147–48
fur and, 202, 210, 215
surveillance, 147, 148
Peregrina. *See* La Peregrina pearl
Perkins, Anne, 55–58, 70, 73
Perlas de Guaymas, 169
Perlas del Mar de Cortéz, 168, 171–73, 175, 176, 180
Persicaria tinctoria (Japanese indigo), 110
pesticides, 34, 38, 121, 232–35
petrochemicals, 46, 217, 232
petroleum-based synthetic fibers, 104, 117, 145, 233
Pharomachrus mocinno (resplendent quetzal), 135, 137, 138
Picotte, Tristan, 157
pigmentation, 123
pigskin, 30, 32
pillows, 138–39, 144, 149
Pinctada fucata martensii, 170
Pinctada maxima, 170
Pinctada mazatlanica (black-lipped oyster), 170, 171
Pinctada sp. *See* pearl oysters
plasmacytosis, 192–93
Plenty Coups, 151, 152
plucking, live, 45, 131, 133, 143, 146–49
plumage, 129. *See also* feathers
plumers, 148. *See also* plucking, live
plumes (feathers), 124, 126–28, 130
poisoning, pledging not to use, 72
Poland, 132, 142, 148, 210
polishing. *See also* finishing
pearls, 159, 179, 182–85
Pollan, Michael, 234, 236
polyester, 68, 117, 225, 231–33
polyester textiles, 231–32
polymers, natural *vs.* synthetic, 232
Polypay, 79
poverty and employment opportunities, 36, 80–81, 90–91, 98–99, 121, 169, 225
poverty eradication, environmental ramifications of, 180
powwows, 150–55
Predator Friendly, 71, 72

predators, 70–72, 144. *See also* coyotes; mountain lions
killing, 71–72, 83, 221
sheep and, 53, 69, 70, 83
predatory fish, 164
pupae, 95–96, 116, 121
"putting on the dog," 8

qasgi (ceremonial house), underwater, 23–24
qiviut, 52
quetzal, resplendent, 135, 137, 138
quill (feathers), 124

rachi (shaft of feather), 124
rainbow-lipped pearl oyster (*Pteria sterna*), 170–71
raincoats, 12–13
Rambouillet sheep, 75
Rana Plaza factory collapse, 234
ranchers, 70–74, 76. *See also specific topics*
ravens, 123, 151
raw skin procurement facilities. *See* slaughterhouses
"raw skins," 33, 34
reciprocity, 24–25, 236
indigenous notions of, 1, 24–25, 235–36
reeling, 95, 96, 98, 99, 112. *See also* Tomioka Silk Mill
defined, 95
women, 98, 99, 112–14, 119–21
reeling machines, 112, 113
Regan, Tom, 230, 231
reindeer. *See* caribou
Reischauer, Haru Matsukata, 90, 93
reproductive behavior, 76–77. *See also* courtship display; mink: breeding/ reproduction
Resnick, Lynda, 185
Responsible Down Standard (RDS), 147, 149–50
"retaliatory killing," 71
Richman, Brent, 42–44, 47
Roman, Joe, 180
Roman Empire, 160
roving, 66
Russia, 128, 208
animal welfare regulations, 205, 222
fur in, 189, 211, 214, 220

Saint-Exupéry, Antoine de, 83–84
Sama-Bajau. *See* Bajau
samurai, 101
silk and, 99, 101, 110, 116, 119–20
Sater, Stephanie, 74–78
Satoh, Fumiko, 109–11

Savar building collapse. *See* Rana Plaza factory collapse
Savino, Carl, 229
Scott, David S., 129–30
Sea of Cortés (Gulf of California), 166, 167, 170, 180, 183. *See also* Cortés pearl
Sea of Japan, 161, 167
seal bans, 207
  EU ban, 205, 207
  and Greenland Inuit, 206–7
seal-gut parkas, 12, 13, 15
seal hunting/sealing, 206–7
  campaign against, 206, 207
  history of commercial, 205
seal products, Kopenhagen Fur and, 205, 207
"seal wars," 205, 206
seals, 9, 11
  bladders, 23, 25
  in literature and folklore, 23–26, 189
  terminology, 17–18
  types of, 12. bearded seals, 17–18, 23; fur seals, 205; harp seals, 205, 206
sealskin market, collapse of, 207
sealskin trade, prohibition against, 207
sealskins, 218
  banned, 205
  colors, 205, 218
  items made from, 9–12, 15, 16, 36
  procured from Greenland natives, 205
  production processes, 12
  "white coat," 205, 207
seashells. *See* shell(s)
Sebald, W. G., 114
Second Sino-Japanese War, 116
seeded oysters, 177, 178
seeding
  mussels, 182
  oysters, 175
  pearls, 176, 177
semiplumes (feathers), 124
sericin, 95
sericulture (cultivation of silkworms), 93–96, 114
  in China, 114, 115
  decline of, 117, 119
  as environmentally friendly, 121
  etymology of the term, 95
  in India, 96, 114, 115, 121
  in Japan, 93, 115–17, 119, 231
  spread across Europe, 113
  women in, 87, 115–16
sericulture farms, 92, 99
  in Japan, 93, 119, 231
sericulture industry, 91
sewing, 217–19. *See also* skin sewing
  furs, 8, 9

shamans, 23, 24
Shanghai Fashion Week, 203
shearers, 61, 62
shearing, 52, 61, 62
  frequency of, 51, 60
  machines for, 28, 39–40
shearling, defined, 34
sheep, 55. *See also* lambs; *specific topics*
  in Africa, 54, 60, 204
  animal welfare regulations, 204
  breeding, 56, 59, 63, 64, 75, 78
  breeds, 54–55, 58–61, 78–79, 204. Shetland, 55, 61–65, 73
  in China, 79, 80
  coats, 55, 59, 61–63, 78
  dyeing, 34
  ecology, 69–81
  evolutionary history, 54
  geographic distribution, 79
  human uses of, 54
  Kopenhagen Fur and, 204
  predators and, 53, 69–72
  species, 54
  water resources used in raising, 66, 68
  wild, 54, 56, 58–59, 61
  wolves and, 75, 83
sheep population, 79
sheepskin, 29, 33–35, 39. *See also* mouton
  colors, 27, 34
  nature of, 27, 29, 40
sheepskin industry, 28, 39
sheepskin pelts, 31
sheepskin tanneries, 32. *See also* Nugget Company
shell beads, 159, 174–76
shell cordovan, 40
shell deposits from ancient times, 166–67
shell(s). *See also* nacre
  cleaning, 169
  colors, 170–71, 184
  Douglas McLaurin-Moreno and, 175–78, 182–84
  historical perspective on, 159
  mantle and, 175–77
  ocean acidification and hardening of, 178
  pearls and, 159, 163, 170–71, 174, 176, 182, 183
  stalls selling ropes of, 168
Shepard, Paul, 56, 82–83
shepherding, 58
shepherds, 69–76
  in American West, 61–62
  idealized/romantic images and characterizations of, 75, 81–83
  Leo Marx on, 81, 82
  overview and nature of the work of, 81–83

in poetry, 81, 82
poverty, 81–82
predators and, 53, 69–73
relationship between sheep and, 83, 231
roles of, 75, 82
terminology, 81
Shetland sheep, 55, 61–65, 73
shibui, 107
shoes, 30, 40, 41, 46–48
Sieban Ranch, 73–78
Siegel, Lucy, 46
silk, 99. *See also* China; Japan; kimonos
banned, 91, 116
Italy and, 113–15
natural-dyed, 235
samurai and, 99, 101, 110, 116, 119–20
the secret of, 85–89
silk artisans, 98, 99. *See also* artisans: in Japan
silk farming. *See* sericulture
silk farms. *See* sericulture farms
silk moth. *See Bombyx mori*; moths
silk production
dyeing, 88, 91, 95, 97, 98, 100–106, 109–11, 116, 121
spinning, 89, 93–95, 97, 98, 117
spread from China to Japan, 87–88
women and, 99, 112, 120, 121
silk reeling. *See* reeling
Silk Road, 86, 87, 118–19
silk textiles, 97, 98, 113, 121
silk workers, 96, 112, 114
silkworm cultivation. *See* sericulture
silkworm eggs, 87, 88, 93–97, 113, 115
silkworm farmers, 116
silkworms, 89, 94–96, 98, 111, 115–16. *See also* caterpillars
breeding, 113
economics and, 91, 119
genetic strains, 113, 116
introduced into Sicily and Spain, 113
in Japan, 99, 113, 115–16, 231
life cycle, 93–94, 96, 97
plants that feed. *See* mulberry trees
Singer, Peter, 229
skin, animal
anatomy, 29–30
nature of, 29
washing, 30, 34, 35, 37
skin sewing, 27. *See also* sewing
scope of the term, 12
secrets of, 9–26
skinning, 30
live, 45, 213. *See also* flaying
skirting, 62
skirting table, 60, 62–63, 65

slaughterhouse work, industrial, 43–44
as one of the most dangerous jobs, 45
slaughterhouses, 41–48, 146. *See also* slaughtering methods
animal welfare and, 44–46, 149–50, 230
terminology and euphemisms for, 33, 42, 47
slaughtering. *See under* animals and humans
slaughtering methods. *See also* slaughterhouses
humane, 44–45, 146
processes and procedures in slaughterhouses, 30, 42–45, 146
US state regulations on, 222
slavery, 83, 185
in Crete, 59
enslaved pearl divers, 164–66
slippers, 27, 35, 36
Slow Fashion movement, 234–35
Smith, Jo, 151, 152
snares, 132, 221, 223
snow leopards, 70–72
sokaku (isolationist foreign policy), 19, 115
sorting, 112, 208, 211
South Africa, 2, 60, 128, 132
Spain
sheep and, 59, 60
silkworms introduced into, 113
Spanish conquest of Aztec Empire, 138, 165, 166
spat (baby oysters), 175
spat collection, 171, 173, 175, 177, 180
speciesism, 229
spinning
cocoons, 93–95
metaphor and fairy tales, 49–50
silk, 89, 93–95, 97, 98, 117
wool, 49–50, 53, 59, 73; ways to prepare for spinning, 66–68
spinning machines, 67, 68
spirituality. *See also* death; shamans
Native American, 150–58, 235
split (finishing), 39
spotted eagles, 153, 155–56
spreaders, 175
states rights, 70
steer, 43–44
Stein, Sarah Abrevaya, 127–29
Steinbeck, John, 166
stole, mink, 195–96, 200
stretching, 22, 35, 67, 201, 219
sukumo ("building indigo"), 110
sustainability, 47, 82, 126, 231–35
defined, 178
sustainable pearls, 178–86

Sustainable Pearls project, 168, 179
Suzuki, Daisetsu Teitaro, 107
Sveinsson, Jon, 143–44
Swakara, 204
sweaters, cashmere, 50–51, 79
Sweden, 204, 231
synthetic indigo, 104, 111
synthetics, 224, 225
  compared with down, 145–46
  compared with wool, 53
  environmental impact, 145–46, 217, 225,
    231–33
  made of natural vs. synthetic polymers,
    232
  petroleum-based, 104, 117, 145, 233
  supply chain for, 233

Taiping Rebellion, 115
takenoko seikatsu ("bamboo shoot exis-
    tence"), 118
taming vs. domestication of animals, 56, 57
Tanaka, Chuzaburo, 98–99
tanneries, 34–40, 44
  ancient, 32
  in China, 34, 36
  conditions at, 33, 34, 36–38, 40, 43, 46
  conditions that have driven them
    overseas, 36–37
  health hazards, 37
  in India, 37–38
  numbers of, 36, 38
  sheepskin, 32. See also Nugget Company
  in Southeast Asia, 34, 36, 37
  water resources used in, 35, 37–38
  workers, 34–39, 128
tanner's guild, 32
Tannery Row, 36
tanning
  defined, 26
  etymology of the term, 32
  vegetable, 35, 37, 40
Tarantola, Andrew, 38
tawing, 32
tea ceremony, 105
Tenochtitlan, 165
  Cortés's invasion of, 138
textile markets, 113, 117, 121, 225
textile materials, 97, 137, 231–33. See also silk
    textiles; wool textiles
  synthetic, 117, 225, 231–32. See also
    synthetics
textile workers, 80, 110, 112, 234
Thirteen Mile Lamb and Wool Company,
    65–69, 71
Thomas, Dana, 235
Thomas, Gary, 27–32, 35

Tissot, James, 120
Tocas, Roberto Enrique Ninahuanca, 76–78
toggling machine, 35
Tokyo, kimonos in, 116, 120
Tomioka Silk Mill (reeling factory), 91, 119
  rise and fall of, 112–13, 117
"Tongue-Cut Sparrow, The" (Japanese
    folktale), 90
tools, history of, 2–3
"Trace-your-down," 150
traceability, 149
traceable down, 235
Traceable Down campaign, 150
Traceable Down Standard, 146
traceable standards, 147
trapping, 12, 214, 220–27
  animal welfare activists and, 187, 225
  bans on, 70, 196, 222–23, 226
  beavers, 220
  Canada and, 188, 189, 220, 222–25
  coyotes and, 220, 222, 224
  and fur clothing, 189
  indigenous trappers in Canada, 188
  opposition to, 196, 214, 231
  packrats, 220
  pledging not to use, 72
  prevalence in rural North America, 220
  problems with and criticisms of, 196, 214,
    223, 225
  reasons for, 220
trapping regulations, 223, 225
traps, types of, 132, 221, 223, 231
  "humane"/quick-kill, 222, 223
triple bottom line, 178–79
Truth in Fur Labeling Act, 226
Tsukiyama, Gail, 112, 119
tusks, 6, 14, 23
Tutankhamun, 32, 48
Twitchell, Sam, 21

undercoats, 50, 52, 63, 78
Uretsky, Daniel, 139–42
Uretsky, Steve, 140, 141
utilitarianism, 229

vats, 34–35, 39, 66, 109–11
  functions, 34
vegetable tanning, 35, 37, 40
vicuñas, 52
Virgil, 81, 82

Walrath, Toby, 224
walrus ivory, 6, 10, 14, 19, 23
walruses, 9, 12, 22, 23
Warsh, Molly A., 164, 167
waste, industrial, 38, 233

water
 recycling, 141
 wool's capacity to absorb, 53
water pollution, 38, 140, 180, 225, 233. *See also* filtering; microfiber pollution
 in China, 140, 183
 cotton and, 121, 231–33
 oysters filtering, 179–80
 pearl farms and, 183
 polyester and, 225, 231
water resources
 used in clothing production, 231–32
 used in down processing, 149
 used in growing cotton, 121, 146, 231–32
 used in pearl farms, 179
 used in processing feathers, 140–41
 used in raising sheep, 66, 68
 used in sericulture, 121
 used in tanning industry, 35, 37–38
 used in washing clothes, 233
 used in wool processing, 79
"water trade," 162
waterproof clothing, 10–12
Wayland Barber, Elizabeth, 49, 50
Weed, Becky, 62, 65–68, 71–72, 78, 233
Weidensaul, Scott, 130
Wheeler, Colin, 31–34, 37–39
"white coat" sealskins, 207
 European ban on, 207
Wilder, Edna, 22
Williams, Alex, 210
Williams, Bud, 74–75
willowing, 128, 129
wolverines, 11, 22, 223
wolves, 9, 70
 humans and, 57, 70, 72–73, 83
 killing, 83
 sheep and, 75, 83
women, 50
 animal metaphors used to characterize, 226
 animal welfare and, 131, 187
 in China, 112, 119, 121
 feathers and, 127–29, 131, 132
 in filature factories, 112, 121
 fur clothing and, 8, 12, 187, 202, 210
 in fur industry, 211
 Inupiaq, 11, 12
 lambs and, 73
 mink and, 210, 211, 214

 pearls and, 6, 186
 silk production and, 99, 112, 120, 121
 Yup'ik, 12, 16, 23
"women of the sea." *See ama*
Women of the Silk (Tsukiyama), 112, 119
Women's Work: The First 20,000 Years (Wayland Barber), 49
wool. *See also* cashmere; mouton; *specific topics*
 characteristics, 53
 China and, 71, 79
 compared with other materials, 53, 68
 contrasted with cotton, 53, 68
 goats and, 50–51, 53, 66, 79
 as patriotic in British Empire, 59–60, 114
 scope of the term, 64
 washing, 66–68, 79, 80
wool making, 60–69. *See also* Thirteen Mile Lamb and Wool Company
 dyeing, 51, 53, 59, 64–67, 79
 spinning, 49–50, 53, 59, 73; ways to prepare wool for spinning, 66–68
wool products, negative consequences of demand for, 78–80
wool textiles, 27, 79
woolen yarn. *See* yarn
World War II, 116
worsted wool, 66. *See also* combing

Xiaoman, Yao, 146

Yamanashi Silk Company, 89
Yamazaki, Akira, 102–5
Yamazaki family, 104–6, 111
Yanagi, Sōetsu, 106–8
Yaqui, 169, 181, 184
yarn, 60–61, 65, 66
Yellow Emperor, 86
Yuho, Shaku (Thomas Kirchner), 97
Yupiit Piciryarit Cultural Center, 16
Yupiit/Yup'ik people, 9, 23, 25, 26, 32
 animals and, 12, 23, 25–26
 clothing, 11–13, 22, 52, 220
 relation to the dead, 23, 25–26
 women, 12, 16, 23
Yup'ik language, 10, 17
yūzen, 104–6

Zen Buddhism, 96–97, 107
Zen priests, 97

Melissa Kwasny is the author of six award-winning poetry collections, among them *Where Outside the Body Is the Soul Today*, *Reading Novalis in Montana*, and *Pictograph*. She is also the author of a collection of essays, *Earth Recitals: Essays on Image and Vision*; the editor of *Toward the Open Field: Poets on the Art of Poetry, 1800–1950*; and the coeditor, with M. L. Smoker, of *I Go to the Ruined Place: Contemporary Poems in Defense of Global Human Rights*. She lives outside Jefferson City, Montana, in the Elkhorn Mountains.